Legalines

Editorial Advisors:
Gloria A. Aluise
Attorney at Law
David H. Barber
Attorney at Law
Robert A. Wyler
Attorney at Law

Authors:
Gloria A. Aluise
Attorney at Law
David H. Barber
Attorney at Law
Daniel O. Bernstine
Professor of Law
D. Steven Brewster
C.P.A.
Roy L. Brooks
Professor of Law
Frank L. Bruno
Attorney at Law
Scott M. Burbank
C.P.A.
Jonathan C. Carlson
Professor of Law
Charles N. Carnes
Professor of Law
Paul S. Dempsey
Professor of Law
Jerome A. Hoffman
Professor of Law
Mark R. Lee
Professor of Law
Jonathan Neville
Attorney at Law
Laurence C. Nolan
Professor of Law
Arpiar Saunders
Professor of Law
Robert A. Wyler
Attorney at Law

CONFLICT OF LAWS

Adaptable to Tenth Edition of Rosenberg Casebook

By Gloria A. Aluise
Attorney at Law

THE
barbri
GROUP

HARCOURT PROFESSIONAL EDUCATION GROUP, INC.
EDITORIAL OFFICES: 111 W. Jackson Blvd., 7th Floor, Chicago, IL 60604

Legalines

REGIONAL OFFICES: Chicago, Dallas, Los Angeles, New York, Washington, D.C
Distributed by: **Harcourt, Inc.** 6277 Sea Harbor Drive, Orlando, FL 32887 (800)787-8717

SERIES EDITOR
Angel M. Murphy, J.D.

PRODUCTION COORDINATOR
Sanetta Hister

TENTH EDITION—2000

Legalines™

**Features Detailed Briefs of Every Major Case,
Plus Summaries of the Black Letter Law.**

Titles Available

Administrative Law .... Keyed to Breyer
Administrative Law .... Keyed to Gellhorn
Administrative Law .... Keyed to Schwartz
Antitrust .... Keyed to Areeda
Antitrust .... Keyed to Handler
Civil Procedure .... Keyed to Cound
Civil Procedure .... Keyed to Field
Civil Procedure .... Keyed to Hazard
Civil Procedure .... Keyed to Rosenberg
Civil Procedure .... Keyed to Yeazell
Commercial Law .... Keyed to Farnsworth
Conflict of Laws .... Keyed to Cramton
Conflict of Laws .... Keyed to Reese
Constitutional Law .... Keyed to Brest
Constitutional Law .... Keyed to Cohen
Constitutional Law .... Keyed to Gunther
Constitutional Law .... Keyed to Lockhart
Constitutional Law .... Keyed to Rotunda
Constitutional Law .... Keyed to Stone
Contracts .... Keyed to Calamari
Contracts .... Keyed to Dawson
Contracts .... Keyed to Farnsworth
Contracts .... Keyed to Fuller
Contracts .... Keyed to Kessler
Contracts .... Keyed to Murphy
Corporations .... Keyed to Cary
Corporations .... Keyed to Choper
Corporations .... Keyed to Hamilton
Corporations .... Keyed to Vagts
Criminal Law .... Keyed to Boyce
Criminal Law .... Keyed to Dix
Criminal Law .... Keyed to Johnson
Criminal Law .... Keyed to Kadish
Criminal Law .... Keyed to LaFave
Criminal Procedure .... Keyed to Kamisar

Decedents' Estates & Trusts .. Keyed to Ritchie
Domestic Relations .... Keyed to Clark
Domestic Relations .... Keyed to Wadlington
Estate & Gift Tax .... Keyed to Surrey
Evidence .... Keyed to Sutton
Evidence .... Keyed to Waltz
Evidence .... Keyed to Weinstein
Family Law .... Keyed to Areen
Federal Courts .... Keyed to McCormick
Income Tax.............................. Keyed to Freeland
Income Tax.............................. Keyed to Klein
Labor Law .... Keyed to Cox
Labor Law .... Keyed to Merrifield
Partnership & Corporate Tax .. Keyed to Surrey
Property .... Keyed to Browder
Property .... Keyed to Casner
Property .... Keyed to Cribbet
Property .... Keyed to Dukeminier
Real Property .... Keyed to Rabin
Remedies .... Keyed to Re
Remedies .... Keyed to York
Sales & Secured Transactions .. Keyed to Speidel
Securities Regulation .... Keyed to Jennings
Torts .... Keyed to Epstein
Torts .... Keyed to Franklin
Torts .... Keyed to Henderson
Torts .... Keyed to Keeton
Torts .... Keyed to Prosser
Wills, Trusts & Estates .... Keyed to Dukeminier

Other Titles Available:
Criminal Law Questions & Answers
Excelling on Exams/How to Study
Torts Questions & Answers

---

*All Titles Available at Your Law School Bookstore,
or Call to Order: 1-800-787-8717*

Harcourt Brace Legal and Professional Publications, Inc.
111 West Jackson Boulevard, Seventh Floor
Chicago, IL 60604

SHORT SUMMARY OF CONTENTS

TABLE OF CONTENTS AND SHORT REVIEW OUTLINE

CONFLICT OF LAWS

I. INTRODUCTION

A. SOURCE OF THE PROBLEMS INVOLVED

Conflict of laws deals with the problems created because humans divide the earth into territorial units with separate legal systems. Purely local problems (those occurring exclusively within one unit) are relatively simple, since the law of the forum controls. Conflict of laws, however, deals with problems having elements in more than one forum (*i.e.*, contact with more than one jurisdiction).

B. THE KINDS OF PROBLEMS CONSIDERED

1. **Jurisdiction.** Which courts can entertain litigation when a problem has "contacts" with more than one jurisdiction? This is largely a constitutional law problem.

2. **Conflict of Laws.** Assuming that one or more states may act, what law will be applied to determine the issues raised?

3. **Judgments.** What effect will judgments of one jurisdiction be given elsewhere?

C. TERMS OF ART USED IN THE COURSE

1. **Conflict of Laws.** Any phenomenon having contact with more than one jurisdiction.

2. **Internal.** A situation having contact with only one jurisdiction. Synonyms: "domestic," "municipal," and "local."

3. **Foreign.** Refers to anything extra-forum; anything outside the court which is adjudicating the case.

4. **Contacts.** Significant attachments to a place or a jurisdiction.

5. **Abbreviations.**

    a. F: The forum state.

    b. X, Y, Z: States having contacts with the cause of action.

    c. X-F: A situation where the transaction occurs in X and the forum is in another jurisdiction.

    d. X-Y-F: Contacts in X and Y; the forum is in a third jurisdiction.

    e. X-YF: Contacts in state X and in the forum state (Y).

    f. F1: State where the judgment is taken.

    g. F2: State where the judgment is sought to be enforced.

II. DOMICILE

This section has two purposes: (i) to give familiarity to the concept of domicile; and (ii) to look at problems that cut across all of the problems in the course.

A. INTRODUCTION TO THE CONCEPT OF DOMICILE

1. **Definition.** "Domicile" is a legal tool or concept used to attach an individual to a particular locality for some particular purpose. It is merely a legal conclusion that there is sufficient "contact" or relationship between the individual and a particular state or country, so that the laws of that state or country may be applied to his affairs or that he may be held subject to the jurisdiction of the courts.

2. **The Importance of the Concept of Domicile.** The concept of domicile is important because courts look to the law of a person's domicile for many purposes, such as to determine personal rights (*e.g.*, in *White v. Tennant, infra*, the law of the intestate's domicile controlled the disposition of his property). Under the Restatement, "domicile" is the place to which the law assigns a person for certain legal purposes.

3. **Types of Domicile.**

    a. **Domicile of origin.** The domicile of origin is acquired at birth, being the domicile of the person's father (if the child is legitimate).

    b. **Domicile of choice.** Subsequent to birth, a person may choose a new domicile.

    c. **Domicile by operation of law.** There are some situations when the law assigns a domicile to a person regardless of his own choice.

B. DOMICILE OF CHOICE

In re Estate of Jones

1. **Intestate Succession--*In re* Estate of Jones,** 192 Iowa 78, 182 N.W. 227 (1921).

    a. **Facts.** Jones, who was born in Wales, immigrated to the United States and became a naturalized citizen. He worked in and was domiciled in Iowa for approximately 32 years. On May 1, 1915, Jones boarded a ship that set sail for Wales. Jones intended to live in Wales with his sister. On May 7, 1915, the ship sank off the coast of the British Isles and Jones drowned. Plaintiff (P) claims that she is the illegitimate child of Jones and as such is his sole heir and entitled to his entire estate. If Jones's domicile at the time the ship sank was legally Wales, then P would have no interest in his estate under British law. However, if his domicile at the time of death was legally Iowa, then the property passed to P as the sole heir under Iowa law. The trial court denied P's claim. P appeals.

    b. **Issue.** Was decedent still domiciled in Iowa at the time of his death?

    c. **Held.** Yes. Judgment reversed.

1) Before the former domicile can be considered lost, the acquiring of a new domicile must have been completely perfected; there must have been a concurrence of both the fact of removal and the intent to remain in the new place.

2) Here, Jones never reached Wales; there was no concurrence of fact and intention.

2. **Intent to Reside Indefinitely.** In *White v. Tennant*, 8 S.E. 596 (W. Va. 1888), decedent (White) was living on a farm in West Virginia, which he sold. He moved his household goods and livestock to a farm in Pennsylvania but did not sleep there because his wife was ill. Instead, they went to a relative's home nearby (in West Virginia). While there, decedent died intestate. The law of domicile controls intestate succession of personal property. Under West Virginia law, the widow took all of the estate. Under Pennsylvania law, decedent's brothers and sisters took one-half. White (P), a brother of decedent, sued Tennant (D), decedent's administrator, to set aside the settlement and distribution of decedent's personal estate under West Virginia law, claiming Pennsylvania law should apply. The trial court dismissed P's complaint. Upon appeal, the court decided that decedent left his former home without any intention of returning and moved his family and property to his new home with the intention of making it his residence for an indefinite time and thus acquired a domicile in Pennsylvania. Therefore, Pennsylvania law controlled.

3. **How Acquired?** *White v. Tennant, supra,* indicated that there are two requirements for acquisition of a domicile by choice.

   a. **Physical presence.** Physical presence in the place where domicile is to be established. The length of time there is not important.

   b. **Intent.** Intent to make a home, to stay indefinitely (although not necessarily permanently), and to abandon one's past home or domicile.

   c. **The purpose of the inquiry.** The two-pronged test for domicile which has been stated above may not apply in the same way in every case. The concept of domicile differs somewhat according to the type of case being decided, or according to the purpose for which the concept is being used. For example, the contact necessary to establish domicile for tax purposes may be different from that contact which is required for divorce purposes.

4. **Validity of a Will--*In re* Estate of Clark,** 288 N.Y.S.2d 993 (1968).

In re Estate of Clark

   a. **Facts.** Clark died while domiciled in Virginia, and his widow continues to reside there. His estate consisted of property in New York and Virginia. Clark's will provided that his testamentary dispositions be construed by New York law. Virginia law provides for a more favorable spousal election. The Surrogate Court found for the executor. The Supreme Court, Appellate Division, reversed.

   b. **Issue.** May a husband domiciled in a foreign state, by selecting New York law to regulate his testamentary dispositions, cut off the more favorable right given to his widow to elect by the law of their domicile?

   c. **Held.** No. Judgment affirmed.

1) The widow's right to take in opposition to the will is statutory in nature and outside of direct contravention to provisions of a will. It must be determined by the law of the domicile of the parties.

2) General principles of choice of law are in accord with our conclusion. The law of the state which has the predominant, if not the sole, interest in the protection and regulation of the rights of the person(s) involved should be invoked.

5. Diversity Jurisdiction--Rodriguez-Diaz v. Sierra-Martinez, 853 F.2d 1027 (1988).

a. **Facts.** Rodriguez-Diaz (P) was injured when his motorcycle collided with an automobile driven by Sierra-Martinez (D). The accident occurred in Puerto Rico, where both parties were domiciled. P was 17 years old at the time of the accident and was living with his parents. P was treated for his injuries at two hospitals in Puerto Rico and claims that he received improper treatment at both hospitals (Ds). Sometime later, P was transferred to a New York City hospital. P alleges that he was living in New York City at the time he brought this diversity action against Ds in the United States District Court of Puerto Rico. P further alleges in his complaint that he intends to remain in New York and make it his permanent home and that he is now domiciled there. Ds moved to dismiss P's complaint for lack of diversity jurisdiction. The district court concluded that P is a minor under Puerto Rico law, and, therefore, his domicile is that of his parents. Since P's domicile at the time of the filing of this action was Puerto Rico, the court dismissed P's complaint for lack of diversity. P appeals.

b. **Issue.** Was P domiciled in New York at the time he brought this action, thereby satisfying the diversity requirement?

c. **Held.** Yes. Vacated and remanded.

1) To establish domicile for diversity jurisdiction, there must be physical presence in the state and the intent to make such state a home.

2) Domicile at the time an action is filed controls, and the fact that P changed domicile with the purpose of bringing a diversity action in federal court is irrelevant.

3) If P meets the requisite factors of physical presence and intent, he is entitled to be a New York domiciliary for diversity purposes notwithstanding his minority status under Puerto Rico law.

6. Judicial Jurisdiction--Alvord & Alvord v. Patenotre, 92 N.Y.S.2d 514 (1949).

a. **Facts.** Alvord & Alvord (P) served Patenotre (D), pursuant to an order for substituted service, by affixing a copy of the complaint to the door of D's New York residence and by mailing a copy the next day. At the time of service, D was in France for a temporary stopover en route to Switzerland. Switzerland is where D intended to establish his new domicile. D moves to vacate the order for substituted service.

b. **Issue.** Was D a resident of New York at the time of service?

c. **Held.** Yes. Motion denied.

1) An existing domicile continues until a new one is acquired. An effective change of domicile requires intent to change accompanied by an actual going to and residing in the new place.

2) Here, D had not yet arrived in Switzerland at the time service was made. D's domicile was still in New York.

7. **Student's Domicile.** Students going away to college do not usually acquire a domicile at the college site.

a. **Eligibility to vote.**

1) **Veterans at college.** In *Robbins v. Chamberlain,* 297 N.Y. 108 (1947), a state statute required domicile in order in vote. The court held that a veteran who had abandoned his parental home and was on his own at school had established domicile to vote.

2) **Test for bona fide residence.** The court in *Ramey v. Rockefeller,* 348 F. Supp. 780 (E.D.N.Y. 1972), found that the only constitutionally permissible test of bona fide residence for voting purposes is one which focuses on the individual's present intention and does not require him to pledge allegiance for an indefinite future. There is nothing constitutionally impermissible in enumerating certain categories of persons who, despite their physical presence, may lack the intention required for voting. There are legitimate state interests in the preservation of the basic concept of a political community and protection of long term residents from control of municipal affairs through the ballot box by an unconcerned body (*i.e.,* by short term residents—students).

b. **Tuition.** In *Seren v. Douglas,* 30 Colo. App. 110 (1971), a person who entered the United States on a student visa was held eligible for "in state" tuition rates even though the visa had expired.

8. **Do the "Presence" and "Intention" Requirements Add Up to a Rational Standard?**

a. **Examining the statutory purpose.**

1) **Hypothetical.** Suppose a California law student wants to be a tax expert. He goes to Washington, D.C. to work for the treasury with the intention of staying there until he learns his trade and then returning to California. The District of Columbia wants to tax him.

2) **Intent to return.** *District of Columbia v. Murphy,* 314 U.S. 441 (1941), held that those in D.C. with specific intent to return to their homes in another jurisdiction, although staying in D.C. for an indefinite period, do not acquire domicile for tax purposes. The court based its decision on its interpretation of the district statute and the supposed intent of Congress in passing it. This was a good decision.

  b. **Multiple domiciles for different purposes.**

   1) **Hypothetical.** Suppose a student who goes to a California law school with intent to remain after graduation, returns for vacation to Washington, D.C., where he dies. What law would govern the disposition of his estate? Without a specific statute the common law rule governs.

   2) **Query.** Does the fact that one harbors a specific intent to return to his old domicile (at some time) mean that he cannot acquire a domicile in a place where he remains for an indefinite period? No. This is called "floating intent"; *i.e.*, intent either to return to an old home or to move on elsewhere at some time in the indefinite future.

   3) **Result.** One can have domiciles at different places, for different purposes, at the same time.

  c. **Mechanical application.** The concept of "domicile" should not be rationalized in terms of "presence" and "intent" in a purely abstract or mechanical manner. Courts should examine the purpose of the statutes involved, and examine the results of their domicile determinations to see that the correct statutory policies are effectuated by the decision concerning domicile. The tendency, however, has been to ignore these considerations and make mechanical applications of the domicile concept.

C. **DOMICILE BY OPERATION OF LAW**

 1. **The Domicile of the Wife Is That of Her Husband.** The common law rule was that the wife acquired, by operation of law, the domicile of her husband. England followed this rule until the 1973 adoption of the Domicile and Matrimonial Proceedings Act, which permits a married woman living with her husband to acquire a domicile of choice in the same manner as anyone else. Cracks also have begun to appear in the common law rule in the United States.

  a. **Public office eligibility.** In *Gladwin v. Power*, 249 N.Y.S.2d 980 (1964), the court held that a wife living amicably with her husband could acquire separate domicile for the purpose of rendering herself eligible to hold public office.

  b. **Husband and wife live apart.** The Restatement (Second) states that the common law rule no longer applies where husband and wife are living apart. It also states that in extremely rare instances a wife who is living with her husband will have a domicile apart from his (when she has closer ties with another state, which she regards as her home).

 2. **The Domicile of a Corporation.** A corporation's domicile is the state of its incorporation. However, some cases have begun to develop the idea that a corporation has a "commercial domicile." This is in the state where the corporation has its business headquarters. The Restatement (Second) indicates that the concept of domicile is not properly applicable to a corporation.

3. People Not Acting of Their Own Free Will.

a. **Prisoners.** A bank robber lives in New York; he takes a plane to San Francisco to pull a job, gets caught, and is imprisoned in California. No domicile is acquired there—an involuntary stay.

b. **Refugees.** In *Roboz v. Kennedy*, 219 F. Supp. 892 (D.D.C. 1963), a Hungarian Jew sent money to the United States with the intent of leaving Hungary and coming here. Before he could, he was imprisoned and killed. His wife and child, who remained in Hungary until 1947 for the sole purpose of trying to obtain his release, were held to be domiciled in the United States before the cutoff date of an executive order (citizens, residents, or subjects of Hungary after 1941 are not entitled to recover confiscated assets) and so were entitled to the property that had been confiscated by the United States government during the war.

c. **People in the armed forces.**

1) Suppose a member of the armed forces is assigned a new place every three years and has the intent to remain indefinitely in each place. Domicile? The general rule has been that she would not establish domicile. She is not a free agent to choose her domicile.

2) Courts do hold, however, that domicile can be obtained in the place stationed if the person forms the requisite intent and intends to return when the tour of duty is over. This is very difficult to prove, however. For example, in *Hammerstein v. Hammerstein*, 269 S.W.2d 591 (Tex. 1954), a Pennsylvania soldier stationed in Texas sought to establish domicile for divorce purposes, but it was held that his domicile was in Pennsylvania since he was not in Texas of his own volition.

3) Note that several states do have statutes providing that service personnel living in the state for a specified period shall be deemed residents for purposes of divorce suits.

4. Domicile of Infants.

a. **Normal rule.** Normally the domicile of an infant is the same as that of his father.

b. **Unusual circumstances.** There are, however, many unusual circumstances when the child may acquire a different domicile—*e.g.*, child is adopted, abandoned, or emancipated or parents are divorced or separated with custody in the mother, etc.

D. JURISDICTION AND THE CONCEPT OF DOMICILE

1. Domicile as a Basis for a State's Power to Act. A state's power to act

vis-a-vis an individual is often said to rest on that individual's domicile in the state. That is, in some instances "domicile" becomes an instrument of constitutional limitations placed on a state's exercise of power (by the Fourteenth Amendment Due Process Clause) on the basis of an individual's domicile or nondomicile in the state.

2. **Legal Significance of a Declaration of Domicile.** In *Matter of Newcomb*, 192 N.Y. 238 (1908), the court found that evidence of a declaration of domicile is admissible; nevertheless, domicile requires "good faith" or actual intent to make a place one's home. A mere declaration of domicile for self-serving purposes, without the good faith intent to make that place one's actual home indefinitely, is insufficient (although with good faith intent, the reason or motive for establishing a domicile is irrelevant). Good faith intent is shown by the individual's actions (also by motives), and by contacts with the individual's intended domicile state. If the individual has significant contacts with two states, then a declared domicile will be nearly conclusive.

    a. **Comment.** The more one wants to control one's domicile for personal reasons which run counter to the policy of the courts (for example, to avoid taxation), the less weight is likely to be given to the declaration of intent. The more nearly the purpose for control accords with favored policies of the law, the greater the weight that will be given the declaration. For instance in *Newcomb*—the law of wills is to give accord to the desires of the testator. Domicile in Louisiana allowed the testator to effectuate her testamentary purposes and thus fulfilled the purposes of the law. Hence, the decedent's declaration of domicile was upheld.

3. **Jurisdiction to Tax.**

    a. **Hypothetical case.**

        1) **Facts.** Suppose that:

State W	State X	State Y	State Z
A is born here in 1900; stays until 1935	In 1935, A makes his winter home here, until 1967, when he dies.	From 1935, A makes his summer home here.	A visits here; has his car garaged here.

        A leaves the following property: Blackacre in X; automobile in Z; and 10,000 shares of stock in B corporation, which is incorporated in Z (the stock certificates are in a safe deposit box in W).

        2) **Question.** Which states have jurisdiction to assess death transfer taxes on the property in A's estate?

            a) **Real property (Blackacre):** State X.

                (1) **Due process limitations.** The constitutional law rule is that only the situs state can tax real property.

b) **Movables (the automobile):** Apportioned by contacts.

   (1) Formulas. Suppose a corporation, incorporated in X, has a fleet of railroad cars which operate throughout several other states. Which states can tax? The Supreme Court has held that every state having sufficient "contacts" with the movables can tax them. However, such states cannot tax the entire value of the cars; each must establish a formula of apportionment, based on the amount of contact the cars have with the state. States can choose their own apportionment formulas, however, subject to the due process requirement that they not be unreasonable or arbitrary.

   (2) Accidental or fortuitous presence. Suppose a New York couple drives to California carrying a large amount of money and is involved in a fatal accident. Can California seize the money and tax it? As yet there is no answer to this question. Best result—No.

c) **Intangible personal property (the shares of stock):** Probably Z (the state of B's incorporation), W (the location of the certificates), X (A's domicile) and possibly Y (since it has sufficient contacts with A).

   (1) Three eras of tax policy.

   (a) Until 1929. Until 1929, there was no constitutional prohibition against multiple taxation of intangibles.

   (b) After 1929. After 1929, only the state of the taxpayer's domicile could tax.

   (c) Now. Now, there is no constitutional prohibition against multiple taxation; any state can tax as long as it has sufficient "contacts" with the intangibles.

b. **Double domicile.** *In re Dorrance's Estate*, 309 Pa. 151 (1932) and 115 N.J. Eq. 268 (1934) concerned this very kind of problem. Pennsylvania and New Jersey both taxed the decedent's (D's) $115 million in intangible personal property (the tax paid to each state amounted to $17 million).

1) **The state courts.**

   a) **New Jersey.** New Jersey viewed the problem as a classic change of domicile case. D had been domiciled in New Jersey and he had not changed his domicile simply because he went to Pennsylvania to stay temporarily. The New Jersey court said that some or conclusive weight should be given to where D wanted his domicile. D wanted it in New Jersey and had maintained a home and other contacts with that state for that very reason.

   b) **Pennsylvania.** Pennsylvania said that intent to stay in a place indefinitely (though not permanently) is enough so that D's domicile could be in Pennsylvania. The question of domicile was determined by where D intended to make his home, not where he intended his domicile to be. If there are two homes, domicile is determined by which is the principal home, a fact determination based, not on D's subjective intent, but on his objective acts. Pennsylvania said D's principal home was in Pennsylvania because D's home there cost more, D spent more time there, etc.

c) **Query.** The Supreme Court denied certiorari in this case. If the Supreme Court had reviewed the *Dorrance* case, which state would have won? There is justification for a tax by both sides.

2) **The Supreme Court.**

a) **Fourteenth Amendment ignored?** When *Dorrance* was decided, only the state of domicile could tax. Two states, however, claimed domicile and imposed death transfer taxes. *Query*: Should not the Supreme Court have reviewed the conflicting determinations of domicile if there is a Fourteenth Amendment requirement that only the domicile state can act?

b) **Why did the Supreme Court deny certiorari?** Possibly the Supreme Court was of the view that multiple taxation should be allowed—this is the position the Court subsequently came to. But the answer might also depend on the Supreme Court's scope of review of state court findings of jurisdictional facts. If the question is only one of fact, the Supreme Court exercises its normal review function. This is what happened when the Supreme Court was requested to review the *Dorrance* decision. There was nothing to review—there was sufficient evidence to support the state court's finding of domicile.

c. **Federal law of jurisdictional domicile.** Refer again to the tax hypothetical, *supra*. If State W attempted to tax on the basis of A's domicile in that state, the Supreme Court would accept on certiorari and reverse because W's definition of domicile is a widely variant one (birth in the state). So in reality the states are allowed to formulate rules of law which fall between certain latitudes. This can be defined in two ways: (i) domicile is a question of state law, within certain federal limits; or (ii) there is a federal law of domicile when state jurisdiction depends on it.

d. **Definition of domicile today.** In the hypothetical, *supra,* State Y can also tax because A's residence in his summer home for four months a year for 32 years would be a sufficient basis for a tax claim. In tax cases today "domicile" means a substantial, regular, continuing connection with a state over a period of time.

e. **Multiple taxation—why not apportionment?** What if several states have significant contacts sufficient for each to levy taxes, which they do, the total amount of which is equal to or in excess of the amount of the estate? This happened in *Texas v. Florida*, 306 U.S. 398 (1939). Somehow the state of Texas was prevailed on to file an original bill in the Supreme Court. Here the Supreme Court found, proceeding on an assumed definition of domicile, that only one state was the domicile and only that state could tax. In these situations of multiple taxation of intangibles, the Supreme Court might require apportionment as a Fourteenth Amendment requirement (the same way it does with movable tangible property). Thus far, however, it has not chosen to do so.

f. **Uniform acts.** Nine states have adopted the Uniform Act on Interstate Compromise of Death Taxes, which authorizes tax officials to enter into compromises in cases of disputed domicile. Additional states have passed the Uniform Act on Interstate Arbitration of Death Taxes, which authorizes state tax officials to submit to arbitration disputes concerning the location of the deceased's domicile.

4. **Jurisdiction for Divorce.**

a. **The *Williams* cases.** *Williams v. North Carolina* (*Williams I*), *infra*, decided that if Nevada had jurisdiction (domicile) over one of the spouses, North Carolina (domicile of the other) had to extend full faith and credit to Nevada's divorce decree.

1) On remand, the North Carolina court refused to recognize the validity of a Nevada decree, finding that the spouse had established no domicile in Nevada (despite the Nevada court's finding to the contrary). When there is no domicile, a state's ex parte divorce decree is not entitled to full faith and credit elsewhere.

2) Plaintiffs went to the Supreme Court again, this time contending that their constitutional rights depended on the finding of domicile. Plaintiffs wanted "domicile" to be a federal question, reviewable de novo. The Supreme Court said no. The question of domicile is reviewable, but only on a limited basis. [Williams v. North Carolina (*Williams II*), *infra*]

b. **Jurisdiction rule.** If F1 makes a determination of jurisdiction, there is a presumption that it had jurisdiction; F2 must overcome this presumption. Therefore, the Supreme Court indicated that when F2 made a finding of nonjurisdiction in F1 it would review the factual findings of F2 to see if: (i) proper instructions had been given the jury, and (ii) there was substantial evidence in the record to support the findings made.

c. **What law is the Supreme Court applying?** In the *Williams* cases the Supreme Court indicated that divorce was a matter reserved to the states. Yet the conclusion seems inescapable that in reconciling the reciprocal respect accorded by the states to their adjudications (judgment law), the Supreme Court is overseeing the boundaries of what it considers acceptable state law. The Supreme Court weighs the facts in the record against what it deems an acceptable domicile standard. For example, if North Carolina's law is that domicile is always in the state of birth, the Supreme Court is unlikely to uphold a North Carolina's court's finding of no domicile in Nevada (if there are contacts with Nevada sufficient to establish domicile under the law of most states). On the other hand, the Supreme Court is unlikely to require North Carolina to accept Nevada's findings if Nevada grants domicile after a 24-hour stay.

1) **Hypothetical.** If Mrs. W went to Nevada to challenge the right of the Nevada court to decide that Nevada is the domicile of her spouse

and she lost, on certiorari to the Supreme Court, the Supreme Court would not reverse. First, it would determine the law applied by the state of Nevada (does it meet the minimum standard?). Then it would determine whether there was substantial evidence to support the findings made. There would be, since the spouse would have entered his testimony in the record that he had stayed in the state six weeks and intended to stay there indefinitely. This is an impeccable record for Supreme Court review. This is what happened in the *Dorrance* decision (*see* 3.b.2)b), *supra*).

III. JURISDICTION OF THE COURTS

A. INTRODUCTION

1. **The Meaning of Jurisdiction.** "Jurisdiction" has diverse meanings, depending on the inquiry which is being made. In conflicts, jurisdiction usually refers to the question of whether a judgment rendered in the courts of one state will be given effect in another state. This depends on whether the first state's courts had proper "jurisdiction."

2. **Jurisdiction May Convey the Following Ideas.** The assertion that a court lacked jurisdiction may convey any one of the following ideas:

    a. **Improper basis.** The state where judgment was rendered did not have a proper basis to go ahead to a decision. That is, it did not have jurisdiction "over the person," "over the res," or "over the thing in the suit." This is a constitutional question.

    b. **Not authorized.** The law of the state where the judgment was rendered did not authorize the court to exercise the state's judicial power in that type of litigation or on the jurisdictional basis that existed in the case. When this happens the court is said to "lack competence." This is a question of statutory interpretation of the forum's internal law.

    c. **Lack of proper notice.** Another possible "jurisdictional" defect is that the defendant was not given proper notice or a proper opportunity to be heard before his interests were affected.

    d. **Error.** The complaint that jurisdiction was lacking may also be asserted on the basis that the court rendering a judgment erred in finding that the requisite facts were present to satisfy the requirements implicit in either a. or b. above.

3. **The Role of the Due Process Clause.** The subject of jurisdiction is a constitutional one. Actually, there is no constitutional provision that specifically refers to the judicial jurisdiction of the states, but the Supreme Court has ruled that the issue is to be governed by the Due Process Clause (Fourteenth Amendment).

4. **Types of Jurisdiction.** Past ideology drew a clear line between three types of jurisdictional bases: *in personam, in rem,* and *quasi in rem* actions. Formerly very important consequences depended on these distinctions (for example, notice to the defendant by publication might be permissible in *in rem* actions but not in *in personam* actions). However, recently the line between these categorizations has blurred to the point where the distinctions may no longer be meaningful. The question now is simply: constitutionally speaking, when does a court have power (jurisdiction) to act?

B. THE COMMON LAW CONCEPT OF JURISDICTION

1. **Introduction.** The vague language of the Due Process Clause is often resorted to in order to resolve jurisdictional questions. This language has

received its content by judicial interpretation. Because American concepts of "due process" and "jurisdiction" evolved at common law, decisions of English courts may be helpful in understanding how our concepts have developed.

2. **Introductory Cases.**

Buchanan
v. Rucker

a. **Common law principles of jurisdiction--Buchanan v. Rucker,** 9 East 192 (K.B. 1808).

1) **Facts.** Plaintiff sued on a foreign judgment he had obtained in Tobago, where the defendant was served by nailing a copy of the declaration of suit on the courthouse door, according to the requirements of Tobago law. Defendant moved for a nonsuit on the basis that he was not present on the island of Tobago at the time of service, nor had he ever been.

2) **Issue.** Which jurisdictional requirements apply, Tobago's or England's?

3) **Held.** England's. The judgment will not be recognized unless the court rendering the judgment had jurisdiction according to the same standards required by the court that is asked to enforce it. Here the English court will not recognize the Tobago judgment.

4) **Comment.** The fact that F1 would not recognize the F2 judgment unless F2 had jurisdiction according to the standards required by the law of F1 meant that a judgment was of little value outside the jurisdiction in which it was rendered.

Schibsby v.
Westenholz

b. **Common law principle that a foreigner was not obligated to travel to the forum--Schibsby v. Westenholz,** 6 Q.B. 155 (1870).

1) **Facts.** Schibsby (P), a Danish citizen residing in France, sues Westenholz (D), a Danish citizen residing in England, in a French court for breach of contract. P signed a contract in English, dated in London, with D for a cargo of Swedish oats to be shipped from Sweden to Caen, France. Payment was to be made on receipt of the shipping documents subject to correction for excess or deficiency according to what might turn out to be delivered at Caen. P claimed that on arrival the cargo was short and damaged. Notice of suit and summons were given to an official of the French government who forwarded them to the French consulate in London, which served D. D had actual notice of the suit in time to defend against it in France but elected not to do so. A default judgment was entered against him. P now brings that judgment to an English court for enforcement.

2) **Issues.** If a defendant has actual notice of a suit against him in a foreign court, does the defendant have a duty to travel to the country of the forum to defend against the action? And if he does not, can a judgment against him rendered by that foreign court be binding and

enforceable in his country of residence if the foreign court never had personal jurisdiction over him?

3) **Held.** No as to both issues. The English court refused to enforce the French court's judgment.

    a)   The court determined that the duty to travel to the country of the forum to defend against the action could be imposed only if the defendant was a citizen of the forum country (this duty would exist even though the citizen resided elsewhere); if the defendant resided in the forum country although not a citizen; or if the contract was executed in the forum country but the defendant left prior to the commencement of the suit.

    b)   Since the defendant was neither a citizen nor a resident of France and the contract was executed in England, the French court was without authority to impose a binding judgment on him.

    c)   Only on the concept of comity could the judgment have been given effect. The court stated that if it held valid a British statute that purported to give English courts jurisdiction over foreign residents to order them to appear to defend suits brought against them, then foreign courts could expect no less in return. Short of comity, however, France can no more pass laws binding the world than can England. If the situation were reversed, the French court could not enforce an English judgment similarly rendered.

4) **Comment.** Comity is that body of rules that states observe toward one another from courtesy or mutual convenience, although not a part of international law.

c.   **Early American view.** The requirements of the Fourteenth Amendment were set forth in *Pennoyer v. Neff,* 95 U.S. 714 (1878). There, a personal action (in personam) was brought against the defendant, a nonresident of the state of Oregon who owned land within the state. Service notifying the defendant was by publication only; the defendant did not appear in the action. After judgment was rendered, the land was sold to satisfy the plaintiff's claim. The defendant claimed the court had no jurisdiction. The issue was whether the jurisdictional requirements of Fourteenth Amendment due process were satisfied. It was held that they were not. Fourteenth Amendment due process of law requires that the defendant be given personal service of process within the state for the courts of the state to render a personal judgment (*i.e.*, one enforceable by other state courts) against the defendant. If, however, the court had first attached the defendant's property, it could have exercised in rem jurisdiction over the property since it was within the territory of the court (even though the defendant-owner personally was not). In this situation (an in rem proceeding) constructive service of process (*i.e.*, process served on the defendant outside the state) would have been constitutionally sufficient. Of course, the in rem judgment would decide only the rights in the land—the court would have power only to the extent of the property attached and could affect no other interests of the defendant (*i.e.*, if plaintiff's claim against the defendant exceeded the amount plaintiff received from the sale of the property, plaintiff could not collect this difference based on the Oregon in rem judgment).

C. BASES OF JUDICIAL JURISDICTION OVER NATURAL AND LEGAL PERSONS—IN PERSONAM JURISDICTION

1. **Presence.**

    a. **Introduction.** The traditional basis of jurisdiction of a court over an individual at common law was the defendant's presence within the territorial limits of the state in which the court sat. [*See* Pennoyer v. Neff, *supra*] *Pennoyer* indicates that the only way to get in personam jurisdiction over the defendant is to serve him while he is present within the state. However, this idea has changed so much that now personal jurisdiction may be obtained over persons who are absent from the state, because of the circumstances, may be "fairly" subject to the courts of the state where the suit is brought.

    b. **Temporary presence.** Section 15, Restatement of Judgments (1942): "A court may acquire jurisdiction over an individual by a proper service of process upon him within the state, although he is only temporarily present within the state." For example, in *Peabody v. Hamilton,* 106 Mass. 217 (1870), the defendant, a nonresident, was en route from Nova Scotia to New York. Service was made on him while he was on board ship in Boston harbor. The court upheld jurisdiction; the jurisdiction of the court is complete if service is on the party while he is in the state, no matter how transiently.

    c. **Rationale inadequate.** The rationale of "presence" proved to be an inadequate single basis for the exercise of jurisdiction. It has, therefore, been supplemented by other theories (which are discussed below).

2. **Domicile, Residence, and Nationality.**

    a. **Domicile.** A state may exercise jurisdiction over persons who are domiciled in the state even though they are absent from the state and never personally served with process there.

    1) **Not physically present in domicile state.** In *Milliken v. Meyer*, 311 U.S. 457 (1940), Milliken sued Meyer (a Wyoming resident) in Wyoming but served him with process in Colorado (in accordance with Wyoming statutes) where he was when the suit was filed. The Wyoming court gave judgment to plaintiff; defendant did not appear. When plaintiff sought to enforce the Wyoming judgment in Colorado, the Colorado court refused on the basis that there was a contradiction between the findings of fact (plaintiff had assigned the claim) and the decree (plaintiff recovers). On appeal, the Supreme Court held that the Wyoming court had jurisdiction and the court of Colorado must give the Wyoming judgment full faith and credit. The Colorado court may not look again into the merits of the action, the logic or consistency of the opinion, or the validity of the rules used to reach a conclusion. This is a very convenient rule since it provides that a person can always be sued in at least one place (his domicile) even if he cannot be found there, provided service of process requirements are met.

2) **Service of process requirements.** The requirements of due process must be met with respect to service of process. In *McDonald v. Mabee*, 243 U.S. 90 (1917) (notice was published only in the forum state) the Supreme Court held that publication was not sufficient notice to satisfy due process requirements.

b. **Residence.** "Residence" must be distinguished from "domicile"; nevertheless, residence in a place also represents a substantial connection with that jurisdiction and may be sufficient to confer jurisdiction on the courts there. The Restatement (Second) supports the concept, "unless the individual's relationship to the state is so attenuated as to make the exercise of such jurisdiction unreasonable." This question has not yet been decided by the Supreme Court, however.

c. **Nationality.**

1) **Jurisdiction of the federal courts.** In *Blackmer v. United States,* 284 U.S. 421 (1932), Blackmer, a citizen of the United States domiciled in France, was required to appear as a witness at a trial in the United States under a statute authorizing service of process abroad, for that purpose. The court upheld the statute. Note that this is primarily a legislative jurisdiction case and did not squarely decide the question of the constitutionality of in personam judicial power against absent citizens.

2) **The exercise of state judicial power against citizens abroad.** In *Skiriotes v. Florida*, 313 U.S. 69 (1941), the Supreme Court upheld the application of state legislation to a state's citizen for acts performed outside the borders of the state (on the sea off the coast of the state).

3) **Reasonableness.** The Restatement (Second) indicates that a state has power to exercise judicial jurisdiction over an individual who is a national or citizen of the state, unless the relationship to the state makes the exercise of jurisdiction unreasonable.

3. **Appearance and Consent in Advance.**

a. **Appearance.**

1) **Restatement (Second) section 33.** A state has jurisdiction over an individual who enters an appearance as a defendant in an action in the state (at least for purposes of that particular action).

2) **Restatement (Second) section 81.** A state will not exercise jurisdiction over an individual who appears in an action solely for the purpose of objecting that there is no jurisdiction over him.

b. **Consent.** A valid *in personam* judgment may be rendered against a person who is neither domiciled in the state nor served there if that person has consented to the exercise of jurisdiction over him.

1) **Contractual consent.** In *Gilbert v. Burnstine*, 255 N.Y. 348 (1931), the court found valid consent to jurisdiction where the parties had

agreed in their contract that any dispute on matters concerning the contract would be arbitrated in England.

2) **Due process requirements of notice in confession of judgment note situations.** In *Egley v. T.B. Bennett & Co.,* 196 Ind. 50 (1924), the court upheld the enforcement of an Illinois judgment, even though such a confession of judgment would not have been upheld in Indiana. Defendant had executed a note in Indiana which provided that he appointed any attorney to appear for him in court and authorized the attorney to waive service of process and confess judgment on the note in favor of the payee. The court found that since the contract was performed in Illinois, Illinois law governed validity, and Illinois permitted such judgments.

   a) **Adequate notice.** Due to the current Supreme Court emphasis on "reasonable notice" (even though the required contacts to exercise jurisdiction are becoming less and less) this case might be overruled as a constitutional violation of a defendant's right to adequate notice.

3) **Service on unknown agent.** In *National Equipment Rental, Ltd. v. Szukhent,* 375 U.S. 311 (1964), the Court upheld service on an agent unknown to the defendant (a similar situation to *Egley*). The agent in fact was the plaintiff's wife. However, in this situation the agent apparently had notified the defendant of the proceedings so that due process requirements were fulfilled.

4) **No notice to defendant.** In *Atlas Credit Corp. v. Ezrine,* 25 N.Y.2d 219 (1969), the court refused to enforce a judgment of F1 where the judgment had been rendered without notice to defendant under a power of attorney by which the defendant had empowered "any attorney of any court of record within the United States . . . to appear for them . . . and confess judgment." The court refused to enforce the judgment on the basis of the Full Faith and Credit Clause since the clause requires that enforcement be given only to "judgments" rendered in a "judicial proceeding" and that enforcement in such a situation would be refused since the "procedures" by which the judgment was rendered were repugnant to New York policy.

5) **Model Choice of Forum Act.** Although withdrawn by the Conference of Commissioners on Uniform State Laws, this act dealt with the question of consent, indicating that if the parties had agreed in writing that the action may be brought in a particular state, and if the agreement was the only basis for the exercise of the court's jurisdiction, then the court will exercise jurisdiction only if the following conditions are met:

   a) State law allows the action.

   b) The state is a reasonably convenient forum.

   c) The agreement on jurisdiction was not obtained by fraud, duress, etc.

   d) Defendant (if in the state) was served as required by state law; or if out of the state, was served personally or by registered mail to his last known address.

6) **Appointed or statutory agents.** The material above does not apply to the appointment of an agent for service pursuant to statute or court order.

7) Uniform Consumer Credit Code section 1.201(8). The following provision applies to consumer transactions in states that have adopted the U.C.C.C.:

    a) Each of the following agreements or provisions of an agreement by a consumer who is a resident of this state at the time of a consumer credit transaction is invalid with respect to the transaction:

        (1) That the law of another jurisdiction apply;

        (2) That the consumer consents to be subject to the process of another jurisdiction;

        (3) That the consumer appoints an agent to receive service of process;

        (4) That fixes venue; and

        (5) That the consumer consents to the jurisdiction of the court that does not otherwise have jurisdiction.

4. Local Actions or Local Effects. The common law rule that a person could not be subject to a court's jurisdiction simply because he had committed certain acts in that jurisdiction has been substantially eroded.

    a. **Implied consent.** In *Hess v. Pawloski*, 274 U.S. 352 (1927), the Supreme Court upheld the validity of a state statute's provision for implied consent. The state statute provided that a nonresident by his use of the state's highways consented to service of process on an official of the state in suits brought in that state for injuries sustained in the operation of the nonresident's car in the state.

        1) In *Doherty & Co. v. Goodman*, 294 U.S. 623 (1935), the defendant carried on the business of selling corporate securities in Iowa through a local agent there. An action growing out of an Iowa transaction was brought against him in Iowa under a state statute which provided for "service of process on any agent of a nonresident individual transacting business in the state" for actions growing out of that business. The Supreme Court affirmed the judgment against the defendant.

    b. **"Doing business" and other theories.**

        1) **In general.** The "implied consent" rationale of *Hess* proved too intellectually cramping to encompass the constantly expanding notion of jurisdiction since in many instances where the exercise of jurisdiction was thought proper the defendant in no way could be said to have consented to the local court's jurisdiction. Thus this rationale of "implied consent" gave way to others, all of which have as their basis the idea that jurisdiction should be permitted when it is "reasonable" and "fair," considering all the circumstances.

2) Minimum contacts with the forum state--International Shoe Co. v. State of Washington, 326 U.S. 310 (1945).

a) **Facts.** International Shoe (D) was a Delaware corporation with its principal place of business in Missouri; it employed salesmen living in Washington who were paid by commissions for sales they solicited in the state (but the orders were accepted in St. Louis and mailed from there). The State of Washington (P) sued to collect unemployment fund contributions which were to be contributed by "employers having employees in the state." Service was made on one of D's salesmen (in the state) and also mailed to D's office in St. Louis.

b) **Issue.** Did D's activities in Washington render it subject to jurisdiction in the state within the limitations of Fourteenth Amendment due process?

c) **Held.** Yes. Jurisdiction is upheld.

(1) Whether jurisdiction is proper depends on the facts of each case; it may be upheld when due process is satisfied, which requires that there be certain "minimum contacts" with the forum state such that the exercise of jurisdiction is "reasonable" and "fair" and "traditional standards of fair play" are not violated.

d) **Comment.** The Court enumerated certain factors to be considered in applying its "contacts" test.

(1) The inconvenience to the defendant in defending the suit in the state.

(2) The nature and quality of the acts done in the state. Are they of sufficient concern to the state so that it is "reasonable" for the state to provide the forum?

(3) How extensive and continuous are the defendant's contacts with the state?

e) **"Doing business."** Note that the *International Shoe* corporation was domiciled in Delaware so that it was a foreign corporation doing business in Washington. A corporation can, of course, be sued in the state of its domicile; and many states require, as a condition of doing business in the state, that foreign corporations consent to jurisdiction there by registering and appointing the Secretary of State as agent for service of process. Finally, *International Shoe* added to these theories of jurisdiction by holding that if a corporation had *sufficient contacts* with the state it would be held to be "doing business" there and thus would be subject to local jurisdiction on this basis.

f) **Query.** Can the rationale of *International Shoe* be used in reverse?

(1) *Example*: A, a New York resident, goes to California for a visit; B follows her and serves process on her in California.

(2) Can A succeed on the argument that even though "presence" is a traditional basis of jurisdiction, in this case such a basis of jurisdiction offends "traditional notions of fair play and substantial justice" as

she does not have "sufficient contacts" with California to be subject to the jurisdiction of its courts? The Supreme Court would probably seriously entertain this argument.

3) Application of the *International Shoe* doctrine to acts committed by nonresident individuals. The approach taken by the Supreme Court in *International Shoe* has been extended by the states to a great number of acts committed by nonresident individuals within the state.

    a) "Long arm" statutes. Many states have passed "long arm" statutes which provide for the exercise of jurisdiction over nonresident defendants committing certain acts in the state (such as tortious acts). For example, in *Nelson v. Miller*, 11 Ill. 2d 378 (1957), an employee of a Wisconsin appliance dealer delivered a stove to plaintiff in Illinois. In the course of the unloading the employee's negligence resulted in plaintiff's loss of a finger. The Illinois court sustained a finding of local jurisdiction under the Illinois statute allowing for jurisdiction over those "committing tortious acts within the state."

    b) Constitutional standards. Since the *Shoe* standard seems equally applicable to foreign corporations or nonresident individuals, the relevant question is simply what contacts with a state will satisfy the constitutional standard of "reasonableness" so that a state may exercise jurisdiction?

c. The parameters of the contacts theory. How few contacts and of what nature will satisfy the constitutional standard of sufficient "minimum contacts?" The trend of the courts is clearly to construe "doing business" more and more liberally and to find that fewer and fewer contacts of less and less substantiality are necessary for jurisdiction. The two cases which follow explore the question of how few contacts are enough.

1) Nonresident corporation with contacts through the mail only--McGee v. International Life Insurance Co., 355 U.S. 220 (1957).

McGee v. International Life Insurance Co.

    a) Facts. By letter, International Life (D) offered to insure plaintiff's decedent, a California resident. Plaintiff's decedent (Franklin) accepted the offer and mailed his premiums to Texas. McGee (P) sued in California to collect the amount of the insurance policy after the death of the policyholder; service was by registered mail to D's principal office in Texas. D had no office and no employees located in California. The California court gave judgment for P. P then sought to enforce the California judgment in the Texas courts. The Texas courts refused to enforce the judgment on the basis that the California court had no jurisdiction (service of process outside California violated Fourteenth Amendment due process). The Supreme Court granted certiorari.

    b) Issue. Were there sufficient contacts to support jurisdiction and was service proper?

    c) Held. Yes. The California court had jurisdiction.

(1)   The foreign insurer voluntarily entered the state, was able to calculate its premiums with regard to the risks of doing so, and substantial inconvenience would accrue to the plaintiff in such a situation if she had to go to Texas to bring suit. In short, the suit was proper since the contract had substantial connection (contacts) with the state of California.

d)   **Comment.** Judging from the *McGee* case, there are very few contacts with a state that would prove to be inadequate as a basis for jurisdiction.

2)   **Limitations on unlimited jurisdiction.**

a)   **Query.** Does *McGee* and the trend of decisions mean that any jurisdiction may exercise power over any defendant? Or less extremely, may a court exercise personal jurisdiction as long as it had some (any) connection with the transaction or the defendant? What are the limits of a court's power?

b)   **Insufficient contacts--Hanson v. Denckla,** 357 U.S. 235 (1958).

(1)   **Facts.** Mrs. Douner (Testatrix) died in Florida where her will was probated. Her estate was comprised of assets located in Delaware and supervised by a Delaware corporate trustee whose only contacts with the state of Florida were to send reports and payments (which he was bound to do by contract) to Florida after the beneficiary had moved there. A dispute arose over a power of appointment in the will, which permitted Mrs. Douner to amend the trust by deed or will. She had done that before her death; she set up another trust of $400,000 for one daughter and left the residue of her estate to two other daughters. The two residuary beneficiaries began a declaratory relief action in Florida, serving the executor under the will personally, but not the Delaware trustee nor the other beneficiaries. The executor began a similar action in Delaware (where everyone appeared but one of the daughters with a residuary interest), but the Florida court was first to reach a judgment and enjoined the Delaware court from proceeding further. The Florida court also held that it lacked jurisdiction over the parties (no personal service) and over the trust corpus (located out of state), but held that it had power to deal with the will, that the power of appointment used by Mrs. Douner was testamentary by state law and its exercise had been invalid. Thus, the $400,000 transfer to the one daughter was invalid, and it passed by the will to the other two plaintiff-daughters. The Delaware court refused to enforce the Florida judgment, holding that under Delaware law the transfer was valid. The two cases (Delaware and Florida) went to the Supreme Court.

(2)   **Issue.** Did Florida err in assuming it had jurisdiction over the nonresident defendants, and did Delaware err in refusing full faith and credit to the Florida judgment?

(3)   **Held.** The Florida judgment is in error and the Delaware decision is correct.

(a)   The Florida judgment invalidating the trust was void because the Delaware corporate trustee lacked the required minimum contacts with Florida. The trustee did not voluntarily enter into contact with Florida but was dragged into contact therewith pursuant to its trust duties. This distinguishes *McGee*, where the defendant's contact with California had been voluntary. Therefore, the Delaware court did not err in refusing full faith and credit to the Florida judgment.

(4) **Dissent** (Black, Burton, Brennan, JJ.). In complex situations some jurisdictions must be able to settle things. Here Florida has a "legitimate interest" in doing so as it has contacts with many of the parties and events involved.

(5) **Dissent** (Douglas, J.). This is a suit to determine the parties' interests, not to impose liability on the Delaware trustee or anyone else. The trustee was in privity with the deceased and the Florida court could say the deceased and her executrix may stand in judgment for the trustee regarding the disposition of the property under the power of appointment and the will. I would hold that California had jurisdiction over the absent trustee.

(6) **Comment.** The theories of the dissent may eventually prevail. It is hard to distinguish the "involuntary" contacts of the majority view from similar contacts held to be sufficient in other cases.

d. **Suits or actions not related to local acts.**

1) **Jurisdiction over a nondomiciliary parent of a child domiciled in the forum.** In *Kulko v. Superior Court of California*, 436 U.S. 84 (1978), the state of California asserted personal jurisdiction over a nonresident, nondomiciliary parent (D) of a minor child domiciled in California in a child custody and support action. The Supreme Court reversed. Just because D agreed to the children's presence in California, the Court said, he could hardly be said to have "purposefully availed himself" of the benefits and protections of the laws of California.

2) **Foreseeable use of a product in foreign states--World-Wide Volkswagen Corp. v. Woodson,** 444 U.S. 286 (1980).

World-Wide Volkswagen Corp. v. Woodson

   a) **Facts.** The Robinsons (Ps) purchased a new Audi automobile from Seaway Volkswagen in New York in 1976. The next year the Robinsons moved to Arizona. On their way they were involved in a collision in Oklahoma. Their Audi caught fire when struck from the rear and Ps claim their resulting injuries were caused by defective design and placement of the gas tank and fuel system. Seaway Volkswagen and World-Wide Volkswagen (D), its distributor, appeared specially to contest Oklahoma's jurisdiction as a violation of Fourteenth Amendment due process requirements of "minimum contacts." The trial court and the Oklahoma Supreme Court rejected D's challenge on the grounds that Ps' use of the car in Oklahoma was foreseeable and that D derived "substantial income from cars which from time to time are used" in Oklahoma. The Supreme Court granted certiorari.

b) Issue. Absent some business activity within Oklahoma, does the fact that the cars sold by D might be driven in Oklahoma satisfy the "minimum contacts" standard?

c) Held. No. Judgment reversed.

   (1) Even if D would not be inconvenienced by having to appear, the forum's law probably applies, and the forum is the most convenient place for litigation, the "minimum contacts" standard must be satisfied to grant personal jurisdiction. In this case there is no showing that D carries on any activity in Oklahoma (it closes no sales and performs no services there) or that D derives any privilege or benefit under Oklahoma law. The "foreseeability" of the car being driven in Oklahoma is, by itself, insufficient to grant personal jurisdiction over D. Foreseeability is relevant when D's "conduct and connection with the forum state are such that he should reasonably anticipate being haled into court there." Such is not the case here. The Oklahoma court's contention that D earns substantial revenue from goods used in Oklahoma is not sufficient to establish "minimum contacts" because the financial benefits come from a "collateral relation" with Oklahoma and "do not stem from a constitutionally cognizable contact with that state."

d) Dissent (Brennan, J.). The interests of the forum state and other parties should not be overpowered by D's right to due process when D would suffer no inconvenience. Modern nationalization of commerce and the ease of transportation and communication have altered the constitutional concepts of fairness such that fairness no longer requires the extreme concern for defendants that once was necessary. In light of commercial reality, defendants should not have veto power over certain very appropriate fora.

e) Dissent (Marshall, Blackmun, JJ.). The Court seems to have drawn an artificial distinction which would allow jurisdiction if the product enters the forum state by a foreseeable chain of distribution but deny jurisdiction if the product enters the state in the course of its intended use. Since commercial activity causes effects in a wide sphere, it is fair to require D to answer in states where the effects are felt. D derives an economic benefit and could readily insure against the cost of defending in a distant forum.

Asahi Metal Industry Co. Ltd. v. Superior Court of California

3) Contacts with a foreign state--Asahi Metal Industry Co., Ltd. v. Superior Court of California, 480 U.S. 102 (1987).

a) Facts. Zurcher's (P) motorcycle collided with a tractor in California, killing P's wife. P claimed the accident was caused by the cycle's defective rear tire. Filed in a California court, P's complaint named Cheng Shin (D), the Taiwanese manufacturer of the tire tube, as one of the defendants. D sought indemnification from Asahi, the Japanese manufacturer of the tube's valve assembly. All claims were settled except for D's indemnity claim against Asahi. Tire valve assemblies were manufactured in Japan by Asahi and sold to D and others. The sales to D occurred in Taiwan and other goods were shipped from Japan to Taiwan. Asahi filed a motion to quash summons, which the trial court denied, finding that Asahi did business internationally. The appeals court disagreed and the state supreme court reversed, sustaining jurisdiction under due process even though Asahi had no offices, property, or agents in California; solicited no business there; and made no direct sales there. Asahi appeals.

b) **Issue.** Did the awareness by a foreign manufacturer of component parts that its product would reach an American state constitute sufficient contacts with the state so that the exercise of personal jurisdiction did not offend due process?

c) **Held.** No. Judgment reversed.

(1) Asahi's awareness that the stream of commerce may or would sweep its product into the forum does not constitute a purposeful act directed at the forum. The placement of a product into the stream of commerce, without more, does not indicate an intent or purpose to serve the market in the forum state.

(2) The tests of "fair play" and "substantial justice" are not met here. Asahi would have to traverse a great distance and submit its dispute to a foreign nation's judicial system.

(3) If minimum contacts were established, often the interests of the plaintiff and the forum in the exercise of jurisdiction will justify serious burdens placed on an alien D. In the present case, these interests are slight; all that remains is the indemnification claim. P is not a California resident. The transaction on which the indemnification claim is based took place in Taiwan. D has not demonstrated that it is more convenient for it to litigate its indemnification claim in California rather than Taiwan or Japan.

d) **Concurrence in part** (Brennan, White, Marshall, Blackmun, JJ.). Asahi's conduct was purposeful; however, minimum requirements of "fair play" and "substantial justice" were not met. However, Asahi's regular and extensive sales to a manufacturer in California who Asahi knew was making sales of final products is sufficient to establish minimum contacts.

e) **Concurrence in part** (Stevens, White, Blackmun, JJ.). Asahi's conduct was purposeful; nevertheless, because the minimum requirements of "fair play" and "substantial justice" were not met, the Court need look no further.

4) **Service of process.** In *Omni Capital International v. Rudolf Wolff & Co.*, 484 U.S. 97 (1987), Omni (P) sued British subjects (Ds) in a Louisiana federal court on a federal statutory claim. Ds sought dismissal on the grounds that service of process was not authorized either by an express provision of federal law or by the Louisiana long arm statute. The federal courts dismissed the action on the grounds advanced by Ds. On appeal, the dismissal was affirmed. The Supreme Court held a legislative grant of authority is necessary for a court to add to the scope of service of summons Congress has authorized. Since Congress has the power to limit service of process, circumspection is called for in going beyond what Congress has authorized. Also, since statutes and rules have always provided the measure for service, courts are inappropriate forums for deciding whether to extend them.

5) **Fourteenth Amendment standards.** In *DeJames v. Magnificence Carriers, Inc.*, 654 F.2d 280 (1981), P, a New Jersey longshoreman, was injured while working on a ship moored in New Jersey. Hitachi (D), a Japanese corporation, had converted the ship in Japan from a bulk carrier to an automobile carrier. P sued D in the United States District Court for the District of New Jersey, alleging that the conversion work was defective. Process was served on D in Japan by the Japanese Minister of Foreign Affairs, in accordance with an international treaty. D filed a motion to dismiss for lack of personal jurisdiction, stating that, after completing work on the ship in Japan, it had no further contact with the ship. D also stated that it does not maintain an office, have an agent, or transact any business in New Jersey. The district court dismissed the complaint against D and the court of appeals affirmed. The court found that when service of process in a non-diversity case must be made pursuant to a state long arm statute, the scope of which is limited by the Fourteenth Amendment, amenability to suit in federal district court is limited by that state statute. Therefore, Hitachi's amenability to suit in the New Jersey District Court must be judged by Fourteenth Amendment due process standards. (This anomaly of a federal court being limited by the due process restrictions imposed on the states by the Fourteenth Amendment can only be rectified by Congress, not by the courts.) Due process requires that the defendant have a reasonable expectation that its conduct is such that it may be "haled before a court" in the forum state. Hitachi had no such expectations. It did not utilize the ship it converted to distribute its own product nor did it receive any economic benefit from residents of New Jersey. Any attenuated or derivative benefits it received were insufficient to support personal jurisdiction in New Jersey.

The dissenting opinion stated that it was foreseeable that ships converted by Hitachi would be used to carry Japanese cars to American and New Jersey ports. The Fifth Amendment, upon which this case hinges, only requires the forum to be fair and reasonable and that the defendant have had notice and an opportunity to be heard. It is not necessary under the Fifth Amendment for the defendant's contacts to relate primarily to the location where the suit arose.

6) **Contractual contacts with a foreign state.** In *Lakeside Bridge & Steel Co. v. Mountain State Construction Co., Inc.*, 445 U.S. 907 (1980), P, a Wisconsin corporation, contracted to provide structural assemblies for D, a West Virginia corporation that was building a dam in Virginia. Telephone and mail communications regarding the contract were D's only connection with the state of Wisconsin. D asserted that some of the products delivered by P were defective and withheld part of the purchase price for which P sued in Wisconsin state court. D removed the case to a Wisconsin federal court which entered summary judgment for P. The court of appeals reversed on the grounds that the "minimum contacts" test had not been satisfied. P petitioned for a writ of certiorari in the United States Supreme Court, but the writ was denied. Justice White's dissent addressed the fact that the court should resolve this issue. He noted that the question of personal jurisdiction over a foreign corporate defendant based on contracts with a resident plaintiff is subject to no uniform response in federal or state courts. Such uniformity would facilitate contractual dealings between purchasers and sellers of different states.

7) **Insufficient contacts.** *Fisher Governor Co. v. Superior Court*, 53 Cal. 2d 222 (1959), held in a wrongful death action that where the cause of action is not related to the corporation's activities, much more substantial "contacts" are necessary before a conclusion that the corporation is doing business in the state will be reached. Here, the corporation had independent contractors acting as agents or manufacturer's representatives in California. The death had occurred in Idaho and the defendant was an Iowa corporation.

8) **Conducting local business.** If a foreign corporation (or a nonresident individual) is found to be "doing business" locally, it may be sued there on any cause of action, whether or not that cause of action is related to activities done within the state. [Perkins v. Benguet Consolidated Mining Co., 342 U.S. 437 (1952)]

9) **General in personam jurisdiction--Helicopteros Nacionales de Colombia, S.A. v. Hall,** 466 U.S. 408 (1984).

Helicopteros Nacionales de Colombia, S.A. v. Hall

a) **Facts.** Helicopteros (D) is a Colombian corporation that provided helicopter transportation for companies in South America. D's helicopter crashed in Peru killing four Americans who worked for a Peruvian company with Texas connections. D's contacts with Texas included its negotiation of a portion of the helicopter transportation contract in Texas (though the stated disputes were to be governed by the law of Peru and the contract stated that the parties' residences were in Peru); its acceptance of checks drawn on a Texas bank; its purchase of helicopter equipment in Texas; and the training of some of its helicopter pilots and other company agents in Texas. D never had a permanent presence in Texas, however. Plaintiffs (Ps), the survivors and representative of the decedents, instituted wrongful death actions in a Texas state court and obtained a verdict, which was sustained by the Texas Supreme Court after D's jurisdictional objections were denied. D appeals.

b) **Issue.** Was it consistent with due process to assert in personam jurisdiction over D in Texas?

c) **Held.** No. Judgment reversed. In-state purchases, even if regularly made, and related trips have been found to be insufficient to sustain general jurisdiction. [Perkins v. Benguet Consolidated Mining Co., 342 U.S. 437 (1952)] D had no significant involvement in Texas because of the use by others of a Texas bank.

d) **Dissent** (Brennan, J.). Increasing instances of corporations engaging in commercial transactions throughout the country should trigger in the states broader jurisdictional capabilities. Here, D's activities in Texas included numerous and frequent commercial transactions resulting in numerous benefits. The "minimum contacts" test was met (causing there to be specific in personam jurisdiction), as D's contacts with Texas were "related to" the lawsuit, though they did not "give rise" to the lawsuit.

10) **Libel action against national publication.** In *Keeton v. Hustler Magazine, Inc.,* 465 U.S. 770 (1984), Keeton (P), a New York resident, had sued Hustler Magazine, Inc. (D) in the United States District Court for New Hampshire, claiming that she had been libeled in five separate issues of D's magazine. P sought to recover, under the single publication rule (damages suffered in all jurisdictions for a libel are determined in one action), for damages suffered in all the states that published the magazines. D is an Ohio corporation with its principal place of business in California. Its only contacts with New Hampshire consisted of the sale of 10 to 15 thousand copies of Hustler magazine in the state each month. P's lack of contacts with New Hampshire and the state's unusually

long statute of limitations caused the district court to dismiss for lack of personal jurisdiction and the appeals court to affirm. The appeals court also expressed concern that, although only a small part of P's injury occurred in the state, the New Hampshire court would be required to award damages for injuries suffered in all states.

The Supreme Court found that D's regular circulation of magazines in New Hampshire was sufficient to support an assertion of jurisdiction in a libel action based on the contents of the magazine. The single publication rule, the length of the New Hampshire statute of limitations, and the other factors cited by the court of appeals did not defeat jurisdiction that was otherwise proper under both New Hampshire law and the Due Process Clause. The Court stated that New Hampshire had a substantial interest in cooperating with other states through the single publication rule to provide a forum for efficiently litigating all issues and damage claims arising out of a libel in a unitary proceeding. Any potential unfairness that might have arisen from applying New Hampshire's statute of limitations in this nationwide suit when the statutes of limitations had run in every other jurisdiction had nothing to do with the court's jurisdiction. The question of the applicability of New Hampshire's statute of limitations to claims for out-of-state damages only arose after jurisdiction had been established.

11) **Insufficient contacts.** In *Bryant v. Finnish Airlines,* 15 N.Y.2d 426 (1965), a Finnish airline was held subject to jurisdiction in New York by a New York resident who was injured in Paris by the alleged negligence of the airline. The basis was that the airline was "doing business in New York." The only activity the airline had in New York was receiving reservations for travel in Europe and advertising the airline's European services. Clearly the airline's activities in New York were unrelated to plaintiff's cause of action.

Volkswagen-
werk Aktien-
gesellschaft
v. Schlunk

12) **"Derivative" jurisdiction over foreign corporations--Volkswagenwerk Aktiengesellschaft v. Schlunk,** 486 U.S. 694 (1988).

a) **Facts.** In 1983, Schlunk (P) filed a wrongful death action in Illinois on behalf of his parents after they were killed in an automobile accident. P alleged Volkswagen of America ("VWoA") had designed and sold the defective automobile that contributed to the deaths. VWoA denied designing or assembling the defective automobile. P then amended his complaint adding Volkswagen Aktiengesellschaft ("VWAG"), a German corporation that wholly owned VWoA. VWAG was served by serving VWoA as VWAG's agent under Illinois law. VWAG moved to quash service, arguing it could only be served in accordance with the Hague Convention, to which both the United States and Germany were parties and which covered complaints transmitted for "service abroad." The Illinois circuit court denied VWAG's motion. The appellate court affirmed and the supreme court denied leave to appeal. The United States Supreme Court granted certiorari.

b) **Issue.** If service on a domestic agent of a foreign corporation in America is valid under state and federal law, does the Hague Convention provide further limits on service?

c) **Held.** No. Judgment affirmed.

(1)   Jurisdiction over VWAG was proper. The Convention did not define what was meant by service abroad, so the internal law of the forum state must be applied. Under Illinois law, even without service abroad, a foreign national is assured of notice reasonably calculated, under all the circumstances, to apprise it of the pendency of the action. The Illinois long arm statute allowed P to serve VWAG by substituted service without sending documents to Germany.

e.   **Summary of jurisdiction.**

1)   **Related activities.** Despite the *Bryant* case, *supra*, if the jurisdictional basis is the doing of a single act in the state, or involvement that does not amount to the doing of business, jurisdiction is generally limited to claims that arise out of, or are closely related to, the act or activity.

2)   **Interest of forum.** The Restatement (Second) indicates that a state has jurisdiction over a person who does any tortious act in the state with respect to a claim arising from the act. As to other acts, the state also has jurisdiction unless the nature of the act and of the individual's relationship to the state make the exercise of jurisdiction unreasonable. Thus, it appears that the existence of jurisdiction depends, at least in part, on the extent of the state's interest in trying a claim arising from an act in the state.

3)   **The basic test.** The basic test is composed of two parts, both of which aim at establishing whether the nature of defendant's activities is such that it is fair and reasonable to expect him to appear in the forum and defend the action.

   a)   **Meaningful contact.** The defendant must have intentionally engaged in some activity in the forum state by which:

      (1)   He obtained benefits from the forum state; or

      (2)   He relied on the protection of the forum's laws.

   b)   **Quality of defendant's acts as well as their number.** In *Buckeye Boiler Co. v. Superior Court of Los Angeles County*, 71 Cal. 2d 893 (1969), defendant's only activity in California was that defendant sold its tanks to a manufacturer in California who used them as sub parts. Plaintiff was injured when one of D's tanks exploded. The court found that defendant was engaging in intentional, foreseeable economic activity in the state and was therefore subject to jurisdiction.

   c)   **Reasonableness.** The forum state must also be a reasonable place for the trial. The same factors considered in a forum non conveniens issue are considered:

      (1)   Hardships to nonresident defendant in having to appear and defend himself locally;

      (2)   Hardships to plaintiff in having to litigate elsewhere;

(3)   Interest of the forum state in the litigation or in regulating the activities involved. *See McGee, supra.*

5.   **Illustrations of Jurisdiction over Natural and Legal Persons.** The following hypotheticals are designed to illustrate the preceding material on jurisdiction.

   a.   **Analysis.** Two questions must always be asked.

      1)   First, is the fact situation covered by the state's statute? That is, is the court, by its own law, authorized to act?

      2)   Second, if it is, does the reach of the state law exceed permissible constitutional limits?

   b.   **Hypothetical.** For example:

Y	X		
A	B		

Facts: A writes B offering to sell him 1,000 widgets. B sends a letter accepting A's offer. A breaches the contract. Can B sue A in state X?

      1)   Does the jurisdictional statute of state X cover the fact situation?

         a)   Suppose that X's "long arm" statute provides that "the transaction of any business within this state" is a sufficient basis for local jurisdiction.

         b)   Suppose B brings suit in X. What can A do? After service of process A can:

            (1)   Make a special appearance before the X court and challenge whether the fact situation is covered by the X statute. If A does this she cannot later collaterally attack the X judgment on the question of jurisdiction. If A loses in the trial courts she can appeal through state X's appellate courts, but no further—state courts are the final arbiters of the meaning of their own state laws.

            (2)   A could refuse to appear and take a default judgment in X. If A does this she loses any chance to contest the case on the merits. But when the X judgment is brought to state Y for enforcement, A can collaterally attack the X courts' finding of jurisdiction under the statute. In this event, Y courts will be interpreting the scope of the X statutes. Therefore, in the event B loses in the trial court he can appear through Y's appellate court structure, and if he loses, the United States Supreme Court will review the judgment as a full faith and credit question. The Supreme Court, while saying it will only review Y's judgment, will actually substitute its own judgment as to what the X law really is.

      2)   Suppose the state X law says: "jurisdiction arises from entering into a contract for services to be rendered or for materials furnished in this

state." There is no question but that here the X statute covers the fact situation. The question is now whether X can constitutionally require A to come in and litigate in state X. Again A can make a special appearance to contest jurisdiction on this question or take a default judgment and then attack the judgment collaterally.

    a)   This hypothetical is closely analogous to the *McGee* case.

    b)   What if B solicited the order from A and then A made the offer which B accepted? Suppose the insurance company in *McGee* had brought an action in Texas for a declaratory judgment of its nonliability? The Texas court would have been exercising jurisdiction over the California beneficiary. Could it? In this situation the *Hanson* case might be a basis for finding no jurisdiction (but probably not).

c.   **Partnerships and associations.** Partnerships raise special points. The Restatement (Second) indicates that if a partnership or association is subject to suit in the firm name in a particular state, that state may exercise jurisdiction over the partnership or association if, under the circumstances, it could exercise jurisdiction over an individual. A valid judgment is a "binding adjudication as to the liability of the partnership or association with respect to its assets in every state." Full faith and credit requires that other states recognize and enforce a valid judgment if the partnership or association is subject to the judicial jurisdiction of the state and may be sued in the state in its firm name.

d.   **Product liability and other tort cases.**

    1)   **Hypothetical.** D, an auto tire manufacturer, gets a bulk order from Sears in Ohio and fills the order. Sears ships part of the tires to its outlet in X, which sells one to P, and P is injured from a defect in the tire. Can P sue D in X?

        a)   Some state statutes purport to cover this situation: "products, materials or things processed by the defendant were used or consumed within this state in the ordinary course of trade."

        b)   A New York state statute was passed that purports to subject to personal jurisdiction a nondomiciliary who, in person or by agent, commits a tortious act outside the state causing injury to person or property within the state, except as to a cause of action for defamation of character arising from the act if he:

            (1)   Regularly does or solicits business, or engages in any other persistent course of conduct, or derives substantial revenue from goods used or consumed or services rendered in the state, or

            (2)   Expects or should reasonably expect the act to have consequences in the state and derives substantial revenue from interstate or international commerce.

        c)   Question: Assuming that events have transpired over a period of time in which there is a causal connection in fact between D in one state and injury to P in another, what is the legal right of the state where P is injured to exercise jurisdiction over D?

(1) There are three kinds of cases:

   (a) D authorizes his agent to act for him in another state (or intentionally sends his product there).

   (b) D can reasonably foresee that his agent might or will end up in another state (or that his product could be sent there) but he never intentionally sends his agent (or product) there.

   (c) However unlikely it is that the agent or product will end up in another state, it does and injury results (D neither intends it nor foresees it).

(2) Query: Where should the line on jurisdiction be drawn? Are there any reasons not to allow jurisdiction in any forum once notice is given? If so, what are these reasons? How are rational lines drawn for allowing or not allowing jurisdiction? More and more courts are permitting jurisdiction in situations such as (c) above.

2) Limitation in defamation cases. First Amendment (free speech) considerations may require a greater showing of "contact" to satisfy the process in defamation cases than in connection with other kinds of torts to protect nonresident publishers from being subjected to personal jurisdiction in every state where their publications are read.

6. Summary. The states, through their jurisdiction statutes and the constitutional cases on the permissible extent of power to exercise jurisdiction, are moving in an ever more liberal trend toward permitting a court to exercise jurisdiction in any case where the required notice has been given the adverse party. Of course, as the cases and comments above indicate, there are still some limitations.

Constitutionally speaking, in view of the Supreme Court's decision in *McGee*, all that seems necessary for a court to exercise jurisdiction is some purposeful, substantial contact between the nonresident and the forum state, regardless of whether the defendant is "present" or has committed any act "within" the state in a realistic sense.

a. If the nonresident's activities are sufficiently continuous and systematic, he can be said to be domiciled or "doing business" locally and he may be held liable in any cause of action whether or not it is related to his activities in the state.

b. If the nonresident's activities are not substantial enough to consider him as "doing business" in the state, the cause of action must be related to whatever activities or contacts were had with the forum state.

Burnham v. Superior Court of California

7. Transient Jurisdiction--Burnham v. Superior Court of California, 495 U.S. 604 (1990).

a. **Facts.** During a trip to California to conduct business and visit his children, petitioner Burnham (P), a New Jersey resident, was served with a California court summons and a copy of his estranged wife's divorce petition. P moved to quash the service of process on the ground that the court lacked personal jurisdiction over him because his only contacts with California were a few short visits for the purposes of conducting business and visiting his children. The superior court denied the motion and the court of appeals denied mandamus relief. The Supreme Court granted certiorari.

b.   **Issue.**   Does the Due Process Clause prohibit California courts from exercising jurisdiction over a nonresident who was personally served with process while temporarily in that state in a suit unrelated to his activities in the state?

c.   **Held.**   No. Judgment affirmed.

   1)   Jurisdiction based on physical presence alone constitutes due process because it is one of the continuing traditions of the legal system which define the due process standard of "traditional notions of fair play and substantial justice." Many recent cases reaffirm in-state service.

d.   **Concurrence in part and in the judgment** (White, J.).   Although the Court has authority under the Fourteenth Amendment to review and declare invalid even traditionally accepted procedures, there has been no showing here or elsewhere that the rule is so arbitrary and lacking in common sense that it should be held in violation of due process.

e.   **Concurrence in the judgment** (Brennan, Marshall, Blackmun, O'Connor, JJ.).   The Fourteenth Amendment Due Process Clause permits the exercise of jurisdiction over a defendant served while voluntarily in a state; however, an independent inquiry is not precluded here merely because the prevailing in-state service rule has a historical pedigree. By visiting a state, a defendant avails himself of health and safety services, benefits from the fruits of the state's economy, and is not denied the protection of its laws. Without transient jurisdiction, the transient would have full benefit of the courts as plaintiff while retaining immunity as defendant.

f.   **Concurrence** (Stevens, J.).   All of the above opinions demonstrate that "this is, indeed, a very easy case."

8.   **Continuance of Jurisdiction.**

a.   **General rule.**   Once personal jurisdiction has been obtained it continues with respect to all subsequent proceedings arising out of the original suit (for example, appeals, etc.).

   1)   **Continuing jurisdiction over probate proceeding--Michigan Trust Co. v. Ferry,** 228 U.S. 346 (1913).

      a)   **Facts.**   William Ferry died in 1867, domiciled in Michigan. Initial probate proceedings were begun in Michigan in 1867; the defendant was appointed executor. Defendant subsequently moved to Utah and became incompetent. In 1903, an action was brought by the residuary legatees in a Michigan court to oust defendant as executor, to appoint the Michigan Trust

Michigan
Trust Co.
v. Ferry

Company as a new executor, and for a final accounting. The Michigan court granted relief to plaintiffs, who then sought to enforce the judgment in the federal district court in Utah, which dismissed the action on defendant's demurrer. The circuit court affirmed, and the case went to the Supreme Court.

b) **Issue.** Did the Michigan court have jurisdiction over the defendant in his role as executor of the estate?

c) **Held.** Yes. Michigan has continuing jurisdiction over the defendant as the executor of the estate until a final judgment is entered in the probate proceeding.

d) **Comment.** *Ferry* is the old common law rule; it is unlikely that it will continue to hold up in all situations under modern conditions.

D. JURISDICTION OVER "THINGS"

1. Types of Jurisdiction.

a. **Introduction.** Every valid exercise of judicial jurisdiction affects the interests of persons. It is possible, however, to affect the interests of persons in different ways and it therefore may be useful to divide the subject of judicial jurisdiction into three main categories: jurisdiction over persons (discussed *supra*), jurisdiction over things, and jurisdiction over status. These are the old common law distinctions.

b. **In personam jurisdiction.** When one or more of the various bases for the exercise of judicial jurisdiction over persons exist (these bases have just been discussed above), a personal judgment can be rendered against the defendant. The effect of such a judgment, if it is one for money, is to make D a judgment debtor of P. This debt can be enforced against any property subject to execution which D then owns or subsequently acquires; an action to recover this debt may likewise be maintained against D, either in the same state or in any other state. A personal judgment may also take the form of an equitable decree ordering the defendant either to do something or to refrain from action. In such a case, D may be punished for contempt if he fails to obey the court's (F1) order.

c. **In rem jurisdiction.**

1) **In general.** Even though personal jurisdiction over D is lacking, the state can affect any interests D may have in things subject to its jurisdiction (because the things are located in the state, even if D is not). A judgment rendered in such a proceeding binds only interests in the specific thing at which it is directed. All that D risks in such a proceeding is the loss of his interests therein. An in personam judgment, on the other hand, can be enforced against any and all of D's property, wherever it is located.

2) **Persons affected.** If a thing is subject to the judicial jurisdiction of a state, an action may be brought to affect the interests in that thing of any and all persons in the world (in rem). Or, as is usually the case, the action may be brought to affect the interests in the thing of particular persons only, in which case it is called a proceeding quasi in rem.

3) **Example.** A proceeding in a court with admiralty jurisdiction to enforce a maritime lien upon a vessel is a proceeding in rem (jurisdiction over a thing), and a valid judgment directing the sale, and the sale in pursuance of the judgment, are binding on the whole world.

d. **Quasi in rem jurisdiction: Two types of proceedings.**

1) **Plaintiff asserts interest in thing.** In the first type the plaintiff asserts an interest in a thing, and seeks to have her interest established against the claim of a designated person or persons. Included in this type of action are actions to recover possession of land or to establish title to land (such as an action of ejectment, or one to quiet title or to remove a cloud on title) if the court has jurisdiction to give the relief asked for because of its power over the land.

2) **Plaintiff asserts claim against defendant personally.** In the second type of proceeding quasi in rem, the plaintiff does not assert that she has an interest in the thing, but asserts a claim against the defendant personally and seeks, by prior attachment or garnishment of some thing, to apply the thing to the satisfaction of her claim against the defendant.

e. **Summary.** Even without personal jurisdiction over the defendant a state can still affect any interests he may have in things which are subject to its jurisdiction. Jurisdiction over these things may be obtained in two ways: (i) in rem, and (ii) quasi in rem. "Things" may take the form of (i) land, (ii) chattels, or (iii) intangibles.

2. **Land.**

a. **Specific performance of sales contracts.** If the court does not have personal jurisdiction over the purchaser of the land, which land is within its jurisdiction, it cannot enforce specific performance (which is an in personam action) against him; it can, however, remove the cloud on the title of the seller in an action in rem since this type of action affects only the land (the thing).

b. **Ancillary determination of personal rights.**

1) **In rem jurisdiction not a basis for affecting personal rights.** In rem jurisdiction will not enable a court to affect personal interests in the parties; this can only be done if the court has a sufficient basis for personal jurisdiction. So, for example, if the court has in rem jurisdiction over property within its borders, this does not permit it to decide, in addition, any personal rights between the parties.

2) Must have personal jurisdiction--Combs v. Combs, 249 Ky. 155 (1933).

   a) **Facts.** Combs (D), a Kentucky resident, was sued in a personal judgment suit for the amount of a debt owing, by his brother (P). D borrowed a substantial amount from P and secured the loan with land situated in Arkansas. P was a resident of neither Kentucky nor Arkansas. P tried but was not able for a period of time to serve personal process on D. In the meantime D filed an equity suit in an Arkansas court against P by constructive process in accordance with the prescribed practices of Arkansas. No personal service was had on P in Arkansas. D set forth the facts creating the indebtedness and petitioned the Arkansas court to allow him to pay to the court the stated amount unpaid on the loan, to be followed by a decree canceling the lien on his land which would remove the cloud on the title. The Arkansas court granted the petition. D then procured a copy of the Arkansas proceeding and filed his answer in the Kentucky action, relying upon the Arkansas judgment to bar recovery. D appeals the disallowance of the defense and the judgment for the amount found to be due.

   b) **Issue.** Must a sister state give full faith and credit to a personal judgment rendered in another state if that state only had in rem jurisdiction?

   c) **Held.** No. The Arkansas judgment is entitled to full faith and credit and has res judicata effect only when the Arkansas court rendering the judgment had competent jurisdiction over the subject matter and the parties.

      (1) The Arkansas court was vested with the authority to release the lien on the land within its jurisdiction thereby clearing the cloud on the title. This is binding on P. Although Arkansas could make a determination of the amount owed by D to P incidental to the lien release, the only binding effect of such adjudication would be that of releasing the lien as an encumbrance upon the title to the property. Such adjudication, insofar as it affected the personal obligations and rights of the parties, was not and is not binding upon P (for lack of personal jurisdiction) and it does not operate as res judicata in any future action.

   d) **Comment.** This is an attempt to enforce a quasi in rem judgment rendered in another jurisdiction. Quasi in rem judgments are not enforceable in sister states unless the court had jurisdiction over the parties. The same is true of in rem judgments.

   c. **Actions when land is outside the court's jurisdiction.** In *Massie v. Watts*, 6 Cranch 148 (1810), Chief Justice Marshall declared that although title to land will normally be governed by the courts of the situs of the land, if the land is the object of a contract action, an action for constructive trust, or an action for fraud, any court having personal jurisdiction over the parties may render judgment that affects title to the land. A court has power to deal with property located in other jurisdictions only if the owner of the property is before the court (*i.e.*, if the court has personal jurisdiction over the owner). Thus, a court with such jurisdiction may order the owner to convey land which is located outside the jurisdiction.

3. **Chattels.**

    a. **Introduction.** The rules here are similar to those for real property. Therefore, if a person has property within the state then the courts of that state can subject this property to in rem jurisdiction (deciding interests or rights in the property) even though the court has no personal jurisdiction over the owner thereof.

    b. **Popcorn--Martin v. Better Taste Popcorn Co.,** 89 F. Supp. 754 (S.D. Iowa 1950).

        1) **Facts.** Martin (P) brought an action in an Iowa state court to partition personal property, located in Iowa, in the custody of Better Taste Popcorn Co. (D), an Indiana corporation. P petitioned the Iowa court for the appointment of a referee to take custody of and preserve 4½ million pounds of popcorn and for an order to determine proper ownership to a portion of the popcorn. P made personal service on D in Indiana pursuant to the state court's order that allowed D five days to appear. No other parties interested in the stored popcorn who did not reside within Iowa were served. D moved the case to federal district court in Iowa. D attacks jurisdiction for insufficiency of process and service under state law and also for lack of jurisdiction of the subject matter because there were owners of interests in the popcorn who had not been joined as parties, also in violation of the requirement of state law.

        2) **Issue.** May the forum court where personal property is located adjudicate ownership of such property without obtaining personal jurisdiction over interested parties?

        3) **Held.** Yes.

            a) Every state has uncontrolled jurisdiction over all property, real or personal, within its borders. Therefore, although a nonresident does not come within the territorial limits of a state, if he owns property therein the courts may acquire jurisdiction thereof which may be exercised on such property. Where property of a nonresident is thus brought within the jurisdiction of the court, notice of the proceedings may be given by publication, since the theory of the law is that the owner is always in possession of his property and that its seizure will warn him to look after his interests. However, personal judgment cannot be rendered against such defendant and the court has jurisdiction only to the extent of adjudicating the interest in the thing itself; that is, in the res or the property located within the state. Before final judgment can be entered, all interested parties having claims in or liens on the property must be joined as plaintiffs or defendants, which can be accomplished by at least actual notice and, if appropriate, constructive notice by publication.

4. **Intangibles.**

    a. **Introduction.** The real problems come in the cases involving intangibles or choses in action (*i.e.*, obligations of one party to another, enforceable by that other, such as a debt). There is no thing involved—just enforceable rights. Hence, there is no situs or physical location as with real property or chattels. Nevertheless, courts have developed certain concepts of jurisdiction, based on fictional situs, by analogy to the concepts used in the real property and chattels cases.

b. Pure intangible interests.

Harris v. Balk

1) A debt follows the debtor: Physical presence of the debtor is where the debt is--Harris v. Balk, 198 U.S. 215 (1905).

a) Facts. Harris and Balk both lived in North Carolina. Harris owed Balk $180. Epstein lived in Maryland and was owed $300 by Balk. Harris came to Maryland where Epstein sued Balk (his debtor) attaching the debt that Harris owed Balk in a quasi in rem cause of action. When Harris returned to North Carolina, Balk sued him for the $180; Harris pled the Maryland judgment.

<table>
<tr><td>North Carolina</td><td>Maryland</td></tr>
<tr><td>Harris</td><td>Epstein</td></tr>
<tr><td>Balk</td><td></td></tr>
<tr><td>(Suit #2) B v. H.</td><td>(Suit #1) E v. B.</td></tr>
</table>

b) Issue. Can a court acquire jurisdiction over a debt through a debtor who is temporarily in the state?

c) Held. Yes.

(1) The North Carolina court must give the Maryland judgment full faith and credit and therefore Balk cannot collect from Harris. The debt follows the debtor wherever he goes, for purposes of garnishment. Therefore the Maryland court had proper jurisdiction over the thing (the debt) when it rendered its judgment. Of course, for due process not to be violated, some type of notice (even if only constructive notice) must be given in the action to the absent party so that he can come in and protect the res (the debt that he is owed and that is being garnished).

2) Seizure of the res. The basis for quasi in rem jurisdiction is the seizure of the nonresident's property or subjecting it to court control through levy of writ of attachment, garnishment, or sequestration.

a) Levy. Normally levy is made at the commencement of the action, although it may be made at any time prior to entry of judgment, provided that other adequate notice of the pendency of the action has been afforded the nonresident defendant.

b) Prejudgment wage garnishment. In *Sniadach v. Family Finance Corp.,* 395 U.S. 337 (1969), Family Finance Corp. (P) instituted garnishment proceedings against Sniadach (D) and her employer under the Wisconsin Garnishment Act, which provided for the freezing of wages of a debtor-defendant without affording her opportunity to be heard or to offer defenses. D moved to dismiss the action on the ground that the statutory procedure failed to satisfy the due process and equal protection requirements of the Fourteenth Amendment. The trial court upheld the constitutionality of the prejudgment statute and the Wisconsin Supreme Court affirmed; D appealed to the United States Supreme Court, which found that a state procedure for garnishing the wages of an alleged debtor prior to a hearing is a violation of Fourteenth Amendment due process. The Wisconsin prejudgment garnishment procedure deprived the defendant debtor of her property without a prior hearing, thus violating the Due Process Clause of the Fourteenth Amendment. The Court reviewed the hardships caused by the prejudgment garnishment and concluded that a prejudgment garnishment of the Wisconsin type may, as a practical matter, "drive a wage earning family to the wall, thus violating the fundamental principles of due process." Here the debtor was deprived of the use of the garnished portion of her wages during the interim period between the garnishment and the culmination of the main suit.

(1) **Comment.** *Sniadach* involved a claim against a resident defendant, who was subject to personal jurisdiction. It is not clear whether the same result would be reached in an action against a nonresident, but lower courts have held that such summary attachment is proper.

(2) **State laws.** In response to *Sniadach*, some states have revised their laws to prohibit prejudgment attachment or garnishment (thus there is no quasi in rem jurisdiction). Most states now restrict attachments against residents, but still permit it in actions against nonresidents.

3) **Determining conflicting claims to a debt--New York Life Insurance Co. v. Dunlevy, 241 U.S. 518 (1916).**

New York Life Insurance Co. v. Dunlevy

a) **Facts.** In 1907, Boggs and Bull obtained a valid personal judgment against Dunlevy in Pennsylvania. During 1909, New York Life became liable for the monetary value of an insurance policy on the life of Gould, Dunlevy's father. Both Gould and Dunlevy claimed the money, Dunlevy claiming it belonged to her because of a valid assignment of the policy to her by her father. Boggs and Bull caused the issue of an execution attachment on their judgment of 1907, and both New York Life and Gould were summoned as garnishees. The insurance company admitted its indebtedness, paid the proceeds into court, and filed a petition for an interpleader to force the parties to interplead and thereby determine who was lawfully entitled to the proceeds. Dunlevy was notified in California, but she failed to appear. The case was tried without her, and the jury found that there was no valid assignment, whereupon the court ordered the proceeds paid to Gould.

Dunlevy, in the present case, brought suit in California against Gould and the insurance company for the value of the policy. The company pleaded that she was barred by the proceedings in Pennsylvania and that the Pennsylvania court had jurisdiction over her by virtue of the original action of 1907 by Boggs and Bull. The district court entered judgment for Dunlevy, and the court of appeals affirmed. New York Life now appeals.

b) **Issue.** Must a court have jurisdiction over a person in an interpleader action for the judgment to be valid against that person?

c)   Held. Yes. Judgment affirmed.

    (1)   Although in garnishment proceedings, the Pennsylvania court, without necessity of personal service on Dunlevy, had power to inquire whether Dunlevy held a valid claim against the insurance company, and, if found to exist, then to condemn and appropriate it so far as necessary to discharge the original judgment against Dunlevy, an interpleader is an altogether different matter. This was an attempt to bring about a final and conclusive adjudication of her personal rights, not merely to discover property and apply it to debts. Unless she was before the court and required to respond to that issue, its orders and judgments in respect thereto were not binding on her.

    (2)   The general rule is that any personal judgment which a state court may render against one who did not voluntarily submit to its jurisdiction, and who is not a citizen of the state, nor served with process within its borders, no matter what the mode of service, is void, because the court had no jurisdiction over the person.

    (3)   The interpleader proceedings were not essential concomitants of the original action by Boggs and Bull against Dunlevy, but plainly collateral; and, when summoned to respond to Boggs's action, Dunlevy was not required to anticipate the interpleader proceedings.

    (4)   The proceedings in Pennsylvania constituted no bar to the action in California.

d)   Comment. Under *Harris v. Balk*, had it been clear that New York Life owed the money to Dunlevy, then Boggs and Bull could have attached the debt by obtaining quasi in rem jurisdiction over the debtor.

4)   Reconsideration of the bases for jurisdiction.

a)   Introduction. Thus far the cases seem to indicate that if a defendant has any substantial contacts with a forum state she is amenable to suit there. However, there are some opinions where the Supreme Court has seemed to draw back from this position.

b)   Applications.

Shaffer v.
Heitner

(1)   The fairness approach--Shaffer v. Heitner, 433 U.S. 186 (1977).

    (a)   Facts. Heitner (P) brought a shareholder derivative suit against the Greyhound corporation, a subsidiary, and 28 officers and directors (Ds) for their actions resulting in damages paid out in antitrust and criminal contempt actions against the corporation. P petitioned to sequester the Delaware property of Ds (stock in the Delaware corporation); the court then "seized" the securities of 21 of the Ds by placing stop orders on transfer, and then the court exercised quasi in rem jurisdiction (based on the "statutory presence" of the securities in Delaware). Ds appeal.

(b) Issue. Does a Delaware court acquire jurisdiction over nonresident Ds solely by sequestering their securities of a Delaware corporation?

(c) Held. No. Judgment reversed. Ds are not subject to Delaware jurisdiction.

    1] *International Shoe's* minimum contacts standard applies here because the property sequestered is unrelated to the action.

    2] The fiduciary duty to a Delaware corporation is an insufficient contact with Delaware to establish jurisdiction absent a state law making acceptance of a corporate position a consent to jurisdiction.

(d) Concurrence (Powell, J.). I reserve judgment only on whether the ownership of some forms of property permanently located within a state may, without more, provide sufficient contacts to subject a defendant to jurisdiction within the state to the extent of the value of the property.

(e) Concurrence (Stevens, J.). The Delaware statute creates an unacceptable risk of judgment without notice. In addition, the statute denies the defendant the opportunity to defend on the merits unless he subjects himself to the unlimited jurisdiction of the court.

(f) Concurrence and dissent (Brennan, J.). Under the minimum contacts analysis, Delaware's interests in insuring a convenient forum for litigating derivative lawsuits potentially involving a multiplicity of defendant fiduciaries do not foreclose it from asserting jurisdiction.

(g) Comment. This case may well signal the end of quasi in rem jurisdiction, at least if "minimum contacts" are not present. If "minimum contacts" are present, the forum court will have personal jurisdiction and will not need to rely on quasi in rem jurisdiction.

(2) Current application of "minimum contacts" as applied to the insurer of a foreign defendant--Rush v. Savchuk, 444 U.S. 320 (1980).

> Rush v.
> Savchuk

    (a) Facts. In 1972, Savchuk (P), a passenger in Rush's (D's) car, was injured in a collision in Indiana, D's state of residence. State Farm Insurance was D's insurer under a policy issued in Indiana. P moved to Minnesota in 1973 and commenced an action for negligence in the Minnesota courts. The Minnesota court had no grounds for personal jurisdiction over D, but P attempted to establish quasi in rem jurisdiction by garnishing State Farm's obligation to indemnify and defend D. P's motion to make State Farm a party to the action was granted, despite D's and State Farm's objection that Minnesota lacked personal jurisdiction over D. The Minnesota Supreme Court affirmed this decision on the grounds that the insurance policy was a "garnishable res" in Minnesota for purposes of obtaining quasi in rem jurisdiction over State Farm, D's liability was limited to the amount of the policy, and Minnesota had an interest in providing a forum for its residents. D appealed to the United States Supreme Court, which vacated the judgment and remanded for further consideration in light of the *Shaffer v. Heitner* case. The Minnesota Supreme Court decided that "due process" requirements had been met since the garnished property was intimately related to the litigation and the state had an interest in "facilitating recoveries for resident plaintiffs." D appeals.

(b) Issue. Absent "minimum contacts" between D and the forum, can a state constitutionally exercise quasi in rem jurisdiction over D by attaching the contractual obligation of an insurer licensed to do business within the forum?

(c) Held. No. Judgment reversed. Minnesota lacked jurisdiction over D.

1] Minimum contacts are required in order to exercise jurisdiction over D. D has no affiliation with Minnesota other than that D's insurer is licensed to do business there. "Mere presence of property in a state does not establish a sufficient relationship between the owner of the property and the state to support the exercise of jurisdiction over an unrelated cause of action." State Farm's business activities in Minnesota are unrelated to P's interest in D's insurance policy. P's contacts with Minnesota should not be decisive in determining whether D's due process rights have been violated.

(d) Dissent (Stevens, J.). The Minnesota statute authorizing jurisdiction is the "functional equivalent" of a "direct action statute" so long as the forum may not exercise any power over D—that is, the judgment can be enforced only against the proceeds of the insurance policy.

(e) Dissent (Brennan, J.). Minnesota is an interested and convenient forum since P is a resident and P's action could be precluded if P were forced to travel to a distant state to prosecute his claim. In addition, D's burden of defending in Minnesota is slight because the real impact is on the insurer who is "concededly amenable" to suit in Minnesota and D's burden is no greater than it would be under a permissible "direct action" statute.

Also, State Farm's business in Minnesota is related to this cause of action because, by purchasing a State Farm policy, D availed himself of the benefits of having an agent in Minnesota who could sue in Minnesota. It is unreasonable to allow D "to take advantage of his nationwide insurance network but not be burdened by it."

E. COMPETENCE OF COURT AND NOTICE

1. Competence.

a. Restatement. A judgment is void if it is not rendered by a court with competency to render it.

1) **Competency.** Even though a state in which a judgment is rendered constitutionally and actually has jurisdiction over the defendant, a court of the state in fact has no jurisdiction to render a judgment if the state has not given its courts the power to entertain the action. In such a case the court has no "competency" to render a valid judgment, and such a judgment will not be recognized or enforced in other states.

2) **Local law.** If a state has jurisdiction, the question of whether a court of the state has competency to render a judgment in an action is a question of the local law of the state in which the judgment is rendered. If by that law the court has power to render the judgment, the judgment is valid and cannot be collaterally attacked (*i.e.*, attacked by the defendant in a separate action to enforce the judgment) in that state or in another state. If, however, the court in F1 is incompetent by its own standards, then any judgment it renders is void and may be collaterally attacked.

3) **Note.** A defendant who does not appear in the F1 action may later collaterally attack the F1 court's finding of its own competency. If, however, defendant appears in the F1 proceedings, the findings of the F1 court on the competency question are res judicata. This is true whether the actual question of competency was raised or not in F1 (as long as defendant had the opportunity to raise the question).

b. **Contesting foreign determination of jurisdictional facts--Thompson v. Whitman, 85 U.S. 457 (1874).**

1) **Facts.** In proceedings brought by Whitman in F2 (New York district court) the finding of jurisdiction made by F1 (New Jersey state court; brought by the Sheriff of Monmouth County, when he had plaintiff's ship seized for illegal fishing), which had rendered a judgment against the now plaintiff in F2, was challenged by attacking the adequacy of F1's findings of fact on which it based its jurisdiction. Jurisdiction depended on the ship being in F1's "territorial waters"; in F2 the court allowed it to be shown that the ship was located in different waters. The jury in F2 found for the plaintiff, and the case was appealed to the Supreme Court.

2) **Issue.** Is the record of F1 a conclusive determination of the facts upon which F1 based its jurisdiction?

3) **Held.** No. Judgment affirmed. The Full Faith and Credit Clause of the Constitution does *not* preclude F2 from inquiring into the jurisdiction of F1.

   a) A recital of jurisdictional facts in the F1 record does not conclude the matter; it is only when this record is not impeached that it is entitled to full faith and credit. Thus in F2 it can be shown that F1 was not competent according to its own standards.

4) **Comment.** The *Thompson* decision only applies if the defendant did not personally appear in the F1 proceeding. If such an appearance was made, then the issue would be res judicata.

2. The Constitutional Requirement of Notice.

a. **Introduction.** Even though the state in which a judgment is rendered has jurisdiction over a defendant, a court of such state has no jurisdiction to render a personal judgment against a defendant who was not given proper notice of the proceedings and an opportunity to be heard. Similarly, a defendant in in rem and quasi in rem actions also must be afforded the same rights. These are constitutional requirements (Fourteenth Amendment due process).

b. **Method of notification.**

    1) Due process requires that a reasonable method of notification be used. What is "reasonable" depends on the circumstances of the case (the best possible method under the circumstances).

    2) A judgment may be void either because a reasonable method of notification is not provided for by the state in which the action is brought, or because the method provided for is not followed.

c. **Method most likely to reach the defendant.** In *McDonald v. Mabee*, 243 U.S. 90 (1917), the plaintiff brought an action in Texas against defendant, who was domiciled there but who had left the state intending not to return (defendant's family was still located there) and service was by publication only (in accordance with the requirements of the Texas statute). The Court held that the judgment rendered by the lower court was void. The Court indicated that a summons left at the defendant's last place of residence in the state might have been sufficient; to "dispense with personal service the substitute that is most likely to reach the defendant is the least that ought to be required if substantial justice is to be done." Here newspaper publication was not good enough.

Mullane v. Central Hanover Bank & Trust Co.

d. **Location of defendants unknown--Mullane v. Central Hanover Bank & Trust Co.,** 399 U.S. 306 (1950).

    1) **Facts.** Central Hanover Bank (D) was trustee of a common trust fund with 113 participating trusts. Pursuant to New York banking law, it petitioned the court for settlement of its first account as common trustee. The court appointed Mullane (P) as special guardian and attorney for all persons known or unknown not otherwise appearing who had or might thereafter have any interest in the income of the common trust fund. In an attempt to discharge its obligations to notify the beneficiaries of the pendency of the petition for settlement, Central Hanover complied with New York law and published notice by newspaper, setting forth merely the name and address of the trust company, the name and date of establishment of the common trust fund, and a list of all participating estates, trusts, and funds. The special guardian objected to the settlement petition on the ground that the notice given by Central Hanover was inadequate to afford due process under the Fourteenth Amendment, thus rendering the court without jurisdiction to render the final decree that would otherwise bind both the appearing and nonappearing beneficiaries. The state court held that service was proper. P appeals.

2) **Issue.** Is notice by publication a violation of due process when the out-of-state parties served are known and have known addresses?

3) **Held.** Yes. Judgment reversed.

a) A fundamental requirement of due process in any proceeding that is to be accorded finality is notice reasonably calculated, under all circumstances, to reach the interested parties and afford them an opportunity to be heard. The method of publication was insufficient with respect to the known beneficiaries with a known place of residence, whose names were not mentioned, and many of whom lived outside of the town where the newspaper was published. However, we disagree with the special guardian's objections to the published notice insofar as it applied to beneficiaries with a known place of residence whose addresses were unknown to the trustee and not reasonably discoverable by due diligence. As to them, the statutory notice is sufficient.

F. LIMITATIONS ON THE EXERCISE OF JURISDICTION

1. **Introduction.** Even though a court may have jurisdiction, sometimes it will not proceed. The following are among the considerations leading courts to decline to proceed.

2. **Limitations Imposed by Contract.**

a. **Hypothetical.** Facts: A and B have a contract with two provisions: (1) A agrees to submit to jurisdiction in state Y in any suit growing out of the contract; (2) Y courts shall have exclusive jurisdiction. The provision giving jurisdiction over A is valid; it is a consent to jurisdiction.

$$\frac{X \qquad Y}{A \qquad B}$$

b. **Exclusive jurisdiction.** But suppose A sues B in state X?

1) **Modern view.** The modern view is that the court has discretionary power to uphold exclusive jurisdiction clauses. Most courts will do so if they are fair to both parties and the jurisdiction stipulated for has some contact with the parties or the transaction.

a) **Freely negotiated clause--M/S Bremen v. Zapata Off-Shore Co.,** 407 U.S. 1 (1972).

M/S Bremen v. Zapata Off-Shore Co.

(1) **Facts.** Zapata, a United States company, entered into a contract with D, a German company, to have Zapata's drilling rig towed by D's ship, the Bremen, from Louisiana to the Adriatic Sea. The contract specified London as the forum for resolving disputes and contained exculpatory clauses concerning any damages that might occur. Shortly after departure,

the drilling rig was severely damaged in a storm in the Gulf of Mexico in international waters and D, on instructions from Zapata, towed the damaged rig to Tampa. Zapata then sued D for $3.5 million damages for negligence in the federal district court in Florida. D responded by invoking the forum clause of the contract and moved to dismiss for lack of jurisdiction on forum non conveniens grounds or, in the alternative, to stay the action pending submission to the London courts. The district court rejected D's motions and the court of appeals affirmed.

(2) Issue. Should the forum selection clause be enforced?

(3) Held. Yes, unless Zapata can clearly show that enforcement would be unreasonable and unjust or that the clause was invalid for reasons such as fraud or overreaching. Remanded.

(a) Here the contract was a freely negotiated international commercial transaction and the forum specified for resolution of disputes was clearly competent in such matters and neutral to both parties. However, if a choice-of-forum clause contravenes a strong public policy of the forum in which suit is brought (either statutory or judicial), it should not be enforced. Here the policy issue was the enforcement by the London courts of exculpatory clauses, which would not be enforced in Florida. On the forum non conveniens issue, Zapata should be given the opportunity to show (i) that the balance of convenience favored Florida (*i.e.*, more inconvenient for Zapata in London than D in Florida) and (ii) a London trial would be so manifestly and gravely inconvenient to Zapata that it would be effectively denied a meaningful day in court.

Carnival
Cruise Lines,
Inc. v. Shute

2) No evidence of bad faith--Carnival Cruise Lines, Inc. v. Shute, 499 U.S. 585 (1991).

a) **Facts.** The Shutes (Ps), a Washington State couple, purchased tickets through a travel agent from Carnival Cruise Lines (D), a Panamanian corporation with its principal place of business in Florida. The tickets, which also constituted a contract, contained a forum-selection clause requiring litigation in Florida of all disputes. Mrs. Shute was injured as a result of a fall when the ship was in international waters. Ps sued in Washington. The court of appeals held that the forum-selection clause was unenforceable. The Supreme Court granted certiorari.

b) **Issue.** Is the forum-selection clause enforceable?

c) **Held.** Yes. Judgment reversed.

(1) The clause was reasonable and enforceable. D was not acting in bad faith in choosing Florida as the forum. There was no evidence that D obtained passengers' accession to the clause by fraud or overreaching, and passengers conceded that they were given notice of the provision.

3) **Defendant lured into jurisdiction--Terlizzi v. Brodie,** 38 A.D.2d 762 (N.Y. App. Div. 1972).

    a) **Facts.** In 1968, Ds, New Jersey residents, were in an automobile collision in New Jersey. Ps, New York residents, were injured in the accident. In 1971, Ds were told that they had won tickets to a Broadway show. Ds attended the show, and while they were in the theater they were served with a summons in this action.

    b) **Issue.** Was the service valid?

    c) **Held.** No.

        (1) It has long been held that if a defendant is lured into a jurisdiction by fraud or deceit in order that he may be served, the service is invalid.

4) **Common situations.** The following are some situations where F1 might retain jurisdiction despite a forum selection clause in favor of F2:

    a) F1 is required by statute to retain the action;

    b) The plaintiff cannot secure effective relief in F2;

    c) F2 would be substantially less convenient;

    d) The agreement as to the place of action was obtained by fraud, etc.;

    e) For some other reason it would be unfair or unreasonable to enforce the agreement.

3. **Limitations Imposed by the Forum.**

    a. **Fraud, force, and privilege.** A court may refuse to exercise jurisdiction over a nonresident brought into the state by the fraud or force of one of the parties to the action (or by someone acting for one of the parties).

    1) **Applications.**

        a) In *United States v. Toscanino*, 500 F.2d 267 (2d Cir. 1974), it was held that a conviction would be void and jurisdiction would be lacking if the defendant could establish that, in addition to being kidnapped abroad, he had also been tortured and interrogated by United States agents and that the United States attorney was at all times aware of such activities.

        b) In *United States v. Gengler*, 510 F.2d 62 (2d Cir. 1975), the defendant had been kidnapped and brought forcibly into the United States but had suffered no acts of torture, terror, or custodial interrogation of any kind. The court affirmed the conviction, apparently limiting *Toscanino* to "conduct of the most outrageous and reprehensible kind by United States government agents."

  b. Immunity of witnesses, counsel, etc. For reasons of public policy, certain persons are exempt from service of process for the purpose of other litigation while they are in a state, *e.g.*, witnesses (so that they will feel free to enter the state to testify), parties involved in the litigation, etc.

  c. Jurisdictional questions or limitations on the exercise of jurisdiction.

    1) Due Process. Some courts treat the questions raised under a. and b. above as ones of jurisdiction. That is, they say that the Due Process Clause of the Fourteenth Amendment prevents a court from exercising jurisdiction if the defendant was fraudulently induced into the state. Other courts (and probably the majority) find no due process violation; *i.e.*, the states can decide these questions for themselves as a matter of state policy, and, of course, as a matter of discretion, refuse to exercise jurisdiction.

    2) Test. The ultimate test of jurisdiction is whether a judgment can be attacked collaterally in F2 after the defendant has taken a default judgment in F1. If a collateral attack cannot be made, then a genuine jurisdictional question is involved. The Supreme Court has never really resolved the question although it came close in *Jaster v. Currie,* 198 U.S. 144 (1905). There, the defendant claimed he was fraudulently induced into Ohio. He had raised the question of jurisdiction in the Ohio court but not on the ground of fraud (he was unaware of it at the time). When the plaintiff sought to enforce the Ohio judgment in Nebraska, defendant pled fraud. However, the court found that there was no fraud, so the constitutional jurisdiction question never arose for decision.

 4. Forum Non Conveniens.

  a. Introduction. Traditionally, a defendant may be sued wherever service can be made. Thus an individual may be served far from home while transiently in a state, and the cause of action involved may have nothing to do with the forum state. This situation provides an opportunity for "forum shopping"; *i.e.*, looking for the forum which is most favorable to the plaintiff, if only for the fact that it might cause the defendant the greatest inconvenience. The doctrine of forum non conveniens has been developed and applied in situations where there is no substantial basis for the plaintiff's choice of forum. In these situations, courts that use the doctrine will dismiss the suit in their forum. Note that in the absence of some constitutional limitation they are free to do so; but note also that there is no constitutional requirement that they do so—it is a matter of discretion with the court.

  b. Considerations leading courts to exercise forum non conveniens doctrine. Suits between nonresidents, considerations of an overcrowded docket, plaintiff's apparent use of the forum to harass defendant or to secure some undue procedural advantage, the belief that the matter can better be tried elsewhere, the inadequacy of the local judicial machinery for effectuating the rights sought to be upheld, or the difficulty of ascertaining foreign law may lead the court to dismiss the suit.

1) **In federal courts--Gulf Oil Corp. v. Gilbert,** 330 U.S. 501 (1947).

a) **Facts.** Gilbert (P) was a citizen of Virginia. Gulf (D) was a corporation domiciled in Pennsylvania and qualified to do business in New York and Virginia. P charged that D had mishandled a shipment of gasoline at P's warehouse in Virginia, burning the warehouse to the ground. P brought suit in New York federal district court on the basis of diversity of citizenship, but the New York court, acknowledging that it had both jurisdiction and proper venue, dismissed the case, noting that the case was better brought in Virginia district court, which also had proper venue.

b) **Issue.** May a federal district court apply the doctrine of forum non conveniens when the factors in favor of another choice of venue outweigh the disadvantages?

c) **Held.** Yes.

(1) The New York court properly dismissed the case according to the doctrine of forum non conveniens. Both New York and Virginia had jurisdiction and venue. But the acts complained of occurred in Virginia, the damage was done there, the cause of action arose there, and all witnesses (with the possible exception of experts) lived there. It would have been extremely prejudicial to the defendant to have had to try its case outside of Virginia, and the added expense of litigation would have been unjustifiable. Therefore, the considerations weighing in favor of the exercise of discretionary abstention from venue were sufficiently weighted in defendant's favor to overbalance plaintiff's original choice of forum.

d) **Comment.** Unless the balance is strongly and clearly in favor of the defendant, the court must sustain the plaintiff's choice of a forum.

2) **Conditional dismissal.** Some courts will exercise forum non conveniens only on the condition that the plaintiff is put in as good a position in another forum as he occupies in F1. In *Aetna Insurance Co. v. Creole Petroleum Corp.*, 23 N.Y.2d 717 (1968), the court dismissed on the condition that defendant consent to jurisdiction in another forum, appear, and agree not to contest jurisdiction.

3) **Jurisdiction available in another forum.** Not all states recognize the forum non conveniens doctrine. Of those that do, many do not recognize conditional dismissals—they say that forum non conveniens is only applicable if the plaintiff could bring suit in another jurisdiction over the defendant's objection.

4) **Procedural matters.** There are many considerations which lead courts not to exercise forum non conveniens. For example, in *Mobil Tankers Co. v. Mene Grande Oil Co.*, 363 F.2d 611 (3d Cir. 1966), the forum provided certain procedural remedies (pretrial discovery) not available in another state.

5) **Domicile.** Many states will not dismiss if either the plaintiff or defendant is domiciled in the state.

In re Union
Carbide Corp.
Gas Plant
Disaster at
Bhopal, India,
in December
1984

6) **Foreign court as alternate forum--*In re* Union Carbide Corp. Gas Plant Disaster at Bhopal, India, in December 1984,** 634 F. Supp. 842 (S.D.N.Y. 1986).

a) **Facts.** More than 2,000 people were killed and hundreds of thousands injured when a lethal gas escaped from a chemical plant operated by Union Carbide India Limited ("UCIL") in Bhopal, India. The Indian government, acting on behalf of the victims, brought this action against Union Carbide Corp. ("UCC"), a Connecticut corporation, which is the American parent of UCIL by virtue of ownership or control of 50% of its stock. UCC moves to dismiss the action on grounds of forum non conveniens.

b) **Issue.** Is the United States the proper forum for this action?

c) **Held.** No.

(1) The Indian legal system is in a better position to determine the cause of the accident and thereby fix liability. The presence in India of the overwhelming majority of witnesses and evidence, as well as claimants, the substantial interest of India in the accident, and the outcome of litigation requires that the case be dismissed on forum non conveniens grounds in favor of an Indian forum.

In re Union
Carbide Corp.
Gas Plant
Disaster, at
Bhopal, India
in December
1984

7) **No shared jurisdiction--*In re* Union Carbide Corp. Gas Plant Disaster at Bhopal, India in December 1984,** 809 F.2d 195, *cert. denied,* 484 U.S. 871 (2d Cir. 1987).

a) **Facts.** (*See* above) The New York court granted UCC's motion to dismiss the Union of India's ("UOI") and victims' complaint on forum non conveniens grounds on three conditions: (i) UCC had to consent to an Indian court's jurisdiction and to a waiver of statute of limitations defenses; (ii) UCC had to agree to satisfy any Indian court judgment, provided it comported with minimal requirements of due process; and (iii) UCC had to be subject in the Indian litigation to discovery under the Federal Rules of Civil Procedure.

b) **Issues.**

(1) With dismissal based on forum non conveniens, can a trial court retain jurisdiction to assure minimal due process?

(2) Did the trial court err in requiring UCC to consent to broad discovery under the Federal Rules of Civil Procedure when there was more limited discovery under Indian law?

c) **Held.** (1) No. (2) Yes.

(1) Once dismissal occurs, the trial court ceases to have any further jurisdiction. The concept of shared jurisdiction is unrealistic. If the Indian court denies due process, UCC can raise the lack of due process as a defense in an attempt to enforce the judgment against UCC in the United States.

(2) The parties in India are limited by the discovery rules of the Indian court where the claims will be pending. Reciprocal agreements on discovery may be agreed upon by the two parties on equal terms under the Federal Rules of Civil Procedure subject to the approval of the Indian court. The district court's order, as modified in accordance with this opinion, should not be a bar to such procedure.

c. **Forum non conveniens in federal courts.** One of the problems was whether, in a diversity suit, state or federal forum non conveniens law controlled. While this question was pending, section 1404(a) of the United States Code was passed. This is a statutory extension of forum non conveniens.

1) *Section 1404(a)*: If a federal district court considers the action to be inappropriately brought, it can transfer the action to any other district where the action "might have been brought."

2) This deals *only with federal courts* and transfers between them.

3) *"Might have been brought"*: *Hoffman v. Blaski*, 363 U.S. 335 (1960), decided that this meant that a federal district court can transfer only to a court where plaintiff otherwise could have secured jurisdiction and venue. Thus no "conditional transfers" are allowed.

4) *Norwood v. Kirkpatrick*, 349 U.S. 29 (1955), decided that a less strong showing is required under section 1404(a) to transfer than to dismiss under the common law rules.

5) *Section 1404(a) probably does not occupy the field*; federal courts probably can still use the common law doctrine of forum non conveniens.

6) *Parsons v. Chesapeake & Ohio Railway*, 375 U.S. 71 (1963), held that in diversity suits in federal district courts, the courts are not bound by the state law where they sit as to forum non conveniens; section 1404(a) is a "federal question."

7) *Van Dusen v. Barrack*, 376 U.S. 612 (1964), decided that when a transfer is made, F2 must apply the same law and policies that F1 would have. All section 1404(a) does is change the location of the suit.

5. **Other Limitations Imposed by the Forum.**

a. **Inability of a court to grant relief.** Note that this is also a factor often considered in forum non conveniens cases. Historically it has been an independent ground for dismissal, however.

1) **Equitable proceedings.** Usually this issue arises in the context of equitable proceedings—*i.e.*, actions for specific relief. A court will usually issue a decree affecting property which is within its own jurisdiction. If the relief sought involves the prohibition of an out-of-state act (*i.e.*, telling a party not to do some act) the court might also

issue a decree. *Example*: Cause of action brought in state X for an injunction to prevent D in state Y from doing something. However, if affirmative relief is asked for (a request that a party do some act) courts are more reluctant and often will not entertain an action if such affirmative acts are to be performed outside the jurisdiction of the court—problems of supervision are involved.

United States
v. First
National
City Bank

a) **Enforced by contempt--United States v. First National City Bank,** 396 F.2d 897 (2d Cir.1968).

    (1) **Facts.** During a grand jury investigation of antitrust violations, First National City Bank (D) was subpoenaed to produce all documents in its office in Frankfurt, Germany that related to particular named customers. D conceded that the federal court had the power to order compliance with the subpoena but refused to comply on the grounds that production of the documents would subject the bank to civil liability from those customers under German law. The federal district court held D in contempt and D appeals.

    (2) **Issue.** Does the possibility of civil action under German law defeat the federal court's power to require production of the documents located in that foreign country if the court has personal jurisdiction over the custodian of the documents?

    (3) **Held.** No. Contempt affirmed. However, no order shall issue if production would subject the custodian to criminal or official sanctions in the foreign country.

        (a) Here no showing has been made that any public policy of Germany would be violated, nor has either the United States government or the German government expressed a view on this case.

        (b) The potential civil liability is too speculative to override the great governmental interest in enforcing United States antitrust laws.

    (4) **Comment.** The apparent problem is whether the federal court can enforce its order to produce the documents that are located outside its jurisdiction. If the court did not have personal jurisdiction over D then it probably could not. But in this case the court may exercise its contempt powers or order posting of a bond because D is subject to personal jurisdiction.

Slater v.
Mexican
National
Railway

2) **Inability to grant relief--Slater v. Mexican National Railway,** 194 U.S. 120 (1904).

    a) **Facts.** Ps' decedent (Slater) was killed in Mexico; D (operating a railroad from Texas into Mexico) was sued in the federal district court in Texas for negligence in the death of its employee (Slater). Ps asked for damages for Slater's death. Ps also asked that Mexican law govern (the situs of death). The relief granted thereunder was unknown at common law (a remedy similar to alimony payments); common law courts gave only lump sum judgments (the case was brought before the merger of law and equity).

The trial court granted a lump sum (jury verdict); the circuit court reversed and dismissed the complaint.

    b)   **Issue.** If the wrong occurred in Mexico, and plaintiff seeks application of Mexican law, but the United States courts have no remedy analogous to Mexican law, can the United States court give its own remedy?

    c)   **Held.** No. Circuit court affirmed. Since the court cannot give the remedy asked for it should not entertain the cause of action.

        (1)   Mexican law provides that an annuity be paid the survivors in a wrongful death action.

        (2)   But defendant is allowed to discontinue the payments on the happening of certain conditions, such as the remarriage of the widow.

        (3)   Thus there is no basis for calculating an annuity under capitalization principles, nor is there a reasonable basis for discounting the annuity into a lump sum figure.

        (4)   There is no basis that is fair to defendant for the court to grant application of Mexican law and apply Mexican law in coming up with the remedy.

        (5)   Therefore the action should be dismissed. Plaintiff can find defendant in Mexico at any time and apply to the Mexican courts for relief.

    d)   **Comment.** This is a rather rigid view. The result might have been different had a Mexican forum not been available. This case was really based on the forum non conveniens idea.

  b. **Dismissal because the cause of action is opposed to the policy of the forum state.** This will be dealt with *infra*.

  c. **Dismissal because the cause of action is a penal one.** This subject is dealt with *infra*.

  d. **Local actions.** "Local" causes of action (as opposed to "transitory" ones) are certain actions relating to real property, such as trespass cases. They may be brought only in the state where the property is located.

6. Limitations Imposed by the State of the Transaction.

  a. **State statutes limiting jurisdiction elsewhere.** Some states have enacted statutes that purport to reserve exclusive jurisdiction on certain causes of action to the state that has passed the legislation creating the cause of action.

    1)   **The general rule.** A state does not have the power to keep other states from adjudicating transitory causes of action that arise within its borders. However, in some instances a state can probably set up certain causes of action so that they cannot be brought elsewhere.

Buttron v. El Paso Northeastern Railway

a) Declaratory relief--Buttron v. El Paso Northeastern Railway, 93 S.W. 676 (Tex. 1906).

   (1) Facts. Buttron (P), a Texas resident, brought suit in Texas against El Paso Northeastern Railway (D) for personal injuries caused by its negligence in the territory of New Mexico. At trial, D produced a judgment holding that it was not liable for the injuries under a New Mexico territorial law that allowed a potential defendant to bring a declaratory action in its state to determine rights of parties involved in an accident there. P had been personally served but did not appear in the New Mexico territorial trial. The Texas court directed the jury to find for D, stating as its reason for doing so that a valid and subsisting judgment of the sixth judicial district court of the territory of New Mexico existed adjudicating the issues involved. P appeals.

   (2) Issue. Is a judgment based on an unorthodox, but constitutionally sound, statute entitled to full faith and credit?

   (3) Held. Yes. Judgment affirmed.

      (a) If a sister state enacts a statute by proper exercise of state powers and the statute does not conflict with the federal Constitution, a valid judgment based on that statute must be accorded full faith and credit. The statute that allows D to bring an action for declaratory relief is a valid procedural rule justified by New Mexico's interest in obtaining prompt adjudication.

Tennessee Coal, Iron & Railway Co. v. George

b) Full faith and credit to substantive provisions only--Tennessee Coal, Iron & Railway Co. v. George, 233 U.S. 354 (1914).

   (1) Facts. Wiley George (P), employed by Tennessee Coal, Iron & Railway Co. (D) as an engineer in Alabama, was seriously injured while under a locomotive repairing the brakes when a defective throttle allowed steam into the cylinder causing the engine to automatically move forward. P brought suit by attachment in a Georgia court, founding his action on an Alabama statute that makes the master liable to the employee when the injury is caused by reason of any defect in the condition of the ways, works, machinery, or plant connected with or used in the business of the master or employer. D prayed that the action be abated because the Alabama statute also requires that such statutory actions be restricted to the state courts of Alabama. P's demurrer to the prayer was sustained and judgment was entered for P and affirmed by the appellate court. D appeals.

   (2) Issue. Does the statutory provision that the action must be brought in the Alabama court preclude P's recovery in the Georgia court?

   (3) Held. No. Judgment affirmed.

      (a) A transitory cause of action can be maintained in another state, even though the statute creating the cause of action provides that the action must be maintained in local courts. The right and the remedy are not so intertwined so that the Alabama court is the only court capable of enforcing the right. In fact, if the parties had moved, Alabama would not necessarily be the most convenient place for adjudication.

(4) Comment—Common law rule. Note that *George* is the common law rule. Today perhaps the Supreme Court would hold that if the state statute creating the right provides for a special tribunal, or a peculiar means for the enforcement of the right, then the "place of suit" requirement could operate as an enforceable limitation. Note, however, that *Crider v. Zurich Insurance Co.*, 380 U.S. 39 (1965), held that the forum court (Alabama) may apply the liability provisions of a statute of another state (Georgia) even when the right given is intended to be afforded only by an administrative agency (the Georgia Workmen's Compensation Board) created by the state statute.

b. Injunctions against suits in foreign courts.

1) Introduction. Equity generally has the power to order the doing or not doing of an act outside the state, including enjoining the bringing of a suit in the courts of another state.

a) Hypothetical. A, a resident of state X, gets jurisdiction and sues B, also a resident of X, in state Y. B goes to X and gets an injunction in one of its courts against A proceeding in Y. The issue raised by B probably should be something more than "inconvenience." If convenience is the sole issue, an injunction is probably not justified (*i.e.*, B should raise his objections in the foreign court on forum non conveniens grounds).

2) Theory. The theory is that such an injunction does not interfere with the jurisdiction of the foreign court (*i.e.*, the foreign court is not enjoined), but it legitimately controls individuals who are subject to the power of the enjoining court (thus the foreign court is not enjoined but the party, A, above, is enjoined from proceeding). However, since the foreign court is not ousted from its jurisdiction the injunction (from the state X court) is not entitled to full faith and credit in the courts of state Y. If A prosecutes her suit in Y (despite the injunction) and wins, the judgment is entitled to full faith and credit elsewhere. A, however, will be subject to a contempt penalty in X for violating the injunction of X's court.

3) Counter injunction--James v. Grand Trunk Western Railroad, 14 Ill. 2d 356 (1958).

James v. Grand Trunk Western Railroad

a) Facts. James, the administrator, (P) sued Grand Trunk Western Railroad (D) in Illinois for the death of her deceased husband (a Michigan resident) under a Michigan statute. Michigan, on D's request in a separate suit, enjoined P from proceeding with the Illinois action. P moved for the Illinois court to enjoin D from proceeding with its Michigan suit. The motion was denied by the trial and appellate courts. P appeals.

b) Issues.

    (1)   Should the Illinois court, having prior jurisdiction of a wrongful death action instituted by a nonresident plaintiff, recognize an out-of-state injunction restraining the plaintiff from proceeding?

    (2)   Should the Illinois court, to protect its jurisdiction of the wrongful death action, issue a counterinjunction restraining defendant from enforcing its injunction against plaintiff in the state of her residence?

c)   Held. (1) No. (2) Yes. Judgment reversed and remanded.

    (1)   Defendant must be enjoined from enforcing its Michigan injunction or else the plaintiff will go to jail (for contempt). Illinois therefore grants the injunction.

d)   Dissent. Illinois has no connection whatsoever with the occurrences out of which the administrator's claim arose.

e)   Comment. The court here seems to indicate that the defendant could have pleaded forum non conveniens in the Illinois court, but instead sought the Michigan injunction.

7.   **Constitutional Limitations.** In some situations the Constitution may compel a court to hear a suit it does not want to hear.

    a.   **The Supremacy Clause.**

        1)   **Federal causes of action in state courts.** The case of *Testa v. Katt*, 330 U.S. 386 (1947), involved treble damage suits under the Office of Price Administration (which provided that suits might be brought in any federal district court or state court). Rhode Island said it would not allow the suit because the underlying cause of action was penal and thus opposed to the state's public policy. The Supreme Court said that the state court must entertain suit when a federal cause of action exists and state courts are made competent to hear the cause of action. Congress can require this result under the Supremacy Clause. (Note that whether a state court can refuse to entertain a federal cause of action is largely a matter of the intent of Congress, a question therefore of statutory interpretation.)

        2)   **Enjoining federal causes of action in state and federal courts.** A state court cannot enjoin a plaintiff from maintaining a federal cause of action in a federal district or a state court in a sister state.

    b.   **Privileges and Immunities Clause.** The argument has been made that this clause requires every state court to hear disputes between citizens of every other state. If this were true then the doctrine of forum non conveniens would be destroyed. In *Missouri v. Mayfield*, 340 U.S. 1 (1950), a minority of the Supreme Court seemed to accept this view; however, the majority has thus far stated that this clause prevents discrimination only on the basis of "citizenship" and not on the basis of "residence" (whatever this means).

c. **Full faith and credit.** Generally, the courts of a state cannot refuse to hear a cause of action of another state on the grounds of offense to the public policy of the state. There may be exceptions (which are discussed *infra*), but this is certainly true if the forum state enforces similar causes of action in its own courts.

d. **The Commerce Clause.**

   1) The Commerce Clause may prevent a state from restricting persons or corporations from exercising the right to sue in its courts. This is true because such a restraint might impose an unreasonable burden on interstate commerce. For example, in *Sioux Remedy Co. v. Cope*, 235 U.S. 197 (1914), the Supreme Court held that it was unconstitutional to require a foreign corporation doing business interstate to appoint an agent for service of process in the state as a condition of the state permitting it to use the state's courts. To have to submit to jurisdiction in the state for all purposes simply to be able to sue in the state's courts is an unreasonable burden on interstate commerce.

   2) Even if a state's courts have jurisdiction, it may be an unreasonable burden on interstate commerce to exercise that jurisdiction. This was the result in *Davis v. Farmers' Co-op*, 262 U.S. 312 (1923). Here a state statute allowed the state courts to exercise jurisdiction over a railroad that was conducting any activity in the state even though such activity was not related in any way to the subject of the suit. On the other hand, on similar facts, the Supreme Court reached a contra result in *International Milling Co. v. Columbia Transportation Co.*, 292 U.S. 511 (1934), which seems to indicate that the imposition on the corporation would have to be substantial before it would amount to an unconstitutional burden.

IV. FOREIGN JUDGMENTS

A. INTRODUCTION

A firmly established principle of Anglo-American law is that foreign judgments, subject to only a few exceptions, are not open to reexamination on the merits when placed in issue before a local court.

1. **Judgments of United States Courts.** The Full Faith and Credit Clause requires that courts enforce sister state judgments.

   a.   Federal court judgments are entitled to the same full faith and credit as those of the state courts.

   b.   Federal courts must give full faith and credit to the judgments of state and territorial courts.

2. **Foreign Country Judgments.**

   a.   **Introduction.** There is no constitutional basis for requiring the enforcement of foreign country judgments in the United States. Therefore, the states have been free to decide whether and to what extent they will enforce them.

   b.   **Applications.**

Hilton v.
Guyot

   1)   **Judgments of foreign countries--Hilton v. Guyot,** 159 U.S. 113 (1895).

      a)   **Facts.** A French plaintiff (Guyot) sued an American defendant (Hilton) in a French court and won, then sought to enforce the judgment in a federal court in the United States. Hilton claimed that the merits of the case should be reexamined since he had valid defenses on which he would have succeeded had the suit been brought in the United States, and furthermore, that a French court would examine the merits of a controversy before enforcing an American judgment. The circuit court entered judgment for the plaintiff without examining the merits.

      b)   **Issue.** If the courts of a foreign country would examine the merits of a case brought to enforce a judgment there, then is a judgment of that foreign country against a United States citizen brought for enforcement in a United States court entitled to conclusive effect without reexamination on the merits?

      c)   **Held.** No. Judgment reversed. Presumptive validity is attributed to foreign judgments; that is, they will be given prima facie effect. But there are limitations:

         (1)   **Jurisdiction.** A United States court will not enforce a foreign judgment unless:

（a）　The foreign court is competent under its own law; and

（b）　The foreign court's basis for exercising jurisdiction meets jurisdictional standards under Fourteenth Amendment due process.

(2) **Public policy.** Note that the forum may refuse to enforce a foreign judgment on the basis of offense to the public policy of the forum.

(3) **Procedure.** The foreign forum must meet certain minimal procedural requirements, although not in exact conformity with what due process requires in this country.

（a）　Its proceeding must be in accord with "the course of civilized proceedings"—there must be a clear and formal record kept, the defendant must be given an opportunity to be heard, etc.

（b）　The system must be "generally fair."

(4) **Reciprocity.** Even though the above requirements are met, we will not enforce the foreign judgment because French courts do not give reciprocal effect to judgments in United States courts against French citizens.

d) **Dissent** (Fuller, C.J., Harlon, J., Brewer, J., Jackson, J.). Res judicata does not rest in discretion. The court's role is to apply our jurisprudence.

e) **Comment.** In enforcing a foreign cause of action, the state court in *Cowans v. Ticonderoga Pulp & Paper Co.*, 219 N.Y.S. 284 (1927), refused to attach the reciprocity requirement.

3. **The Underlying Rationale.** Public policy dictates that there be an end of litigation, that those who have contested an issue shall be bound by the result of the contest, and that matters once tried shall be considered forever settled as between the parties. This is the principle of res judicata.

4. **Enforcement.** The effect an F1 judgment receives in F2 is determined by F1 law; however, the enforcement procedures are always those of F2 (it is immaterial that additional enforcement methods would have been available in F1).

B. **GENERAL RECOGNITION AND ENFORCEMENT**

1. **In Personam Judgments.**

a. **Introduction.** An in personam judgment has one of the following uses:

1) Affirmative relief. A judgment on the merits for the plaintiff can be used to obtain affirmative relief. For example, if the cause of action is an equitable one the defendant might be compelled to do or not do something.

2) Passive or negative use. A judgment for the plaintiff or the defendant on the merits can be used by either party as a defense to any further litigation on the same cause of action.

3) Collateral estoppel. In a judgment on the merits, any issues actually litigated, decided, and necessary to the decision in the first cause of action between the parties (and those in privity with them) are res judicata on those same issues in any other cause of action. This means, of course, that the doctrine of collateral estoppel does not require that res judicata effect in F2 be given to default or consent judgments from F1.

4) Direct estoppel. Even if the first cause of action is not decided on the merits, those issues which were or might have been conclusively adjudicated are res judicata in any further litigation on the same cause of action.

    a) Merger. Plaintiff's original cause of action is merged into the final judgment. Thereafter, she can no longer sue on the original cause of action. She can sue only on the judgment itself. The original claim, however, is not merged in a judgment that orders the doing of an act other than the payment of money.

    b) Bar. A judgment for the defendant terminates the original cause of action.

    c) Note. Merger and bar together result in the first final judgment being conclusive as to all matters that were or could have been litigated in the first proceedings.

b. Note. In the area of judgments, much depends on how narrowly or broadly the term "claim" is defined. The broader the definition, the more the plaintiff will be required to consolidate her actions (complaints against defendant) and seek relief in a single action. An important question is, which forum's (F1 or F2) law decides the definition of claim?

c. Judgment on the merits. Note that for the doctrine of collateral estoppel to apply, or for the plaintiff to use a judgment as the basis for affirmative relief, or the defendant with a judgment to use it as the basis for a defense, a judgment must be on the merits.

1) This means that F1 must have decided the issues raised by the case and not disposed of the case on the basis of some collateral matter.

2) This distinction is not always an easy one to draw; however, generally a judgment that dismisses a case on the basis of F1's statute of limitations will not bar a suit in F2 on the same cause of action, nor will dismissal on a demurrer bar suit in F2 if the party properly alleges a cause of action.

3) Whether the F1 judgment is on the merits will be decided according to the law of the F1 forum.

d. **The effect of the foreign judgment in F2.** It has never been true that the F1 judgment must be given the same effect in F2 that it is given in F1. The F1 judgment is not a judgment in F2—it is just an unimpeachable cause of action. Therefore the party with the judgment must go to F2, bring his cause of action for a judgment there, get a judgment and then have process served there for enforcement of that judgment. The Uniform Enforcement of Foreign Judgments Act (1964) attempts to change this, but only a few states have adopted it.

    1) **Enforcement devices.** The enforcement devices used are those provided for by F2—they need not be the same as those afforded by F1.

    2) **Defense.** A party using an F1 judgment as a defense to a suit can set it up as a defense without first getting a judgment in F2.

    3) **The federal system.** A party with a judgment in the federal courts can register it elsewhere and get enforcement without bringing a second suit for judgment.

e. **Applications.**

    1) **A suit to enforce a sister state's decree of alimony--Lynde v. Lynde,** 181 U.S. 183 (1901).

Lynde v.
Lynde

        a) **Facts.** Mrs. Lynde (P) obtained a New Jersey divorce from Mr. Lynde (D). Four years later P asked the court to amend the divorce decree to provide for alimony, which had been inadvertently omitted from the original judgment. D, now remarried and living in New York, appeared generally in the proceedings to contest the alimony. The court awarded P $7,840 back alimony, $80 per week future alimony, and $1,000 attorney's fees, and the decree provided for security and an injunction against disposal of property to evade the decree. D has no assets in New Jersey to secure the judgment so P sues to have the judgment enforced.

        b) **Issues.**

            (1) May the judgment be enforced both as it relates to back alimony and as it relates to future payments?

            (2) Will New Jersey's enforcement rules apply to enforcement in New York?

        c) **Held.**

            (1) No. Future payments of alimony are modifiable and therefore are not final judgments entitled to full faith and credit in sister states. On the other hand, the lump sum judgment for payments past due is a final judgment entitled to full faith and credit in New York.

            (2) No. When P seeks enforcement in New York, New York's enforcement procedures apply, not New Jersey's.

2) **Suit to recover attorney's fees--Emery v. Hovey,** 153 A. 322 (N.H. 1931).

    a) **Facts.** Emery (P), a New Hampshire attorney, rendered services for Hovey (D) in New Hampshire and Maine. P sued D in Maine for the fees arising from the services rendered. D successfully defended the suit on a Maine statute prohibiting the recovery of attorney's fees in that state by an attorney not licensed there. P then sued D in New Hampshire on the same claim. D successfully asserts the Maine judgment as a defense. P makes exception to the court's ruling.

    b) **Issue.** Is the judgment of a court of record having jurisdiction over the parties and the cause of action entitled to full faith and credit in a sister state's courts no matter how erroneous in law or in fact the judgment of F1 may be?

    c) **Held.** Yes.

        (1) The judgment of a court of record (F1), having jurisdiction over the parties and the cause of action, is conclusive of the issues litigated and is entitled to full faith and credit in the courts of every other state or the federal government. P's only remedy when jurisdiction was proper is appeal in F1, not relitigation in F2.

2. **Judgments In Rem and Quasi In Rem.**

    a. **Introduction.** Judgments of this sort do not impose a personal obligation on the defendant and hence, unlike in personam judgments, cannot be enforced by action in other states. The full effect of such judgments has been set forth *supra*. Nevertheless, the doctrine of collateral estoppel indicates that issues determined in a suit in F1 are res judicata between the same parties in a suit on a different cause of action in F2 (*i.e.*, the F1 judgment itself is not res judicata). Be careful to remember that collateral estoppel requires that the issues must have been actually raised, litigated, and decided in F1.

    b. **Example of in rem effect.**

X	Y
D's Property	D
Suit 1	Suit 2

In a suit by P in X to foreclose a mortgage with $10,000 owing, the X court may seize D's property in X and sell it to satisfy the debt. However, if the sale nets only $7,500, the court may not give P a deficiency judgment for $2,500. The doctrine of merger, however, does not prevent P from going to Y and bringing a cause of action there for the deficiency (*i.e.*, a cause of action on the debt). In this second suit in Y, D could defeat P's claim by showing that his debt to P was only for $5,000 or that there was no debt. The judgment in X decides only the issues of the ownership of the property in X.

c. **An exception to the general rule--Harnischfeger Sales Corp. v. Sternberg Dredging Co.,** 189 Miss. 73 (1939).

   1) **Facts.** Harnischfeger (P) sold Sternberg (D) a dredge, taking notes secured by chattel mortgage. P sued in Louisiana to foreclose the mortgage and for a personal judgment on the notes. D appeared to contest jurisdiction and lost; he then defended on the merits, urging a breach of warranty. The trial court foreclosed the mortgage and gave a personal judgment on the notes. The Louisiana Supreme Court reversed the in personam part of the judgment (Louisiana had a rule that the defendant could come and defend property in an in rem proceeding without being exposed to personal liability). Plaintiff then went to Mississippi to enforce his judgment and sue for the deficiency. Defendant set up breach of warranty as a defense. The trial court held in favor of D on the merits of the defense. P appeals.

   2) **Issue.** May a defense asserted by a party in a previous in rem proceeding in another state be relitigated in a suit in the forum between the same parties over issues arising out of the same set of facts?

   3) **Held.** No. Judgment reversed.

      a) Even though the suit in Louisiana was in rem, nevertheless, the Louisiana court allowed defendant to appear and contest the suit, in the course of which he raised the same defense (*i.e.*, breach of warranty); therefore, it is res judicata here.

   4) **Comment—the effect of the Full Faith and Credit Clause.** The Full Faith and Credit Clause puts a floor under the res judicata concept. F2 must give as much effect to the F1 judgment as F1 does. Does it also require that F2 give the F1 judgment no more effect than F1 would? Sternberg indicated that it does not.

3. **Particular Effects.**

   a. **Persons affected.**

   1) **Hypothetical.** A, B, C, and E in one car, are injured in an auto accident with a car negligently driven by D.

      a) Four suits are brought:

         A v. D; B v. D; C v. D; E v. D

      b) D wins suits 1-3; in the E v. D suit D wants to set up these other judgments as a bar to E's suit (since it will try the very same issue—*i.e.*, D's negligence). However, D cannot do this—due process declares that E must "have his day in court."

   2) **Same situation, except plaintiffs win.** If in suits 1-3, however, A, B, and C won and E wanted res judicata on the issues decided in these cases, such a result would not violate due process (D has had his day in court).

a) Generally courts do not allow this, however, due to the doctrine of mutuality—if the judgments are not binding in suits if the results favor a party (that is, D), they should not be binding if the results are not favorable.

b) Note, however, that some courts have shown a propensity to depart from the doctrine of mutuality.

Sovereign Camp v. Bolin

3) Class suits: An exception to the general rule--Sovereign Camp v. Bolin, 305 U.S. 66 (1938).

a) **Facts.** Sovereign Camp (D), a fraternal benefit association organized under the laws of Nebraska, authorized the issuance of life memberships to those who paid dues for 20 years upon entering the order after 43 years of age. Beneficiaries of members were entitled to death benefits. Bolin (P) joined (after age 43) and paid dues for 20 years; after his death his beneficiaries sued D in Missouri state court for death benefits. D said that the association's law, making membership fully paid after 20 years, was ultra vires the association and had been so held by the Nebraska Supreme Court in earlier litigation with one Trapp. D asked for full faith and credit for that judgment. The Missouri court applied its own law (the contract was made there) and held that the certificate was not ultra vires or if it was that D was estopped to so claim.

b) **Issue.** Must a state give full faith and credit to another state's decision defining the rights of membership in a fraternal benefit society, even if the certificate of membership was issued in the forum state?

c) **Held.** Yes. Judgment reversed.

(1) **Choice of law.** In fraternal benefit association cases the law of the association's domicile (Nebraska) governs.

(2) **Full faith and credit in "class" actions.** The suit by Trapp in Nebraska was a "class action"; therefore, P is bound by that judgment and the Missouri court must give it full faith and credit.

d) **Comment.** In *Hansberry v. Lee*, 311 U.S. 32 (1940), the Supreme Court indicated that the forum could not arbitrarily define a "class" and thus affect at will the rights of people not before the court and who have not received personal service of process. Minimum standards required by due process of law must be maintained—the procedure adopted must fairly insure protection of the interests of absent parties who will be bound by the judgment. The Supreme Court, in the last analysis, will determine what these procedures must be.

4) The problem of privity.

a) **Constitutional question.** The problem of privity is closely related to that of class actions. A judgment in the F1 court binds the parties before the court and all other persons that are in "privity" with those parties. F1 law determines who these persons are; however, by due process, no party is bound by a judgment unless the court which renders it has proper jurisdiction. Therefore ultimately the question of privity (and what persons are privies) is a constitutional question of jurisdiction.

b) **Due process limitation--Riley v. New York Trust Co.,** 315 U.S. 343 (1941).

  (1) **Facts.** The parties are litigating in Delaware for administrative control over stock in the name of a decedent located in Delaware in a Delaware corporation. The New York Trust Company was appointed the decedent's administrator by the state of New York; the Georgia executor was appointed by a Georgia court in probate proceedings that had already decided ownership of decedent's property in Georgia (having determined for that purpose that decedent had been domiciled in Georgia). The Delaware Supreme Court decided domicile for itself and held that New York was the domiciliary administrator. The Georgia executor relies on the judgment of the Georgia court, which had determined that Georgia was the testator's domicile, and asks that full faith and credit be given this determination.

  (2) **Issue.** May the issue of domicile be litigated in one state if that issue has been determined by another state and the party to the second suit was not a party to the first suit?

  (3) **Held.** Yes. There was no denial of full faith and credit by the Delaware court.

    (a) The Georgia court did not claim that its judgment had res judicata effect on the New York administrator; such a claim would be unconstitutional as a denial of due process. The Georgia court had no in personam power to bind the New York administrator (he was not present or in privity with a party who was).

    (b) The Georgia judgment was in rem as to the assets in Georgia, and therefore as to those assets it was binding on the whole world.

c) **Res judicata effect of state decision in federal court--Kremer v. Chemical Construction Corp.,** 456 U.S. 461 (1982).

  (1) **Facts.** Kremer (P) filed a complaint with the Equal Employment Opportunity Commission under Title VII of the Civil Rights Act of 1964. As required by the Act, P's claim was referred to the New York Division of Human Rights ("NYDHR"). The NYDHR rejected the claim as meritless and on appeal the Appellate Division of the New York Supreme Court affirmed. P then brought a Title VII action in federal district court. The district court dismissed on res judicata grounds and the court of appeals affirmed. P brought this appeal claiming that in cases brought under Title VII, Congress did not intend that federal courts would be required to grant finality to state court decisions.

  (2) **Issue.** Should the state court decision be given res judicata effect in the federal court?

  (3) **Held.** Yes. (5-4 decision.)

    (a) 28 U.S.C. section 1738 requires federal courts to give the same preclusive effect to state court judgments that those judgments would be given in the courts of the state from which the judgment emerged. Under section 1738, the state proceedings need do no more than satisfy the minimum procedural requirements of the Fourteenth

Amendment's Due Process Clause in order to qualify for full faith and credit. There is no question that the decision by the Appellate Division of the New York Supreme Court precludes P from bringing any other action based upon the same grievance in New York courts, and because the procedures provided in New York for determination of such claims offer a full and fair opportunity to litigate the merits, section 1738 precludes P from relitigating the same question in federal court.

Marrese v. American Academy of Orthopaedic Surgeons

d) **Exclusive federal court authority--Marrese v. American Academy of Orthopaedic Surgeons,** 470 U.S. 373 (1985).

(1) **Facts.** Orthopaedic surgeons (Ps) sued in Illinois, claiming an academy of surgeons had infringed rights protected by Illinois law in denying their admission applications. After Ps were denied relief, they sued in federal court, filing an antitrust claim they could not have raised in their earlier suit. Ps were again denied relief on the ground that under federal law their claims were precluded by the earlier state court judgment.

(2) **Issue.** Did the state court judgment have a preclusive effect on a later federal antitrust claim which could not have been raised in the state proceeding?

(3) **Held.** No. Judgment reversed and case remanded.

(a) Under 28 U.S.C. section 1738, the preclusive effect of the Illinois judgment should be determined under Illinois law. Assuming Illinois law precludes the federal court claim, it must then be determined if an exception to section 1738 should apply (with congressional intent the primary consideration). Since this has not been done below, the case is remanded.

b. **Issues affected.**

1) **Introduction.** The Restatement (Second) indicates that the issues that are determined by a valid judgment are determined by the local law of the state where the judgment was rendered; subject, of course, to constitutional limitations.

2) **Res judicata effect given to decisions on the same issue.**

a) **Query.** In *Riley, supra*, if all of the parties in the Delaware cause of action had been before the Georgia court, would the Georgia judgment have been res judicata in Delaware?

(1) Note that everyone seemed to assume that the definition of "domicile" was the same in Georgia and Delaware.

(a) If the domicile rules were verbally similar and the respective states gave the same content to their rules, then the

Georgia judgment would have been res judicata on the question of domicile in Delaware.

    (b)   The issue to be decided in Delaware would have been precisely the same as the one already decided in Georgia.

  (2)   If the Georgia conception of domicile (for example, "the wife's domicile is that of her husband") was different from Delaware's ("domicile is established by intent") then Georgia judgment would not be res judicata in Delaware.

    (a)   The question in both forums is the same—where was testator domiciled?—but the factual issue is not the same since the states have different questions to answer in determining domicile.

    (b)   Before collateral estoppel applies, the issue in F2 must be precisely the same as that decided in F1.

b)   **Question of fact.**

  (1)   **Hypothetical.**

	X	Y
	P	D
	Accident	F2
	F1	

    (a)   P brings suit in F1 for damages to his automobile. F1 decides that X law applies (contributory negligence—P is barred from recovery in his suit).

    (b)   P then brings a suit in F2 for personal injuries.

      1]   If F2 decides that X law applies, the decision on contributory negligence in F1 is res judicata in F2.

      2]   If F2 applies Y law but its contributory negligence law was the very same as that of X, then the decision in X on this issue is still res judicata.

      3]   If, however, F2 applies Y law and the contributory negligence law of Y is different from X (for example, X law: "stop, look, and listen"; Y law: "the reasonable person" test) then the F1 determination is not res judicata in F2.

  (2)   **Determination of fact.** If, for example, liability depends on who was driving the car, a determination of fact, and F1 decides that P was driving and this determination is relevant in determining an issue in F2 litigation, (even though the law being applied in F2 is different from that applied in F1) the factual determination is still res judicata.

c)   **Questions of law.**

  (1)   **General rule.** Res judicata is said always to apply to questions of fact but not to questions of law.

(a) For example, A in 1996 claims a tax deduction that is disallowed. In 1997, A claims the same deduction under the very same provision of the Internal Revenue Code. However, the IRS has promulgated a new regulation that allows the deduction.

(b) Since questions of law are generally not res judicata, A can recover in 1997 and is not bound by the 1996 judgment.

(2) Choice of law questions. Note, however, that a choice of law made for an issue decided in F1 forecloses a different choice as to precisely that same issue in F2. F2 will be allowed to make a new choice of law only if a new issue is involved.

(3) Decision on the merits. In *Warner v. Buffalo Drydock Co.*, 67 F.2d 540 (2d Cir. 1933), *cert. denied*, 291 U.S. 678 (1934), plaintiffs filed a libel action in federal court in Ohio, which was dismissed because of laches. The second action in federal court in New York, to recover for damages to plaintiffs' steamer caused by defendant's servants, based upon the same cause of action was not barred. A dismissal based upon a statute of limitations is not a decision on the merits.

3) Compare. While the Restatement requires that the law of F1 be applied to determine the effect of a judgment, not only by way of merger or bar, but also by way of collateral estoppel, there are somewhat analogous cases where F1's determination is not determinative.

a) In *Hart v. American Airlines, Inc.*, 304 N.Y.S.2d 810 (1969), the New York court held that the issue of defendant's negligence in causing an air crash was res judicata as a result of a Texas judgment brought by other plaintiffs. Texas would not have treated the issue as res judicata in its courts. The New York court indicated that no question of full faith and credit was involved, because this was not an action to enforce the Texas judgment.

4. Limitations on Full Faith and Credit.

a. Decrees affecting title to land.

1) Hypothetical case.

a) **Facts.** Suppose that:

State X	State Y
Seller/Buyer Contract F1	Situs of Property F2

S contracts with B to sell his land located in Y, then defaults on the contract. B sues S in X—F1, having in personam jurisdiction, commands S to convey title to B. S fails to comply with the decree; F1 has its clerk issue a deed for S in B's name. B brings a quiet title action in Y, relying on the deed made in F1.

b) **Question.** Must F2 give full faith and credit to the F1 judgment? If S had obeyed the F1 decree and executed a deed to the land in F2, this deed would be given full effect. However, courts are split over the effect to be given the F1 decree executing a deed on S's behalf.

2) **F2 may relitigate title issue--Fall v. Eastin,** 215 U.S. 1 (1909).

a) **Facts.** Sarah Fall (P) sued E.W. Fall (D), in an action for divorce. Both were residents of Washington. The divorce decree awarded P Nebraska land and ordered D to convey title to her. D did not comply with the decree, and a commissioner appointed by the Washington court executed a deed to the Nebraska land to her. Subsequently D executed a mortgage on the land and a deed to the land to third parties (including Eastin). P then brought suit in Nebraska to quiet her title to the land and cancel the mortgage and the deed executed by D. D was never served personally in the Nebraska proceedings nor did he appear, although the third parties were served. The trial court found in favor of P. The Nebraska Supreme Court first affirmed, but on rehearing, it reversed the decree of the trial court. P appeals.

b) **Issue.** Must a deed to land situated in Nebraska, made by a commissioner under the decree of a court of the state of Washington in an action for divorce, be recognized in Nebraska under the full faith and credit clause of the Constitution of the United States?

c) **Held.** No.

   (1) The courts of one state cannot directly affect title to real property in another state. That is, the Washington court can order a party over which it has personal jurisdiction to convey title to out-of-state property, but the state where the land is located is not obligated to recognize Washington's disposition of the property. Washington's remedy for failure to comply is contempt of court, since technically it does not have jurisdiction over the property.

d) **Concurrence** (Holmes, J.). The Nebraska court based its decision on the view that the Washington court's decree was an in rem order made without valid jurisdiction over the Nebraska land. If the Nebraska court had viewed the Washington court's decree as an in personam order against the husband, the order would be entitled to full faith and credit in Nebraska if valid jurisdiction over the husband could be had. But, viewed in the light of an in rem order, the Nebraska court's decision is not reviewable by this court.

3) **Better view.** The better view is that if the defendant is before the court in F1 then the court has power to order him to convey foreign land and such a decree should be an effective judgment and determine his obligation to convey—the decree ought to be given full faith and credit at the situs of the land (F2).

b. **Other circumstances in which F2 may be excused from giving full faith and credit to sister state judgments.**

Yarborough
v.
Yarborough

1) **An overriding F2 interest--Yarborough v. Yarborough,** 290 U.S. 202 (1933).

   a) **Facts.** Sadie (P), Yarborough's daughter, living with her grandfather in South Carolina, sued her father (D), a resident of Georgia, for support payments. D pled an earlier Georgia judgment, given at the time he divorced P's mother, that set a fixed sum (which he had paid) for Sadie's support. The trial court ordered D to pay. The judgment was affirmed by the Supreme Court of South Carolina. The United States Supreme Court granted certiorari.

   b) **Issue.** Must the courts of F2 (South Carolina) give full faith and credit to the judgment of F1 (Georgia) if that judgment affects vital interests of F2 that were not in existence at the time of the F1 judgment?

   c) **Held.** Yes. Judgment reversed. The Georgia judgment is a bar.

      (1) Plaintiff's cause of action merged with the Georgia judgment; South Carolina must give full faith and credit to this judgment. No further cause of action exists for child support.

   d) **Dissent** (Stone, J.).

      (1) F2 may relitigate an issue if it has an interest that overrides the notion of giving res judicata effect to the decision of that issue in F1. The Full Faith and Credit Clause does not prevent this. South Carolina has such an interest—Sadie is now domiciled there, and the state, as a measure of self-preservation, may seek to secure the adequate protection and maintenance of its citizens.

      (2) Furthermore, Georgia only meant to control the father-child relationship within Georgia; therefore, the Georgia judgment does not operate beyond the borders of that state.

   e) **Comments.**

      (1) The decision may rest, in part, on the view that F2 did not have legislative jurisdiction to give a judgment for child support against the father domiciled in Georgia.

      (2) In *Elkind v. Byck,* 68 Cal. 2d 453 (1968), the facts were similar, except the husband moved from Georgia to California and the wife moved to New York. Despite the Georgia settlement, the wife sought additional support payments in a California action. The court consented, distinguishing *Yarborough* on the basis that the husband had left Georgia and had a substantial relationship with California.

      (3) In *Kubon v. Kubon*, 51 Cal. 2d 229 (1958), a Nevada court with jurisdiction over both parents gave custody of the children to the

mother (later modifying its order to allow the husband physical custody in the summer), ordered the father to pay child support, and reserved jurisdiction to make further orders involving custody and support. While in California with the children during summer vacation, the father petitioned a California court seeking appointment as guardian. Following a temporary restraining order restraining the mother from taking the children pending the hearing, the mother took the children back to Nevada. The Nevada court modified its order granting husband summer custody. The father ceased paying child support. After notice to the husband, the Nevada court entered judgment for payments and fees. The mother filed suit in California on the Nevada judgment. The supreme court of California upheld the husband's defense that by violating the California restraining order, the mother was in contempt of the court from which she sought relief.

2) **Workers' compensation cases.**

a) **Rehearing in F2 after F1 has made award--Magnolia Petroleum Co. v. Hunt,** 320 U.S. 430 (1943).

   (1) **Facts.** Hunt (P), a Louisiana domiciliary, was injured while working for Magnolia Petroleum (D) in Texas. P received a Texas workers' compensation award but later sued in Louisiana under the statute there—it allowed greater awards than the Texas statute. The Louisiana court gave judgment for the amount fixed by the Louisiana statute after deducting the amount of the Texas payments. The Louisiana court of appeals affirmed. The Supreme Court of Louisiana refused review. The United States Supreme court granted certiorari.

   (2) **Issue.** Is F2 barred by full faith and credit from rehearing under its own laws a workers' compensation case if F1 has previously heard the claim and made an award?

   (3) **Held.** Yes.

      (a) Once one state (Texas) has made an award, this precludes a subsequent award in another state (Louisiana).

   (4) **Dissent.** Texas did not intend to foreclose any other actions on the same cause of action, but only to settle matters under Texas law. Even if Texas did intend to settle all other causes of action, Louisiana has an interest (social responsibility for the results) and should be able to make an additional award.

   (5) **Comment.** Justice Stone wrote both the dissent in *Yarborough* and the majority opinion in *Magnolia*. If F2 ought to be able to make a supplementary award in child support cases, why not also in workers' compensation cases? And why not in tort cases? If in tort cases, why not in all cases? And if the interest of F2 is thought to be overriding in all cases then F2 can decide for itself whether it will give full faith and credit to the judgments of F1. If F2 does this, then there is nothing left to the Full Faith and Credit Clause.

Industrial
Commission
of Wisconsin
v. McCartin

b) **Additional award by F2--Industrial Commission of Wisconsin v. McCartin,** 330 U.S. 622 (1947).

(1) **Facts.** Kopp worked for McCartin (D); both were residents of Illinois. While on a job in Wisconsin, Kopp was injured. He filed claims with the Wisconsin and the Illinois industrial commissions; he settled the Illinois claim and then proceeded in Wisconsin under the Wisconsin statute. These benefits were denied on the basis that the Illinois award was final and exclusive. The Supreme Court granted certiorari.

(2) **Issue.** May F2 grant an additional benefit after the employee has received benefits from F1 if F1's statute does not explicitly preclude an additional award?

(3) **Held.** Yes.

(a) There is nothing in the Illinois statute or decisions indicating it was meant to preclude any recovery from proceedings in another state for injuries received there in the course of an Illinois employment. This distinguishes the *Magnolia* case where Texas purported to grant an exclusive award.

(4) **Comment.** While the Wisconsin commission seemed to indicate that it would deduct from its award the amount received under the Illinois award, there is nothing in the Supreme Court decision that would compel it to do this. In settling the Illinois claim the parties, however, stipulated for this result.

Thomas v.
Washington
Gas Light Co.

c) **Successive awards not precluded by full faith and credit--Thomas v. Washington Gas Light Co.,** 448 U.S. 261 (1980).

(1) **Facts.** Thomas (P), a resident of the District of Columbia, was hired by Washington Gas Light Co. (D) in the District of Columbia. While employed by D, P worked in the District of Columbia, Maryland, and Virginia. In 1971, P was injured while working in Virginia. Two weeks after the accident, P entered into an agreement with the Virginia Industrial Commission under which he would receive $62 per week in compensation for the injury. In 1974, P notified the Department of Labor of his intention to seek a supplemental award from the District of Columbia. D objected on the ground that, under Virginia law, P was excluded from any other recovery stemming from the injury in Virginia. D contended that the District of Columbia's obligation to give full faith and credit to the Virginia award precluded any further award by the District. A second award was granted to P in the District of Columbia. The United States Court of Appeals reversed. The United States Supreme Court granted certiorari.

(2) **Issue.** Does full faith and credit preclude successive workers' compensation awards?

(3) **Held.** No. Judgment reversed.

(a) In holding that the Full Faith and Credit Clause does not preclude successive awards, we overrule *Magnolia Petroleum Co. v. Hunt* in favor of *Industrial Commission of Wisconsin v. McCartin* and conduct a fresh examination of the full faith and credit issue. We find that Virginia has an interest in placing a limit on the potential liability of companies transacting business in the state and that both states have an interest in the welfare of the injured employee. In addition, we find that Virginia has an interest in having the integrity of its formal determinations of contested issues respected by other states. Because P could have sought an award in the first instance in either state, D and its insurer would have had to measure their potential liability by the more generous of the states' compensation schemes. Therefore, the state's interest in limiting potential liability of business within the state is not of controlling importance. We also find that because both jurisdictions have a common interest in providing adequate compensation to the injured worker and because this interest would be fully served by allowing successive awards, there is no significant conflict in this area. Therefore the ultimate issue is whether Virginia's interest in the integrity of its tribunals' determinations foreclosed a second proceeding in the District of Columbia. We hold that workers' compensation awards are not entitled to the same effect as court judgments. The jurisdiction of the Virginia workers' compensation commission is limited to questions arising under Virginia's workers' compensation act. The commission could only apply Virginia's law. It could not determine P's rights under the law of the District of Columbia. Because the commission had no power to determine P's rights under District of Columbia law, there can be no constitutional objection to a supplemental award by the District of Columbia.

(4) Concurrence (White, J., Burger, C.J., Powell, J.). The plurality's analysis does not appear to be limited to state workers' compensation boards. However, I see no difference insofar as full faith and credit is concerned between a statute that prescribes a forum-favoring choice of law rule and a common law doctrine stating the same principle. The plurality's rationale substantially undercuts the purpose of the Full Faith and Credit Clause, *i.e.*, to act as a nationally unifying force.

(5) Dissent (Rehnquist, Marshall, JJ.). Balancing of state interests is not appropriate here, but would be appropriate in determining questions of constitutional control of choice of law.

d) Workers' compensation cases—sui generis?

(1) The usual approach. The hypothesis proceeded on in X-YF cases (*i.e.*, cases where there are contacts with the transaction in two states and the forum is in one of these states) thus far has been that the forum should decide which one body of law (either X or Y) should apply to the entire transaction and that all of the rights of the parties should be decided by that law. The assumption has been that if X law is applied then Y can give the plaintiff no additional rights.

(2) Workers' compensation cases. These cases seem to adopt a different approach. There is nothing in them to suggest that both X and Y could not give plaintiff a judgment in the full amount allowed by each of them.

    (a) It can be argued that these cases are sui generis. In *McCartin*, for example, constitutionally the Illinois commission could have considered the Wisconsin law and given a recovery thereunder (*i.e.*, made a choice of law). However, characteristically state industrial commissions have a legislative mandate to adjudicate cases only under their own state statutes—they have no competence to make a choice of law.

(b) While these cases are probably sui generis, they do suggest ideas of broad implications—*i.e.*, that in any type of case, wherever P can get jurisdiction and a different law applied he can get a separate judgment.

3) Modification by F2 when modification is allowed in F1. In *People of New York ex rel. Halvey v. Halvey*, 330 U.S. 610 (1947), a New York court modified a Florida divorce decree since Florida, due to changed circumstances, would allow modification of its decree. The New York court only modified the decree to the extent a Florida court would—keeping the custody of the child with the mother, but giving the father visitation rights. However, this court action provokes the question whether, on the basis of changed circumstances, F2 might be able to go beyond the modifications allowed by F1.

4) Res judicata. Res judicata is a harsh doctrine; its rationale—it is better to settle litigation rather than to continue to pursue the truth. Of late this rationale has been subject to question, and the questioning suggests that there may be several ways in which to avoid res judicata effects in F2.

    a) Restrictive interpretation of the F1 judgment.

        (1) Interpret the issue before F1 as not being precisely the same issue.

        (2) Interpret the F1 decree as being subject to modification.

        (3) Interpret the F1 decree as only adjudicating the rights of the parties under F1 law—this does not prevent F2 from deciding rights under F2 law.

    b) Supreme Court created exceptions to full faith and credit—If F2 has an overriding interest. This argument was unsuccessful in *Yarborough* (7-2) and *Magnolia* (but note that this latter was a 5-4 decision).

C. DEFENSES

1. The Nature of the Original Proceedings. A prerequisite to recognition of a judgment at common law and under the Full Faith and Credit Clause is that it be rendered in the course of proper "judicial proceedings." Such proceedings comprehend all action taken in the name of a state by a duly authorized representative in the settlement of an individual controversy after notice to the parties and after having afforded them an opportunity to be heard.

a.   A state may exercise judicial jurisdiction through its courts, its legislature, or its administrative bodies.

b.   But note that just because something is termed a "judgment" by the state of rendition does not entitle it to full faith and credit. For example, a commissioner's report appraising the value of property for probate purposes, even though denominated a judgment in F1, was denied the constitutional protection required for its enforcement in F2. [Taylor v. Barron, 30 N.H. 78 (1855)]

2.   Errors in F1.

a.   A judgment of a court having proper jurisdiction of the parties and the cause of action is conclusive in the courts of every other state and in the federal courts, regardless of the fact that the court rendering it may have made an error of fact or law in pronouncing it. Such mistakes must be rectified by action (such as appeal) where the judgment was rendered (*i.e.*, in F1). [Emery v. Hovey, *supra*]

b.   Similarly, the fact that there is an irreconcilable inconsistency between the factual findings of F1 and the decision rendered by that court is no excuse for the F2 court not enforcing the judgment. [Milliken v. Meyer, 311 U.S. 457 (1940)]

3.   **Jurisdiction.** The lack of jurisdiction in the F1 court may be shown as a defense to the judgment's enforcement by the courts of F2. This is true both if the F1 court lacked jurisdiction over the person or over the subject matter.

a.   **F2 may inquire into the question of F1 jurisdiction.** F2 may inquire into the jurisdiction of F1. A recital by F1 that it had proper jurisdiction does not preclude such an inquiry. See the discussion of *Thompson v. Whitman, supra*, page 43, where the Supreme Court held that the Full Faith and Credit Clause does not preclude this inquiry and that the record of F1 may be impeached as to its recital of jurisdictional facts.

b.   **General, special, and no appearance.** If the defendant did not appear in the F1 action but instead took a default judgment, then the question of jurisdiction of the F1 court may be collaterally attacked in F2. On the other hand, if the defendant made a general appearance before the F1 court to defend on the merits and actually litigated the question of jurisdiction, or had the opportunity to do so, or if she made a special appearance to contest F1's jurisdiction, then the issue of jurisdiction is res judicata and binding on F2. This is true of both personal jurisdiction and competency (*i.e.*, subject matter jurisdiction).

1)   **Standards for service of process--Adam v. Saenger,** 303 U.S. 59 (1938).

Adam v. Saenger

a)   **Facts.** Adam (P) sued Saenger (D) in California. On a cross-complaint (process was served only on plaintiff's attorney) D got a judgment. D then sued in Texas to enforce the judgment.

The Texas court refused the judgment full faith and credit because it claimed (i) the California court was not competent by its own state statutes, and (ii) it did not meet Fourteenth Amendment due process standards for exercising jurisdiction over P (*i.e.*, service was only on plaintiff's attorney).

b) **Issue.** May F2 use its own standards for proper service of process to ascertain whether service in F1 was proper for jurisdiction purposes?

c) **Held.** No. Reversed. The California judgment must be accorded full faith and credit.

(1) The Supreme Court will be the final arbiter as to whether F1 was competent under its own jurisdictional statutes.

(2) However, in deciding this question, the Supreme Court will be controlled in determining the content of F1 law by the procedure used in F2 for this determination. Therefore, if F2 requires that F1 law be pleaded and proved (*i.e.*, F2 will not take judicial notice), then the Supreme Court will follow this procedure.

(3) Since the plaintiff put the machinery of the California court in motion, he should be subject to any setoffs, etc., which grow out of the same action and which the forum provides are proper defenses. California demanded as a condition of using its courts a submission by plaintiffs to in personam jurisdiction on any claims by the defendant. Therefore, constitutional standards are not offended here by service on P's attorney.

2) **Contesting foreign determination of jurisdictional facts--Thompson v. Whitman,** *supra*, page 43.

3) **Jurisdictional issue litigated in special appearance.** In *Baldwin v. Iowa State Travelling Men's Association,* 283 U.S. 522 (1931), when a corporation, sued in F1, raised the question of jurisdiction in a special appearance (on the basis of faulty service of process), it lost, failed to plead further, and a default judgment was rendered against it. The judgment was sought to be enforced in F2 and the corporation defended on the basis that F1 lacked jurisdiction. The court found that the issue of jurisdiction was res judicata; it was litigated and decided in F1.

c. **Real estate.**

1) **Uncertain jurisdictional location of land.** In *Durfee v. Duke*, 375 U.S. 106 (1963), the Supreme Court upheld a Nebraska court judgment that land in the Missouri River was actually located in Nebraska. The Missouri claimant had brought another action in Missouri courts, which had found the land to be in Missouri and hence had argued that they need not give the Nebraska judgment full faith and credit since the Nebraska court did not have subject matter jurisdiction.

It had been argued that the courts of one state could not exercise jurisdiction and affect title to land in other states. But the Supreme Court indicated that the question here was "where the land located?" Once Nebraska courts decided this, the issue was res judicata.

4. **The Judgment Must Be Final.** The traditional view has been that a judgment must be final and not subject to change before F2 must enforce it. The more recent cases, however, indicate that this is probably no longer the case. The question is simply whether the prior litigation sufficiently covered the same issue before the court so that the issue has been disposed of.

    a. **Conflicting judgments--Treinies v. Sunshine Mining Co.,** 308 U.S. 66 (1939).

Treinies v.
Sunshine
Mining Co.

        1) **Facts.** Pelkes's wife died testate, leaving Pelkes and his daughter Mason (Ds). The estate was probated in Washington; Ds ignored the will and divided the property by agreement. Part of the estate consisted of shares of stock in Sunshine Mining Co. (P), at that time thought to be worthless but which later became valuable. Ds then differed over the agreement with respect to the stock. In 1934, Mason sued Pelkes in Idaho, claiming one-half the stock; she also opened the probate proceedings in Washington to replace Pelkes as administrator—Pelkes filed a cross-claim claiming full ownership. Mason said the court had no jurisdiction to decide the issue. The Washington court decided for Pelkes. Mason appealed to the Washington Supreme Court and lost. In 1935, Pelkes tried to enforce his judgment in Idaho, but in 1936 Mason got a judgment in her Idaho suit (the Idaho court refused to enforce Pelkes's Washington judgment, saying the courts there lacked jurisdiction of the subject matter). Finally, P brought an interpleader action in federal court in Idaho (F3) to decide which of the conflicting judgments it was bound to uphold. The court found in favor of Mason and the court of appeals affirmed. The Supreme Court granted certiorari.

        2) **Issue.** If the issue of subject matter jurisdiction has been litigated in the courts of two states by courts of limited jurisdiction, is this a bar to a new determination of the issue by a federal court?

        3) **Held.** No. Decree affirmed. The Idaho (the latter) judgment prevails in F3.

            a) Pelkes's Washington judgment should have been enforced by the Idaho court since the Washington courts had decided the jurisdictional question (res judicata). However, Pelkes petitioned the Supreme Court for review of the Idaho Supreme Court decree immediately after it was entered and under Idaho law it did not become "final" until it was sent back to the Idaho trial court for new findings of fact and conclusions of law and entry of the trial court's final decree. Therefore, the Supreme Court would have given res judicata effect to the Washington judgment. Just because F2 (the Idaho trial court) failed to recognize Pelkes's constitutional rights is no basis in civil causes of action not to give full faith and credit to the F2 judgment. Pelkes's recourse was to correctly appeal the F2 judgment. The last judgment in time will be enforced in F3.

4) **Comment.** The Second Restatement recognizes the *Treinies* rule, except that this rule should not be applied in situations where it is not possible to obtain review by the Supreme Court of the second inconsistent judgment (*e.g.*, where the second judgment is that of a foreign country or where the Supreme Court denies certiorari).

b. **If the judgment is subject to appeal.**

1) Many courts hold that the appeal in F1 of the F1 judgment is not a bar to proceedings in F2. That is, a judgment in a lower court in F1 is final (even though it is being appealed) and thus it must be given full faith and credit in F2. In *Paine v. Schenectady Insurance Co.*, 11 R.I. 411 (1877), F2 recognized an F1 judgment that was then being appealed; however, it stayed an entry of judgment awaiting the outcome of the F1 appeal—this is a sensible way to handle such situations.

2) The policy of the F1 state controls the question, and this policy varies among states. If F1 statutes seem to make the lower court judgment conclusive or final, then F2 may proceed despite an appeal in F1. If F1 makes its lower court judgments inconclusive and an appeal serves to vacate the judgment, then the F1 judgment is not entitled to full faith and credit in F2.

c. **Alimony and child support cases.**

1) **Hypothetical.** W sues H for divorce in New York in 1950. The New York court awards her a divorce and $1,600 alimony (accrued) to the point of the entry of the decree plus $150 per month thereafter. The husband does not make any payments. In 1955 the wife brings a second cause of action in New York for accrued alimony installments and gets a judgment for $9,000. Again the husband pays nothing. Finally in 1963 the wife brings a third cause of action, this time in California for back alimony in the amount of $25,000 (the amount of the two previous judgments plus eight years' accrued alimony at $150 per month) and future alimony.

   a) **Enforceability in F2 of modifiable F1 judgment.** Problems as to "finality" are present when an F1 alimony decree is sought to be enforced in F2 and it appears that the decree is subject to modification in F1.

      (i) The California court is bound to give full faith and credit to as much of the New York awards as are not subject to modification under New York law at the time of the California proceeding. The first judgment ($1,600) and the second ($9,000) probably fall in this category.

      (ii) But are the already accrued back installments ($14,000) still capable of modification under New York law? If some or all of these payments are subject to modification under New York law then arguably California need not give full faith and credit.

      In *Lynde v. Lynde, supra*, page 61, the Supreme Court held that a decree of F1 for future alimony, modifiable by F1, did not have to be enforced and given full faith and credit in F2 since it was not final in F1.

b) **F1 judgment for accrued installments--Barber v. Barber,** 323 U.S. 77 (1944).

Barber v. Barber

(1) **Facts.** Mrs. Barber brought suit in Tennessee on a North Carolina alimony decree against Mr. Barber. He had stopped paying after 12 years and had not paid for eight years. The chancery court held in favor of Mrs. Barber. The Tennessee Supreme Court reversed and found that the North Carolina judgment (a lump sum for the accrued installments) was still modifiable under F1 law and hence not a final judgment. Thus it was not required to give the North Carolina alimony decree full faith and credit. The United States Supreme Court granted certiorari.

(2) **Issue.** If the decree in F1 is not made retroactively modifiable, must F2 give it full faith and credit?

(3) **Held.** Yes. Judgment reversed.

(4) **Concurrence** (Jackson, J.). The North Carolina judgment was entitled to full faith and credit in Tennessee even if it was not a "final" judgment in North Carolina. "Finality" ought not to be a requirement or a relevant inquiry under full faith and credit—neither the constitutional clause nor its implementing statute says anything about it.

(5) **Comment.** The defense of lack of finality is in an uncertain status today. Furthermore, the Supreme Court, even if it finds the defense acceptable, will be the one to determine what "finality" amounts to.

2) **Modifiability.** Note that most courts, even if not constitutionally required to do so, will enforce decrees of F1 that are modifiable in F1.

a) **Modification by F2.** However, *People of New York ex rel. Halvey v. Halvey* (discussed *supra*) held that with respect to either prospective or retroactive enforcement of F1 decrees, F2 can modify them to the same extent that F1 could. But *Griffin v. Griffin*, 327 U.S. 220 (1946), has held that if obligations involved in an F1 decree are enforced in F2 when modifiable in F1, due process requires that at least as to accrued arrearages, the defendant be given an opportunity to litigate the question of modification (as he would have received in F1).

b) **Alimony--Worthley v. Worthley,** 283 P.2d 19 (Cal. 1955).

Worthley v. Worthley

(1) **Facts.** Mrs. Worthley (P) sued Mr. Worthley (D) to recover accrued alimony arrearages under a New Jersey judgment decree that was both prospectively and retroactively modifiable. P wanted the New Jersey decree established as a California judgment as to future installments. The trial court entered judgment for D. P appeals to the California Supreme Court.

(2) **Issue.** Even when full faith and credit is not constitutionally required, may the court in its discretion recognize and enforce sister state alimony and child support decrees both as to modifiable installments past due and future installments?

(3) Held. Yes. Judgment reversed.

(a) The courts of one state are not constitutionally bound to enforce the modifiable decree of a sister state nor are they constitutionally bound not to do so. A state may choose to give such credit to the previous decree as it would receive in the state where it was rendered. California courts recognize and give prospective enforcement to a foreign alimony decree even though it was subject to modification under the law of the state where it was originally rendered, by establishing it "as the decree of the California court with the same force and effect as if it had been entered in California, including punishment for contempt if the defendant fails to comply."

(4) Dissent. The majority decision will cause confusion because any state will be able to modify the judgment. Judgments should not be enforceable in F2 until they become final in the forum.

(5) Comment. Before a foreign judgment is entitled to full faith and credit there is a requirement that the foreign judgment be a "final" judgment "on the merits." However, a problem as to finality is present when an F1 alimony or child support decree is sought to be enforced in F2 and the F1 decree is subject to modification. Past due accrued installments that are no longer modifiable under the law of F1 will be treated as sufficiently "final" for full faith and credit purposes so that they can be enforced in F2. However, full faith and credit is not constitutionally required to be given to future modifiable installments under an F1 alimony or child support order. In 1994, the Full Faith and Credit for Child Support Orders Act was enacted. Under the Act, full faith and credit must be given to another state's child support order if the parties had reasonable notice and an opportunity to be heard. [28 U.S.C. §1738B] In addition, the Uniform Interstate Family Support Act ("UIFSA") simplifies collection of child support, or sometimes spousal support, when the support order was issued by F1, but the obligor or the child now resides in F2. Under UIFSA, an F1 order may be enforced in F2 via income withholding by the obligor's employer or an F2 state enforcement agency, or the F1 order may be registered in F2. After registration, the order is subject to the same enforcement procedures as if it had been issued in F2.

5. The Defense of Fraud.

a. The old view. Fraud is no defense in a state on a judgment of a sister state. If fraud was practiced on the court that rendered the judgment, the one alleging the fraud can reopen the judgment in the courts of that state and have it set aside. But one cannot attack a judgment collaterally on this basis in the courts of another state. [Christmas v. Russell, 72 U.S. 290 (1866)]

b. **The modern view.** Later Supreme Court cases conflict as to whether, under full faith and credit, the defense of fraud can be raised against the enforcement of a sister state judgment. The better view is represented by the case that follows.

c. **F1 fraud asserted in F2--Levin v. Gladstein,** 142 N.C. 482 (1906).

   1) **Facts.** Gladstein (D), a North Carolina resident, tried to return merchandise purchased from Levin (P), a Maryland resident. P refused to accept the returned goods and D went to Maryland to discuss the issue with P. While in Maryland, P served process on D who failed to answer the complaint. P promised not to continue the Maryland action if D would accept the merchandise. D agreed, but P obtained a default judgment, which P sought to have enforced by the North Carolina court. The North Carolina court allowed the defense of fraud and P appeals.

   2) **Issue.** May a party assert jurisdictional defenses in F2 (such as fraud in the procurement of judgment) that would be available in F1?

   3) **Held.** Yes. Judgment affirmed.

      a) Since a judgment obtained by fraud is subject to being set aside in F1, it should be impeachable in F2. Full faith and credit requires only that the judgment be given the same effect in F2 as it would receive in F1.

   4) **Comment.** Early cases held that fraud in the procurement of the F1 judgment was not a legal defense to its enforcement in F2. However, the injured party could seek equitable intervention to enjoin enforcement of the judgment. Since law and equity have been merged in most jurisdictions the better view is that if the judgment is subject to the equitable defense of fraud in F1, fraud will be a defense to recognition or enforcement of the judgment in F2 as well.

6. **Nature of the Original Cause of Action.** Another ground of attack on a foreign judgment might be that its recognition or enforcement would be contrary to the forum's public policy.

   a. **Penal causes of action.** The traditionally stated rule was that penal obligations imposed by one state would not be enforced by the courts of another state.

      1) **Definition of penal--Huntington v. Attrill,** 146 U.S. 657 (1892).

         a) **Facts.** Huntington (P), a New York resident, loaned the Rockway Beach Improvement Company, Limited (a corporation under the laws of New York) $100,000. Attrill (D), a Canadian resident, incorporator and director of the New York corporation, falsely certified that the corporation had received all of its pledged capital. A New York statute held an officer (so falsely certifying) personally liable to the corporation's creditors. After the New York corporation became insolvent, P got a New York judgment against D for the $100,000. D then transferred his security holdings in a Maryland corporation into trust for his wife and three daughters. P then filed suit in a Maryland court asking that the transfer of securities made by D be set aside as a fraud of his creditors and that the securities be charged with the payment of the judgment obtained by P under the New York statute. D defended on the grounds that the New York statute which imposed liability is penal in nature and therefore unenforceable outside the state. The trial court held for P. On appeal, the decision was reversed. The United States Supreme Court granted certiorari.

b) **Issue.** Does a statute which imposes a penalty necessarily qualify as a "penal statute" for the purpose of denying foreign enforcement?

c) **Held.** No. Judgment reversed.

(1) The statute is not penal and therefore the New York judgment against D is entitled to full faith and credit. Designation of a statute as penal depends on whether its purpose is to redress an offense against the public (in which case it is penal) or to afford a private remedy to an injured private property (in which case the statute is enforceable in foreign jurisdictions). The purpose of the New York statute is to grant a private remedy to corporate creditors not to redress a public offense.

d) **Comment.** A "penal law" in the conflict sense is one which is designated to punish (by fine and or imprisonment) an offense against the public justice; a wrong to the public as a whole. A judgment for "punitive" (exemplary) damages, recovered by an individual as a remedy for a wrong done to him individually or as a member of a group, is not a "penal" judgment in the conflict sense and full faith and credit applies.

This case indicates that the Supreme Court will decide which causes of action are penal and which are not. Furthermore, the fact that civil causes of action must be enforced does not necessarily indicate that penal ones will not be (the Supreme Court said that penal causes of action are those where it appears to the court asked to enforce it that the essential character of the law is to punish for an offense against the public), so the case is inconclusive as to whether F2 can refuse to enforce penal causes of action.

b. **The defense of public policy.**

Fauntleroy v. Lum

1) **Full faith and credit due an F1 decision that violates F2 public policy-- Fauntleroy v. Lum,** 210 U.S. 230 (1908).

a) **Facts.** Lum (P) and Fauntleroy (D), residents of Mississippi, engaged in a gambling transaction in Mississippi that was made illegal by a Mississippi statute. P then asserted that D owed him money—they submitted their differences to arbitration. P won and then sued D in a Mississippi court for enforcement of the award. The court, learning of the illegal nature of the transaction, dismissed. P then sued D in Missouri, got a judgment based on the arbitration award, and sought to return and enforce this judgment in Mississippi. The court there refused to give the judgment full faith and credit. The Supreme Court granted certiorari.

    b) **Issue.** Must the courts of F2 give full faith and credit to and enforce a judgment of F1, which is based on an agreement that violates the public policy of F2?

    c) **Held.** Yes. Judgment reversed.

        (1) Mississippi must give full faith and credit to the Missouri judgment. Public policy is not a defense to a suit on a sister state's judgment.

    d) **Dissent** (White, Harlan, McKenna, Day, JJ.). Under the rules of comity recognized at the time of the adoption of the Constitution, and which at this time universally prevail, no sovereignty was or is under the slightest moral obligation to give effect to a judgment of a court of another sovereignty, when to do so would compel the state in which the judgment was sought to be executed to enforce an illegal and prohibited contract, when both the contract and all the acts done in connection with the performance had taken place in the latter state. This seems conclusive of this case.

    e) **Note.** This is not to say that it is not a defense to not entertaining a sister state's cause of action. [*See* Hughes v. Fetter, discussed *supra*]

    f) **Comment.** In effect this decision means that there is a double standard—full faith and credit may not require the enforcement in all cases of a foreign cause of action if the forum objects on the grounds of public policy, but no such objection is open to F2 when enforcement of an F1 judgment is at issue. This notion may provide the answer to the "penalty" question. "Penalty" objections by F2 can really only be considered public policy objections—perhaps then this objection is not open to F2.

  c. **Judgments for taxes.** In *Milwaukee County v. M.E. White Co.*, 296 U.S. 268 (1935), the Supreme Court required that F2 give full faith and credit to the judgment on a claim for taxes which had arisen and been decided in F1. The F1 judgment included an item for a 2% delinquency penalty.

7. Matters Subsequent to F1 Judgment.

  a. **Introduction.** A judgment's effectiveness can be destroyed by events taking place afterward.

1)   **Example.** For example, the forum's (F2) statute of limitations on bringing actions on a judgment may run out. For example, in *M'Elmoyle v. Cohen*, 38 U.S. (13 Pet.) 312 (1839), the Supreme Court held that F2 may enforce its own statute of limitations applicable to suits on judgments even though the judgment would still be enforceable in F1.

2)   **Statute of limitations--Watkins v. Conway,** 385 U.S. 188 (1966).

    a)   **Facts.** Watkins (P) secured a $25,000 tort judgment against Conway (D) in a Florida court. P sought to have the judgment enforced by a Georgia court, but Georgia law precluded enforcement of foreign judgments not rendered within five years. Since P waited five years and a day, the Georgia court granted summary judgment in favor of D. P appeals claiming that the longer limitation period allowed by the Georgia statute on domestic judgments was inconsistent with the Full Faith and Credit and Equal Protection Clauses of the federal Constitution.

    b)   **Issue.** Does a statute that imposes a shorter statute of limitations on enforcement of foreign judgments than would apply to domestic judgments necessarily violate full faith and credit?

    c)   **Held.** No. Judgment affirmed.

        1)   Because P may revive the judgment in Florida so long as the Florida statute of limitations has not run, the statute does not discriminate against foreign judgments. Once the judgment is revived in Florida, the Georgia statute grants P five years from the date of revival to enforce the judgment in Georgia.

    d)   **Comment.** The traditional view was to treat statutes of limitations as procedural and therefore governed by the law of the forum. Forum statutes of limitations applied not only to causes of action arising under foreign law but also to suits to enforce foreign judgments. However, the modern trend rejects the "substance-procedure" distinction in favor of applying the statute of the state with the "most significant relationship" or "interest."

b.   **Payment or other discharge.** Payment, release, and accord and satisfaction are valid defenses to the enforcement of a judgment. If a second judgment is rendered on the first, then discharge of the obligation created by either of these judgments in one of the foregoing ways will also operate to extinguish that created by the other.

c.   **Reversal of earlier judgments.** What is the effect on the F2 judgment of a subsequent reversal of the earlier F1 judgment on which it was based?

Assuming that F2 had jurisdiction, its judgment was a valid exercise of judicial power and therefore remains res judicata as to the issues involved despite the reversal of the F1 judgment. The judgment debtor, however, is not without remedy. Depending on the particular law of F2, he can in that state either have the second judgment vacated or reversed on appeal or else have its enforcement enjoined by means of an independent action in equity.

8. **Lack of a Competent Court.**

   a. **Introduction.** If there is really not a court that is competent to enforce an F1 judgment, then this is a valid ground for not enforcing the judgment. However, full faith and credit must be given to an F1 judgment if the Supreme Court finds that F2 is merely trying to evade its responsibility to give full faith and credit to sister state court judgments.

   b. **Cannot deny forum--Kenney v. Supreme Lodge of the World, Loyal Order of the Moose,** 252 U.S. 411 (1920).

      1) **Facts.** Kenney (P) obtained a judgment in Alabama against the Loyal Order of the Moose (D) for wrongful death. When P went to Illinois to enforce the judgment, Illinois refused, relying on an Illinois statute that local courts could not entertain a suit for wrongful death occurring outside the state. The Illinois Supreme Court affirmed on the grounds that the original action could not have been brought in Illinois and Illinois was not required to provide a forum. P appeals.

      2) **Issue.** Must F2 enforce a valid F1 judgment that could not have been initially brought in F2?

      3) **Held.** Yes. Judgment reversed.

         a) Illinois cannot evade its constitutional duty to afford full faith and credit to sister state judgments by statutorily denying jurisdiction to Illinois courts that otherwise are competent to hear the case. The Illinois statute violates full faith and credit because it attempts to close Illinois courts to enforcement of valid judgments rendered by sister states.

      4) **Comment.** The rationale expressed here is really an extension of *Fauntleroy v. Lum, supra*; F2 must give the same effect to an F1 judgment as it would have received in F1, regardless of how much this offends F2 public policy.

9. **Foreign Country Judgments.** How do the defenses available to the recognition of sister state judgments compare to those available against judgments of a foreign country? See *Hilton v. Guyot,* 150 U.S. 113 (1895), and *Cowans v. Ticonderoga Pulp & Paper Co.*, 219 N.Y.S. 284 (1927), both discussed *supra*, for the basic framework required in this area.

   a. **Note.** It is apparently true that the expanding ideas of jurisdiction in the United States have caused United States courts to be more liberal in granting or recognizing jurisdiction claims by foreign courts.

   b. **Res judicata and collateral estoppel.** Another question is the extent to which these doctrines will be applied in United States courts when they are claimed based on foreign country judgments. In *Bata v. Bata*, 163 A.2d 493 (Del. 1963), the court indicated that collateral estoppel would apply—but found that case to be "not a proper case."

V. CHOICE OF LAW

A. AUTHORITATIVE SOURCES OF CONFLICT OF LAWS—CONSTITUTIONAL LIMITATIONS

It is important at the outset to understand what limitations are imposed on a court in applying a choice of law rule. The Constitution places some restrictions on what state conflict of laws rules may provide. This is very important to the enforcement of foreign based rights, to the limitations on the use of the local law of the forum, and to the problem of choosing between competing foreign laws.

1. The Enforcement of Foreign Based Rights: The Obligation to Provide a Forum.

a. Hypothetical.

X	Y
B	Forum
G	G v. B.
Promise	

Facts: B and G are domiciled in state X; B promises to marry G and then repudiates. G sues B in state Y. The Y statute allows "no cause of action for breach of promise to marry." X allows such actions.

Question: Can Y refuse to hear and decide the case? (Note that this is an X-F type case.)

b. Can courts constitutionally refuse to entertain a cause of action arising in another state?

Hughes
v. Fetter

1) Enforcement of foreign based rights and the local law of the forum--Hughes v. Fetter, 341 U.S. 609 (1951).

Illinois	Wisconsin
Accident	Forum

a) Facts. Hughes, an Illinois resident, was killed in Illinois in an auto accident by Fetter, a Wisconsin resident. Hughes's administrator (P) brought suit against Fetter and his insurance company (Ds) in Wisconsin. Both states had wrongful death statutes that precluded suits for deaths occurring outside the state. The trial court, on motion, entered summary judgment for Ds, dismissing the complaint on the merits. The trial court held that the Wisconsin statute, which creates a right of action only for deaths caused in that state, establishes a local public policy against Wisconsin entertaining suits brought under the wrongful death acts of other states. The Wisconsin Supreme Court affirmed, denying the argument that the statute so construed violated the Full Faith and Credit

Clause of article IV, section 1 of the Constitution. P appeals.

b) **Issue.** Can Wisconsin close the doors of its courts to a cause of action created by the Illinois Wrongful Death Act?

c) **Held.** No. Judgment reversed.

(1) Under the Full Faith and Credit Clause, the Wisconsin court must hear this action. Sometimes the statutes of one state need not be enforced in another (*i.e.*, on occasion foreign based causes of action need not be enforced), if the forum's "public policy" is against enforcement. But here Wisconsin had no real feeling of antagonism against wrongful death actions, since it allowed such actions when they arose within its own borders.

d) **Dissent** (Frankfurter, Reed, Jackson, Minton, JJ.). In the present case, the defendant was a resident of Wisconsin. The corporate defendant was created under Wisconsin law. The suit was brought in Wisconsin. No reason is apparent, and none is vouchsafed in the opinion of the court, why the interest of Illinois is so great that it can force the courts of Wisconsin to grant relief in defiance of their own law.

e) **Comment.** Courts today are not free to refuse to enforce a foreign right unless to enforce it would violate some "fundamental principle of justice, good morals or a deep-rooted tradition of the local jurisdiction" (and even here, as *Hughes* points out, there are limitations on such refusals). Note that when federal causes of action are involved, the Supremacy Clause is also in issue, not merely the Full Faith and Credit Clause. If Congress intends state courts to hear these causes of action, state courts cannot refuse on grounds of public policy.

f) **Limitation on refusal to enforce.** The *Hughes* case does not really decide the hypothetical, *supra*. Under the *Hughes* principle, one state cannot discriminate against a cause of action arising in another if the forum enforces similar causes of action arising in its own state. *Query*: How much different does the forum cause of action have to be before the forum can deny enforcement on public policy grounds?

2) **Enforcement of the forum's statute of limitations to preclude foreign causes of action.**

a) **Introduction.** The modern view is to allow a forum to apply its own rules of law as long as a *reasonable relationship* exists between the forum and the parties or the transaction, so that the forum has a legitimate interest in doing so.

b) **No violation of full faith and credit--Wells v. Simonds Abrasive Co.,** 345 U.S. 514 (1953).

Wells v. Simonds Abrasive Co.

(1) **Facts.** Wells (P), a resident of Alabama, was killed by an exploding grinding wheel while in Alabama. The wheel was manufactured by Simonds Abrasive Co. (D) in Pennsylvania. P's administrator, unable to serve process on D in Alabama, brought a wrongful death action in the federal courts of Pennsylvania under the Alabama

statute, which had a two-year statute of limitations. Pennsylvania had a wrongful death statute, but it had a one-year statute of limitations. The suit was filed between the first and second year. The Pennsylvania conflict of laws rule called for the application of its own period of limitations. The district judge felt bound by the Pennsylvania conflicts rule and granted summary judgment for D. The court of appeals affirmed. P appeals.

(2) **Issue.** Does the application of the forum's statute of limitations to a foreign cause of action violate full faith and credit requirements?

(3) **Held.** No. Judgment affirmed.

(a) It is a well-established principle of conflict of laws that if an action is barred by the statute of limitations of the forum, no action can be maintained although the action is not barred in the state where the cause of action arose. [Restatement, Conflict of Laws §603 (1934)] The court appropriately applied the forum statute of limitations to a foreign cause of action.

(4) **Dissent** (Jackson, Black, Minton, JJ.). The statute of limitations of the state where the cause of action arose ought to apply.

(5) **Comment.** Note the overlap with the "substance-procedure" distinction discussed *supra*. Cases have generally held that statutes of limitations are procedural (the forum's statute applies) despite their material effect on the outcome of the case. But the modern trend is to apply the statute of the state with the "most significant interest" in having its statute applied.

2. **Constitutional Limitations on the Choice of Law.** In the above hypothetical (*see* V.A.1.a., *supra*) possibly state Y does not have to hear the case; but suppose it does anyway and applies its own state law (no cause of action exists for breach of promise to marry), finding for the defendant B? This is a question concerning constitutional limitations on a state applying its own law.

a. **Fourteenth Amendment due process limitation in the X-F case.**

1) **Introduction.** It is a violation of the Fourteenth Amendment Due Process Clause for the forum to apply its own law when the only contact it has with the problem being litigated is that it is the forum. Therefore, if all the other contacts are with another state or states, the forum cannot constitutionally refuse to make reference to the appropriate foreign law. Due process requires "fundamental fairness"; thus if there is no reasonable relationship between the forum and the parties or cause of action, application of forum law would be fundamentally unfair—*i.e.*, it is not something which the parties could have foreseen or intended.

2) Insufficient contacts--Home Insurance Co. v. Dick, 281 U.S. 397 (1930).

    a) Facts. Dick (P), a citizen of Texas residing in Mexico, purchased a fire insurance policy from a Mexican insurance company to cover his tugboat operated in Mexican waters. Home Insurance Co. (D), a New York corporation, reinsured by contract with the Mexican insurance company for part of the risk it had assumed on the tugboat. The reinsurance contract was executed in Mexico. P paid his premiums in Mexico and any loss sustained was payable in the city of Mexico in current funds of the United States of Mexico or their equivalent elsewhere. At the time the policy was issued and until after the loss of the tugboat, P resided in Mexico, although his permanent residence was in Texas. More than a year after the loss of the tugboat by fire, P brought suit in a Texas court to recover on the reinsurance agreement. Jurisdiction was asserted in rem through garnishment by ancillary writs issued against D. The insurance policy contained a clause that required that suit be brought within a year of the loss. Texas had a statute that required that such a clause in a contract could not be shorter than two years. Texas applied its statute and found for P. The Texas supreme court affirmed. D appeals.

    b) Issue. May a state apply its own law to alter the terms of a contract entered into and to be performed outside the state?

    c) Held. No. Judgment reversed.

        (1) Application of Texas law to this contract violates Fourteenth Amendment due process because there are not sufficient contacts between the forum and the subject matter of the case. A state may vary the terms of a contract made within its borders or to be performed there, or if the forum state has some other contact with the transaction; but the only connection here is P's citizenship in Texas.

    d) Comment. Note the similarity between the "due process" contact requirements necessary to allow a forum to apply its own law and the "minimum contacts" necessary to give the forum jurisdiction over the parties. Be careful to distinguish the two because *International Shoe* "minimum contacts" cases do not apply to "due process" conflict of law questions.

    In *Dick*, the insurance policy was issued in Texas, the cause of action occurred in Mexico, and P was living in Mexico. However, if P's residence had been in Texas at the time the cause of action arose, presumably there would have been sufficient contacts for Texas to have applied its law.

b. Early application of due process limitations on the choice of law.

    1) Introduction. In a series of insurance cases, the Supreme Court suggested that the Due Process Clause required application of the law of the place where the contract was made to determine the validity and consequences of the contract. Had this suggestion been followed, it would have written the "vested rights" theory of choice of law into the Constitution.

New York
Life Insurance
Co. v. Dodge

a) **Application in an X-YF case--New York Life Insurance Co. v. Dodge,** 246 U.S. 357 (1918).

(1) **Facts.** P's husband (both were Missouri residents) took out an insurance policy with a New York insurance company. Later he borrowed on it (from the insurance company) and when he defaulted on the premium payments, the company appropriated the policy reserve to satisfy the loan.

(2) **Issue.** Can the Missouri state court apply its nonforfeiture statute so that the insurance receives some recovery from the policy, or must the court apply the New York statute, which allows forfeiture and thus bars recovery?

(3) **Held.** The court must apply New York law; it cannot apply its own state's statute.

(4) **Dissent.** The dissent focused on the "contacts" of the entire transaction (the insurance policy and the loan transaction) and decided that the transaction had sufficient contacts with Missouri for the Missouri court to apply its own law.

(5) **Comment.** The "vested rights" theory, which this case represents, requires that formation of contracts be governed by the law in the state where the contract was formed and that performance of contracts be governed by the law of the state of performance. But, modern conflict interpretations recognize that such rigid rules may well deny enforcement of valid statutes in states which have a greater interest in resolution of the contract than the state of formation or performance.

(6) **Note.** *Dodge* is an X-YF case. *Dick* was an X-F case (*i.e.*, all contacts were with state X. There were no significant contacts with the forum state).

The *Dodge* court (majority) substituted its judgment for the judgment of the Missouri state court, under the notion of Fourteenth Amendment due process. This led some to conclude that choice of law was a federal constitutional question. However, subsequent Supreme Court decisions make it clear that the court now would have allowed the Missouri state court's decision to stand, since constitutionally there were sufficient contacts (*i.e.*, with the forum state) to allow the forum (Missouri) to apply its own law.

c. **Full faith and credit limitation on the choice of law.**

1) **Earlier view.**

a) **Introduction.** If the weight of public policy behind the foreign law clearly outweighs the public policy behind the law of the forum, full faith and credit would compel reference to foreign law.

b) **Uniformity--Order of United Commercial Travelers v. Wolfe,** 331 U.S. 586 (1947).

Order of United Commercial Travelers v. Wolfe

   (1) **Facts.** Wolfe (P), an Ohio citizen, sued a fraternal benefit society (D) (incorporated in Ohio) to recover benefits claimed to have arisen under the constitution of that society as a result of the death of an insured member who had been issued a policy in South Dakota and who was a citizen of South Dakota during his membership. The South Dakota statute of limitations was six years; an additional statute stated that any provision in a contract limiting the time for enforcing rights thereunder was void. The defendant's constitution required that actions be brought within six months. The South Dakota court recognized its own statute, contrary to D's constitution, and rendered judgment in favor of P. D appeals on the grounds that South Dakota owed full faith and credit to the Ohio law, which allowed D's six-month limitation.

   (2) **Issue.** Even though South Dakota has contacts with the case, does full faith and credit require that South Dakota recognize the law of the state where the fraternal benefit association was incorporated?

   (3) **Held.** Yes. Judgment reversed.

      (a) Even though South Dakota had many contacts with the transaction, the South Dakota court must apply the law of the state of incorporation because this was a fraternal benefit association case, and these cases require uniformity.

   (4) **Dissent** (Black, Douglas, Murphy, Rutledge, JJ.). The rationale of this case could lead to dominance of the laws of states where major corporations are incorporated.

   (5) **Comment.** Undoubtedly if this had been an ordinary insurance case the Supreme Court would have allowed the South Dakota court to apply its own law.

      Note that in other cases subsequent to *Dodge*, the Supreme Court held that in the X-YF situation (such as existed in this case) if there is sufficient contact with a state (as there was here with South Dakota) to avoid Fourteenth Amendment inhibitions to that state applying its law, the Full Faith and Credit Clause does not require anything more. But the *Commercial Travelers* case stands for the proposition that public policy considerations may on occasion alter the "constitutional minimum" test.

2) **Modern view.** A forum may constitutionally apply its own rules of law as long as a reasonable relationship exists between the forum and the parties or the transaction, so that the forum has a legitimate interest in doing so. This point has arisen several times in cases in which the forum has applied its own limita-

tions statute as to causes of action arising under the laws of another state (as a matter of "procedure"). [*See* Wells v. Simonds Abrasive Co., *supra*]

The modern thrust of the Full Faith and Credit Clause has been to narrow the scope of the local public policy defense to the application of foreign law (*Hughes v. Fetter, supra*). It has not been used much to compel reference to any particular foreign law. As an example, examine the evolution of the workers' compensation cases.

a) **Worker on assignment in another state.** In *Bradford Electric Light Co. v. Clapper*, 286 U.S. 145 (1931), a Vermont domiciliary was employed by a Vermont employer working on an assignment in New Hampshire. His widow brought an action for the employee's death; the Supreme Court required the New Hampshire court to apply the Vermont law (the place of employment) on the workers' compensation question.

b) **Relative interests.** In *Alaska Packers Association v. Industrial Accident Commission of California*, 294 U.S. 532 (1935), the Supreme Court recognized alternative choice of law rules where the interest of the place of employment was outweighed by the interest of the place of injury.

Pacific Employers Insurance Co. v. Industrial Accident Commission

c) **Full faith and credit requirement--Pacific Employers Insurance Co. v. Industrial Accident Commission,** 306 U.S. 493 (1939).

(1) **Facts.** A Massachusetts employee of a Massachusetts employer was injured while on company business in California. The employee successfully petitioned the California Industrial Accident Commission (P) for workers' compensation under California law. Now P seeks to enforce the judgment against the employer's insurance company (D). D claims that full faith and credit requires California to recognize Massachusetts law, which grants jurisdiction to Massachusetts over contracts entered into within the state.

(2) **Issue.** Does California have a sufficient interest in applying its own law so that full faith and credit will not be violated if California does not recognize Massachusetts law?

(3) **Held.** Yes. California may apply its own law.

(a) California has a valid interest in protecting employees injured in California. A ruling to the contrary would deny a state enforcement of its own public policy expressed in valid statutes.

d) **No constitutional requirement.** In *Crider v. Zurich Insurance Co.,* 380 U.S. 39 (1965), an Alabama resident, injured in Alabama while working for a Georgia employer during the course of employment covered by the Georgia workers' compensation act, secured a default judgment against the employer in an Alabama state court on the Georgia workers' compensation claim. He then brought suit in Alabama federal court on the state court judgment. The Georgia employer's defense was that the Alabama state court was without jurisdiction to hear the first suit because the Georgia act under which it was brought prescribed an exclusive remedy before the Georgia compensation board. The Supreme Court held, however, that a forum state need not give full faith and credit to a sister state's statute that after creating a right purports to limit its enforcement to local tribunals. The Alabama court had jurisdiction over the parties, and while most courts would choose not to exercise jurisdiction over a sister state workers' compensation claim, there is nothing in the federal Constitution to prevent their hearing such cases nor to invalidate judgments rendered in them. Note that *Crider* is the reverse of *Hughes, supra.*

3) **Conclusion.** The Supreme Court has retreated from its position of involvement expressed in the *Dodge* case era. It now speaks in terms of constitutional minima; it no longer requires complete uniformity in state choice of law rules, policies, and criteria. Thus, in the X-YF situation, if there is sufficient contact to avoid Fourteenth Amendment inhibitions, the forum can probably apply its own law notwithstanding anything in the Full Faith and Credit Clause.

a) **Interests vs. contacts.** Does a state today have to have not only "contacts" but also an "interest" in order to constitutionally justify the application of its law? That is, does a state have sufficient interest to apply its own law simply on the basis of having some contact, any contact, even if wholly fortuitous, with the transaction?

b) **The balancing test--Carroll v. Lanza,** 349 U.S. 408 (1955). Carroll
v. Lanza

   (1) **Facts.** Carroll (P), an employee of Lanza's (D's) subcontractor, was injured while working in Arkansas. P and his employer were residents of Missouri, the state where the employment contract was entered into. Unaware of any cause of action available in Arkansas, P received workers' compensation under Missouri law, which also stated that workers' compensation was the exclusive remedy available under employment contracts formed in Missouri. P later recovered damages from a federal court in Arkansas, but the court of appeals reversed on the basis of full faith and credit. P appeals.

   (2) **Issue.** Can Arkansas refuse to give a Missouri statute full faith and credit and thereby apply its own statute (which also purported to be exclusive) because the place of injury is a sufficient contact to justify a forum's application of its own law?

   (3) **Held.** Yes. Judgment reversed.

      (a) The state where a personal injury occurs has sufficient interest in the case so that full faith and credit will not be violated if that state chooses not to enforce the foreign "exclusive remedy" statute. Arkansas does not have to limit P's remedies to those arising under Missouri law.

   (4) **Dissent** (Frankfurter, Burton, Harlan, JJ.). If Arkansas is going to hear the case it should decide the rights of the parties by Missouri law, not because Arkansas does not have the constitutional requirement of minimum contacts, but because Missouri has a much greater interest.

   (5) **Comment.** Essentially the position of the dissent is that Missouri had the greatest interest so its law should apply. But the majority holds that Arkansas can apply its law as long as it has the constitutionally required "minimum contacts." The dissent weighs the relative state

interests. The dissent's view has never prevailed, but it may in the future.

    c) **Note.** While there appear to be some precedents for the interest weighing approach, they do not seem to have carried a majority for a long time. Thus, constitutionally speaking, minimum contacts are all that is required for the forum to apply its own law.

    d) **Scope of the Full Faith and Credit Clause.** The Full Faith and Credit Clause requires that one state give "full faith and credit" to the "public acts, records and judicial proceedings" of every other state.

        (1) **Public acts.** "Public acts" has been interpreted to mean the statutes of sister states. But this does not mean that all foreign statutes are to be given effect in each case. The question is still which state's laws (including its statutes) are to be applied.

        (2) **Judicial proceedings.** "Judicial proceedings" is construed as meaning judgments of state courts. Query as to other state administrative acts?

        (3) **Conclusion.** Today there are some constitutional limits on a forum's choice of law rules, but not many. Recently the Supreme Court has drifted away from use of the Fourteenth Amendment due process idea and used the Full Faith and Credit Clause almost exclusively. Even here, however, there are not many limits imposed.

  d. **Application of due process to compel recognition of foreign law.**

    1) **Introduction.** Back in the era of *Dodge, supra*, the Supreme Court often substituted its own judgment for that of the states on choice of law rules, under the notion of Fourteenth Amendment due process. It now appears settled that due process cannot be invoked to compel the forum to apply any particular choice of law rule—*i.e.*, there are no affirmative choice of law rules compelled by the Due Process Clause.

    2) **Applications.**

Watson v.
Employers
Liability
Assurance
Corp., Ltd.

    a) **Due process denied as grounds for application of foreign law-- Watson v. Employers Liability Assurance Corp., Ltd.,** 348 U.S. 66 (1954).

        (1) **Facts.** Watson (P), a resident of Louisiana, brought suit in that state against a British liability insurer (D) for injuries sustained in Louisiana through use of a product manufactured by an Illinois subsidiary (Toni) of a Massachusetts corporation (Gillette) and covered by insurance written by D. The court permitted the action under a local "direct action" statute (permitting a victim to sue the defendant's liability insurer directly) despite a provision in the insurance contract to the contrary. D argued that due process required the Louisiana court to refer to the laws of Massachusetts and Illinois to enforce the "no direct action" provision of contracts entered into in those states. The trial court dismissed P's case and the court of appeals affirmed.

(2) Issue. Does due process require the Louisiana court to refer to the laws of Massachusetts and Illinois when Louisiana has significant contacts with the case?

(3) Held. No. Judgment reversed.

(a) Some contracts made locally, affecting nothing but local affairs, may well justify denying other states the power to alter those contracts. However, Louisiana's direct action statute is not a mere intermeddling in affairs beyond its boundaries. Persons injured or killed in Louisiana are most likely to be Louisiana residents, and even if not, Louisiana may have to care for them. Louisiana has manifested its natural interest in the injured by providing remedies for recovery of damages.

(b) Louisiana courts provide the most convenient forum for trial of these cases. It is difficult to serve process on wrongdoers who live in or do business in other states. In this case, if not for the direct action law, P might have to go to Massachusetts or Illinois to get her case tried, although she lives in Louisiana and her claim is for injuries from a product bought and used there.

b) **Contact at the time of suit--Clay v. Sun Insurance Office, Ltd.,** 377 U.S. 179 (1964).

Clay v. Sun Insurance Office, Ltd.

(1) Facts. Clay (P), while a resident of Illinois, purchased a contract of insurance from a British company giving worldwide coverage of all risks of loss to plaintiff's personal property and requiring that suit for loss be brought within one year after discovery. P moved to Florida where some of his property was destroyed. A Florida statute made contractual statutes of limitation void if shorter than the state's own five-year limit. Three members of the Supreme Court went on record as willing to let Florida apply its own law (contact at time of suit), but the case was remanded to the court of appeals pending resolution of local law questions by the Florida Supreme Court. After resolution of these questions in P's favor, the court of appeals held it was incompatible with due process to apply Florida law. P appeals.

(2) Issue. Does Florida have sufficient contacts with the case to allow application of its law even though the case involves the validity of a contract provision entered in a foreign state?

(3) Held. Yes. Judgment reversed.

(a) Florida law can constitutionally be applied despite the contract's original contacts with Illinois. The presence of the insured's residence there at the time of loss, all with the insurer's knowledge, provides Florida with "ample contacts" permitting application of its law.

(4) Comments.

(a)   A forum is free under due process and/or the Full Faith and Credit Clause to apply its own law, or the law of any other state with which the transaction has a reasonable relationship.

(b)   Of course, an issue raised by *Clay* is (assuming that a state must have contact to apply its law) when is the critical time to assess whether a state has the necessary contact—at the date of the transaction or at the date of suit?

c)   **Employment; change of residence prior to suit--Allstate Insurance Co. v. Hague,** 449 U.S. 302 (1981).

(1)   **Facts.** Hague's (P's) husband was killed in a motorcycle accident in Wisconsin. P, her husband, and the operators of both vehicles were all Wisconsin residents at the time of the accident. P's husband had been employed in Minnesota for 15 years and after the accident P moved to Minnesota, where the Minnesota Registrar of Probate appointed P personal representative of her husband's estate. P brought this action in a Minnesota court seeking a declaration that the decedent's three insurance policies should be "stacked" to provide for $45,000 worth of coverage instead of $15,000. Allstate Insurance Co. (D) argued that Wisconsin law (which prohibits stacking) should apply because the policy was delivered in Wisconsin, the accident occurred in Wisconsin, and all parties were Wisconsin residents. The Minnesota Supreme Court affirmed the Minnesota district court's decision to apply Minnesota law and award P $45,000. D appeals.

(2)   **Issue.** Does Minnesota have sufficient contacts to apply its own law?

(3)   **Held.** Yes. Judgment Affirmed.

(a)   A state, in order to constitutionally apply its own law when there is a choice of law, must have a significant contact or a significant aggregation of contacts creating state interests. The Minnesota contacts with the parties and the occurrence are obviously significant. Three contacts are crucial for determining jurisdiction: the decedent was a member of Minnesota's work force, having been employed there for 15 years; D was present and doing business in Minnesota, and might have known that it might be sued there and that the state courts would apply their own law; last, P became a Minnesota resident prior to this suit, and in connection with P's residence in Minnesota she was appointed personal representative of her husband's estate by the Minnesota Registrar of Probate. The sum of these contacts with the parties and the occurrence is significant and Minnesota's application of its law was not arbitrary or fundamentally unfair.

(4)   **Concurrence** (Stevens, J.). Although I regard the Minnesota court's decision to apply that state's law as unsound as a matter of conflicts law, I concur in the plurality's judgment. The Minnesota court's decision poses no threat to Wisconsin's sovereignty, does not frustrate Wisconsin's reasonable expectations, and is not fundamentally unfair.

(5) Dissent (Powell, J., Burger, C.J., Rehnquist, J.). The Court has found significant what appear to me to be trivial contacts between the forum state and the litigation.

d) *Allstate* **revisited--Phillips Petroleum Co. v. Shutts,** 472 U.S. 797 (1985).

(1) Facts. Petitioner (P) is a Delaware corporation with its principal place of business in Oklahoma. During the 1970s P produced or purchased natural gas from land leased in 11 states and sold its product throughout the country. Respondents (Rs), 28,000 royalty owners who reside throughout the United States and foreign countries, brought a class action against P in Kansas state court to recover interest on delayed royalty payments. Rs recovered in both the trial court and the state supreme court. P petitioned the Supreme Court for certiorari regarding both jurisdictional and choice of law claims. The Supreme Court granted certiorari.

(2) Issues.

(a) Does the Due Process Clause of the Fourteenth Amendment prevent Kansas from adjudicating claims of all the respondents?

(b) Do the Due Process and Full Faith and Credit Clauses of Article IV of the Constitution prohibit the application of Kansas law to all of the transactions between P and Rs?

(3) Held. (a) No. (b) Yes.

(a) Due process requires that class plaintiffs be given (i) notice of the action, (ii) an opportunity to appear in person or by counsel, (iii) adequate representation, and (iv) an opportunity to "opt into" the class. Rs here were notified by mail, invited to attend in person or through counsel, and had the opportunity to "opt out" of the action by returning a "request for exclusion." Rs' interests were sufficiently protected.

(b) Kansas law differs in material aspects from the laws of other states.

(c) In *Allstate* we noted that for a state's substantive law to be selected in a conflict of law situation in a constitutionally permissible manner, the state must have significant contact or aggregation of contacts, creating state interests such that its choice of law is not arbitrary or fundamentally unfair.

(d) The state court's analogy that this suit was similar to a suit against a common fund located in Kansas is not founded. P commingled the suspended royalties with general corporate accounts. There is no specific, identifiable res in Kansas.

(e) Rs who failed to opt out of the action cannot be said to have shown a desire to be bound by the Kansas law. Even if Rs did desire Kansas law, a plaintiff's desire for forum law is rarely, if ever, controlling.

(f) Kansas's lack of interest in claims unrelated to that state and the substantive conflict with jurisdictions such as Texas cause us to conclude that Kansas does not have significant contact or aggregation of contacts to Rs' claims "creating state interests" in order to ensure that choice of Kansas law is not arbitrary or unfair.

(4) **Concurrence in part; dissent in part** (Stevens, J.). Exercise of jurisdiction was proper. However, the Full Faith and Credit Clause requires only that a state accord "full faith and credit" to other states' laws—that is, acknowledge the validity and finality of such laws and make a good faith attempt to apply them when necessary. The Kansas court attempted to give careful consideration to any conflict of law problems. There is no demonstration here that the state court impaired the legitimate interests of any other states. The standard applied by the Court to evaluate choice of law conflicts is erroneous. Rather than potential, "putative," or "likely" conflicts, I would require demonstration of an unambiguous conflict with the established law of another state as an essential element of a constitutional choice of law claim.

3. **Unreasonable Discrimination.** The traditional notions concerning which law applies are giving way to numerous new approaches. As long as the forum fulfills the constitutional requirement of "minimum contacts," it may apply the law of any number of states in a lawsuit having contacts with many jurisdictions.

This diversity of applicable laws has given rise to the possibility that in the same lawsuit the forum might apply the law of one state to decide one person's claims and the law of an entirely different state to decide another person's claims (even though both claims grow out of the same transaction—for example, the same car accident).

Thus the Privileges and Immunities Clause (Article IV, section 2) and the Equal Protection Clause (Fourteenth Amendment), which provide that a state cannot unreasonably discriminate against persons within the court's jurisdiction, may become increasingly important in the years ahead.

Supreme Court of New Hampshire v. Piper

a. **Privileges and immunities--Supreme Court of New Hampshire v. Piper,** 470 U.S. 274 (1985).

1) **Facts.** Petitioner Piper applied to take the New Hampshire bar examination and indicated her intention to become a New Hampshire resident since the state had a residency requirement for admission to the bar. P took and passed the examination and requested a dispensation from the residency requirement. P was denied and petitioned the New Hampshire Supreme Court, which also denied P's request.

2) **Issue.** Do the rules of the Supreme Court of New Hampshire that limit bar admission to state residents violate the Privileges and Immunities Clause of the Constitution?

3) **Held.** Yes. Judgment of appeals court affirmed.

a) The Privileges and Immunities Clause was intended to create a national economic union that has as a benefit the opportunity for the citizens of one state to do business in another state on terms of substantial equity.

b) The clause does not preclude discrimination against nonresidents if: (i) there is a substantial reason for difference in treatment; and (ii) the discrimination practiced against nonresidents bears a substantial relationship to the state's objective. The New Hampshire justifications (*e.g.*, nonresident bar members would be less likely to do pro bono work) do not meet this test.

B. INITIAL PROBLEMS OF THE FORUM IN CHOICE OF LAW CASES

1. **Whether To Consider the Action or Defense: Local Public Policy, Penal Laws, and Revenue Laws.**

   a. **Local public policy.**

      1) **Traditional approval.**

         a) **General rule.** The First Restatement provided that the forum state was not required to entertain actions in its courts that were founded on foreign causes of actions that were contrary to its strong public policy. Since this entire approach was based on the theory that courts would enforce rights that had "vested" under the law of another state, the Restatement attempted to minimize this public policy exception by stating that it was extremely limited. "Courts today are not free to refuse to enforce a foreign right unless to enforce it would violate some fundamental principle of justice, good morals, or deep-rooted tradition of the local jurisdiction." [*See* Loucks v. Standard Oil Co., *infra*]

            (1) **Effect.** Thus, forum courts generally permit recovery on debts arising from gambling activities that were legal where performed (*e.g.*, Nevada, Puerto Rico), even though had such activities taken place in the forum they would have been criminal acts—*i.e.*, the traditional contract choice of law rule directs the court to apply the law of the place of performance to determine the enforceability of a debt, and the fact that the debt is opposed to local law or public policy is no defense to application of the appropriate foreign law. [Intercontinental Hotels Corp. v. Golden, *infra*]

            (2) **Limited application.** Nevertheless, courts have refused to enforce rights arising under foreign law on the grounds that they violate local public policy. [*See* Mertz v. Mertz, *infra*]

(3) **Compare—dissimilarity of laws.** The lack of any similar cause of action in the forum would not justify its refusal to enforce a foreign right. If the forum's choice of law rule required reference to a foreign law for determination of the case, the fact that the foreign law creates rights which are different from or dissimilar to those recognized in the forum is immaterial.

(4) **Comment.** The application of the "local public policy" doctrine is necessary only when courts feel compelled to employ rigid choice of law rules to the problem at hand. If the forum's choice of law rules are flexible, local public policy may be relied upon in the process of selecting, rather than in correcting, the rule to be applied. This point is increasingly recognized by the courts and, therefore, it is only when the conflicts rules remain rigid (*e.g.*, title to land) that this defense need survive at all.

b) **The most significant relationship approach.** The Second Restatement continues the flat prohibition against the forum's enforcement of foreign law contrary to its own strong public policy. Again, the rule has a narrow application and the court should not refuse to entertain a foreign cause of action, in Judge Cardozo's terms, unless it violates a "fundamental principle of justice, some prevalent conception of morals, some deep-seated tradition" of the forum.

c) **Policy-oriented approaches.** These approaches do not use public policy as a "defense" against the enforcement of foreign law. Instead, "public policy" is used affirmatively to determine whether forum law should be applied in the first place.

b. **Penal laws.**

1) **Traditional approach.** Historically, the forum refused to enforce claims arising under the "penal" laws of another state. A "penal" law in the conflicts sense is one in which a penalty is awarded to the state as compensation for some public wrong, as distinguished from redress for private wrongs. Whether the foreign statute is penal is determined by the forum, and the forum is not bound by the enacting state's characterization.

2) **The most significant relationship approach.** The Restatement (Second) continues the prohibition against the enforcement of foreign penal laws and the distinction between punishment for public wrongs and compensation for private injuries.

c. **Revenue laws.** Claims arising under revenue laws were traditionally treated the same as those arising under "penal" laws—*i.e.*, they were not enforceable in another state. This rule developed in England and it originally applied only to the revenue claims of foreign nations. But a number of state courts today are willing to entertain an action brought by another state to collect taxes—stressing the need for reciprocal relations among the states. In fact, more than half of the states have enacted "reciprocal" statutes, which require their courts to entertain foreign tax claims if the sister state extends the same privilege to the forum.

d. **Applications.**

1) **Denial of local public policy as a defense to the application of foreign law-- Loucks v. Standard Oil Co.,** 224 N.Y. 99 (1918).

   a) **Facts.** P is the administrator for a New York domiciliary who was killed while in Massachusetts due to the negligence of D's agent (a New York corporation). P brings an action in New York for wrongful death. The Massachusetts statute provided for recovery, the amount to be determined in accord with D's culpability. D argued that the Massachusetts statute was (i) "penal" and the universal rule is that the courts of one jurisdiction do not enforce the "penal" laws of another; and (ii) dissimilar from New York law; and that the court should dismiss on grounds of public policy.

   b) **Issue.** May courts of one state refuse to enforce a right created under foreign law if such enforcement would not "violate some principles of fairness, some prevalent conception of good morals, some deep-rooted tradition of the common weal"?

   c) **Held.** No. Massachusetts law applies.

   (1) The statute is not penal in the relevant, international sense. A statute is "penal" only if it awards a penalty to the state as an atonement for a crime, or to an individual suing to redress a "public" wrong.

   (2) The forum's choice of law rule requires reference to some foreign law; the fact that the foreign law creates rights that are different from or dissimilar to those recognized in the forum is immaterial.

   (3) The court adopted a liberal view towards "public policy" as a defense: "The courts of a state are not free to refuse to enforce a foreign right at the pleasure of the judges. . . . They do not close their doors unless help would violate some fundamental principle of fairness, some prevalent conception of good morals, some deep-rooted tradition of the common weal."

   d) **Comment.** The public policy defense to the application of foreign law may be applied differently in the various jurisdictions. However, the fact that the laws of the forum are dissimilar to those of the foreign state does not necessarily mean that the public policy defense is available.

2) **Refusal to enforce rights arising under foreign law--Mertz v. Mertz,** 271 N.Y. 466 (1936).

   a) **Facts.** Wife was injured in Connecticut while a passenger in an auto owned and driven by her husband. Wife and Husband were New York residents. Connecticut allowed interspousal suits for tort damages, while New York did not. Wife appealed from a dismissal of her suit in the New York court.

   b) **Issue.** May the forum state apply its own law in a case if its residents are injured in another state and wish to apply the law of that state (which conflicts with forum law)?

   c) **Held.** Yes. Judgment affirmed.

(1) The law of the state of New York attaches to marital status a reciprocal disability that precludes a suit by one spouse against the other for personal injuries; it recognizes the wrong but denies a remedy and the disability to sue cannot be removed by the laws of another state.

d) **Dissent.** In situations where the law of a sister state is dissimilar to forum law, the forum must look to the underlying rationale of its own statute. If such rationale does not offer good reason for imposing the forum law over the law of the sister state, then the appropriate law of the sister state ought to apply.

e) **Comment.** The dissent in this case seems to be consistent with *Loucks* in that it requires more than dissimilar statutes to invoke the public policy defense to the application of the appropriate foreign law.

Intercontinental Hotels Corp. v. Golden

3) **Foreign enforcement of gambling debts--Intercontinental Hotels Corp. v. Golden,** 15 N.Y.2d 9 (1964).

a) **Facts.** P sued in New York on a check and several I.O.U.'s which D, a New York resident, had given in Puerto Rico in return for money (which he subsequently lost gambling in P's casino). The gambling debts were valid under Puerto Rican law, but the contracts involved would not have been valid under New York law (although not all gambling contracts are invalid under New York law).

b) **Issue.** Will local public policy preclude local enforcement of foreign gambling debts?

c) **Held.** No. Puerto Rican law will be applied and P may recover.

(1) Public policy as a ground for denying access to local courts will be restricted to transactions "inherently vicious, wicked and immoral, and shocking to the prevailing moral sense." Public policy, therefore, is not to be discovered by past precedent but by currently prevailing community attitudes.

d) **Dissent.** These debts should not be enforced since they are unenforceable at common law, unenforceable even in states that allow gambling, and violative of New York public policies.

Wong v. Tenneco

4) **Violating the laws of another country--Wong v. Tenneco,** 39 Cal. 3d 126 (1985).

a) **Facts.** Wong (P), a United States citizen residing in California, conducted farming operations in Mexico through a local front man in order to get around Mexican law. The venture failed and P sued Tenneco's subsidiary (D), a California produce broker, for breach of contract and other causes of action. D cross-complained for money owed by Wong. After trial and verdict with damage awards to both P and D, the verdict was set aside and all claims were dismissed; the trial court held the underlying transaction illegal under Mexican law. The California district court of appeal reversed.

b) **Issue.** Will a contract made with a view of violating the laws of another country, though not otherwise obnoxious to the law of the forum, be enforced?

c) **Held.** No. Trial court affirmed. The whole venture was illegal, but D may keep $108,816 from escrowed funds to cover expenses.

  (1) The standard is not that the law is contrary to California's public policy, but that it is so offensive to our public policy as to be "prejudicial to recognized standards of morality and to the general interests of the citizens."

  (2) A fundamental principle of the law of conflicts is that questions relating to control of real property are to be determined by the law of the jurisdiction in which the property is located. Mexican policy differs, but that does not mean our principles should be abandoned. Furthermore, Mexican law is not so antagonistic to California public policy interests as to preclude the extension of comity to the present case.

5) **Local public policy applied to cause to action from a foreign country--** **Holzer v. Deutsche Reichsbahn-Gesellschaft,** 277 N.Y. 474 (1938).

Holzer v.
Deutsche
Reichsbahn-
Gesellschaft

a) **Facts.** An employment contract was entered into in Germany, by a German plaintiff (P) and the defendant German corporation (D), to be performed in Germany and other locations outside the forum state. D did not perform the contract but dismissed P (on orders from the German government) because P was a Jew. The second cause of action involves a clause in the contract in which D promised to pay P a lump sum if P could not perform the contract due to no fault of his own (he was imprisoned by the Germans).

b) **Issue.** May a defense available under German law be used in the New York court even though the result may violate New York public policy?

c) **Held.** Yes. German law governs.

  (1) P's second argument states a good cause of action. P's first argument, that he should be awarded damages for unlawful dismissal, fails—D had no choice but to dismiss him, it was a government order. (This is the act of state doctrine.)

d) **Comment.** Rather than treat this case as a "public policy" case, the court chose to apply German law for other reasons. The contract was entered into and to be performed in Germany. Also, it appears that P went "forum shopping" in violation of the basic principle of the law of conflicts.

e. **Note on public policy.** "Public policy" grounds are important in two different situations: (a) If the forum asserts this as a basis for dismissal of the suit without prejudice (as in the *Loucks* case); and (b) if the forum asserts this as a basis for application of its own law and thereby decides the case on the merits. Careful analysis is required in the latter situation. Infrequently, a court having no contacts with the suit will assert its public policy as a ground for applying its law; more frequently, a state having some or significant contacts will do the same. In the first instance, the application of the forum state's law may be unconstitutional. In the latter, it is important to decide whether the forum decided the case on the merits, thus giving its holding res judicata effect, or dismissed on grounds of public policy.

2. Proof of Foreign Law.

a. Traditional rule. Traditionally, the content of foreign law—even that of a sister state—was considered a question of fact. If a party, therefore, asserted a claim or defense under foreign law, he was required to plead and prove that law as if it were a fact (*e.g.*, by bringing in an expert witness to testify).

b. Modern practice.

1) State and federal law. In modern practice, however, American courts are empowered, by statute, to take judicial notice of the law of sister states or that of the United States.

2) Laws of other nations. When considering the laws of a foreign nation, some states will require pleading and proof of the foreign law as if it were a factual issue; while other states have adopted the Interstate and International Procedure Act, which permits their courts to determine the foreign law on their own, as a matter of law.

c. Consequences of failure to prove foreign law. The law of the forum determines the consequences of the failure to prove foreign law. As mentioned above, only the content of a foreign nation's law is subject to proof requirements. Thus, in an international case, the forum may:

1) Dismiss the suit.

2) Presume similar law in the foreign state. Rather than dismiss the suit, the forum may resort to a presumption that the law of the other state is similar to its own and then apply its own law. This presumption has been extended to include "rudimentary principles of justice" in non-common law states.

3) Apply forum law. Finally, a few courts and some writers advocate the application of the forum's law, since no other law has been established in its place, on the theory that the parties either acquiesced in the forum law or that they waived the right to rely on the foreign law by failing to prove it.

d. Applications.

Walton v. Arabian American Oil Co.

1) Dismissal for failure to prove the law of a foreign country-- Walton v. Arabian American Oil Co., 223 F.2d 541 (1956).

a) Facts. Walton (P) sued Arabian American Oil Co. (D) on a tort committed by D's agents in Saudi Arabia. When neither party pleaded or proved Arabian tort law, the trial court refused to take judicial notice of the law of Arabia, but hesitated to dismiss the suit.

b) **Issue.** May the court dismiss an action which arose under tort law of a foreign country for failure to plead or prove the appropriate foreign law?

c) **Held.** Yes, directed verdict for D.

    (1)   Under New York's conflicts principles, the substantive law of the place of the tort must be applied. Since P deliberately refused to establish foreign law and failed to prove that Saudi Arabia had no system of laws upon which the court could rely, the court dismissed P's complaint.

2) **Application of forum law when the law of the foreign country was not pleaded or proved--Leary v. Gledhill,** 8 N.J. 260 (1951).

Leary v.
Gledhill

a) **Facts.** Leary (P) sued Gledhill (D) in New Jersey to force repayment of a loan allegedly made in France. When neither party pleaded or proved French law, the court applied New Jersey law. D appeals on the grounds that P had no case without proving French law.

b) **Issue.** In the absence of proof of law of a foreign country, may the court apply the forum's law to agreements entered into in a foreign country?

c) **Held.** Yes. Denial of D's motion to dismiss is affirmed. Certain common law presumptions may be applied to cases where foreign law is not proved:

    (1)   That the foreign law is the same as the forum's law;

    (2)   That the common law applies in foreign jurisdictions; and

    (3)   That parties who fail to plead or prove foreign law acquiesce to the application of the forum's law.

d) **Comment.** The consequences of failure to prove foreign law vary among jurisdictions. The New York courts would probably have dismissed this case according to the principle in *Walton, supra.* However, New Jersey decided to recognize certain presumptions and the "acquiescence theory" as described above.

3) **Modern trend: The Federal Rules of Civil Procedure.** In *Loebig v. Larucci,* 572 F.2d 81 (1978), Loebig (P) sued Larucci (D) in federal court for injuries resulting from a traffic accident in Nuremberg, Germany. P, a resident of New York temporarily stationed in Germany, was injured while a passenger on D's motorcycle with D. P requested that the judge instruct the jury as to New York's statute requiring "appropriate speed" while entering an intersection. The judge denied the request and gave an instruction regarding general negligence because he felt New York statutory law should not apply to an accident in Germany. The jury decided in D's favor and on appeal, judgment was affirmed. The court found that New York law required the application of the law of the situs or German law. Under Rule 44.1 of the Federal Rules of Civil Procedure, a court may make its own determination of foreign law based on its own research, but such research is not mandatory. Appellant (D) described German

law in his brief and German law was not in conflict with the given instruction. In Germany there was no statutory requirement that would require a different standard of care while approaching an intersection. Therefore, denial of such an instruction was appropriate.

James v. Powell

4) Validity of conveyance determined by the law of the situs--James v. Powell, 19 N.Y.2d 249 (1967).

a) **Facts.** James (P) was granted a $41,500 libel judgment against Powell (D). Shortly before the decision was rendered, D's wife transferred to relatives real property located in Puerto Rico that otherwise would have been available to secure the judgment. P alleged that D attempted to defraud her of her award. The trial court granted $75,000 compensatory damages as well as punitive damages of $500,000 against D and $25,000 against D's wife. On appeal, the court reduced the judgment to compensatory damages of $56,000 and punitive damages against D of only $100,000.

b) **Issue.** Will the issue of whether a transfer of real property is fraudulent be governed by the law of the situs of the property?

c) **Held.** Yes.

(1) Both courts above mistakenly applied the law of New York to the issue of the validity of the conveyance. Whether a conveyance of land is fraudulent will be decided according to the law of the situs, which is Puerto Rico. However, the issue of punitive damages will be governed by the "law of the jurisdiction with the strongest interest" in protecting against the object or purpose of the wrongdoing. Since New York has the strongest interest in protecting its judgment creditors, if there is a cause of action under Puerto Rican law, the issue of punitive damages will be governed by New York law. However, under New York law, punitive damages are not justified.

3. **The Local Law of the Forum: "Substantive" vs. "Procedural" Rules.**

a. **Introduction.** One of the objectives of conflict rules is uniformity of result wherever a lawsuit is brought. When foreign law is referred to, the reference should be to that law for everything that might influence the outcome of the case. However, such a complete reference is rarely made; to do so would throw too great a burden on the forum state. Phases of a case which make administration of the foreign law by the local tribunal impracticable, inconvenient, or violative of local policy are generally conducted under local rules and classified as "procedural" matters as opposed to "substantive" matters.

b. **What is "substance" and what is "procedure"?**

1) **Intrinsic test.** The traditional test says that substantive law is that law that speaks to the parties, telling them at the time they act what

their obligations are. Procedural law is that law which speaks to lawyers, judges, and juries at the time of litigation, directing them in the effectuation of the substantive law (*e.g.*, rules prescribing how litigation should be conducted).

   2) **Outcome test.** The "outcome" test says that the forum should apply its procedural rules unless they affect the outcome of the litigation.

c. **Contexts in which the question arises.**

   1) **State cause of action in a state court.** In this situation the courts have usually applied the intrinsic test. For example, the statute of limitations applied has characteristically been that of the forum.

   2) **Federal cause of action tried in a state court.** Here primarily the outcome test has been used, in the interest of the uniform enforcement of national law.

   3) **State cause of action tried in federal court.** The outcome test is predominant. But the uniformity of outcome requirement has not been carried as far as it has in the reverse—*Erie* situations (federal cause of action tried in a state court).

   4) **Evaluation.** The intrinsic test is not very helpful; and the outcome test will nearly always require that the forum apply foreign law.

      a) **Analysis.** One could call those rules that can be complied with by effective lawyering (and thus potentially would not affect outcome) "procedural." For example, service of process rules, the differences in which can affect the outcome, are nevertheless "procedural" since they can be complied with through effective lawyering. However, **the** outcome test may force the forum to significantly alter its legal system.

d. **Direct action statutes--Noe v. United States Fidelity & Guaranty Co.,** 406 S.W.2d 666 (Mo. 1966).

   1) **Facts.** P sued D insurance company in Missouri under a Louisiana statute giving a right of direct action by a person injured in Louisiana against a liability insurer for damages sustained. P said the law was substantive; D contended the statute was procedural only and had no extra-territorial effect.

   2) **Issue.** Are "direct action" statutes that provide an alternative remedy but do not create a separate cause of action enforceable as substantive law outside the enacting state?

   3) **Held.** No.

      a) The forum decides whether a foreign law is substantive or procedural, but in making the decision gives consideration to the interpretation of foreign law by the courts of that state. Here the court held that the statute was procedural, largely because this was the predominant theory in the previous Louisiana cases. No new remedy was created against the insurer—simply a method of proceeding in Louisiana courts.

4) Comment. Had the statute been worded such that it created a cause of action that did not previously exist, the outcome may well have been different.

e. Presumptions and burden of proof: Substantive or procedural?

1) Burden of proof. The "burden of proof" may require one party to either (i) raise the issue and go forward with the evidence; or (ii) present certain elements of evidence as to a particular issue or lose thereon.

a) The burden to raise the issue and go forward with the evidence.

(1) Introduction. If the burden of proof means the burden to raise the issue and go forward with the evidence, the failure to meet the burden generally does not have any profound effect on the case. Accordingly, there is no compelling reason to apply the foreign law at all, and thus it may be treated as "procedural" to justify application of the law of the forum.

Levy v. Steiger

(2) Procedural rule--Levy v. Steiger, 233 Mass. 600 (1919).

(a) Facts. Ps, Massachusetts citizens, were injured in a car accident in Rhode Island and sued D in Massachusetts. The court applied Rhode Island negligence law but used the forum's own law in assigning the burden of proof of contributory negligence to D, who appealed the ruling.

(b) Issue. Did the court err in applying its own burden of proof law while applying the substantive law of a foreign state?

(c) Held. No. Judgment affirmed.

1] Ps still had to prove negligence under Rhode Island law. Massachusetts properly applied its "procedural rules," which required D to bring forth evidence on the issue of contributory negligence.

b) The burden to raise certain elements of evidence or lose the issue.

(1) Introduction. If the burden of proof is of this type, it will clearly have a profound effect on the outcome of the case and thus should be governed by the law under which the cause of action arises. Thus, "burden of proof" in this sense is clearly a "substantive" matter.

(2) Contributory negligence. In *Fitzpatrick v. International Railway Co.*, 252 N.Y. 127 (1929), P, an employee of International Railway (D), was injured in Ontario allegedly as a result of D's negligence. P sued in New York, the state of D's incorporation. The New York court applied Ontario's law of comparative negligence, which placed the burden of proving contributory negligence on D. New York law treats the issue of burden of proof as to contributory negligence as part of the substantive cause of action, the absence of which must be proved by P for a cause of action to arise. D appealed, claiming that the law of contributory negligence was "procedural" and therefore to be governed by the law of the forum. The court of appeals affirmed the lower court, saying that the law of comparative negligence in the forum where the injury occurred created a new cause of action that did not exist at common law. It was therefore more than a "procedural matter" and New York was not required to apply its own law.

2) **Presumptions.** The same problems are involved here as with burden of proof. If a presumption relates merely to the manner in which facts may be proved, it is clearly "procedural." However, if a presumption would materially affect the outcome of the case (*i.e.*, conclusive presumptions), then it should be governed by the appropriate foreign law, up to the point that such application becomes impractical or unduly inconvenient for the forum.

3) **Another approach: state interest analysis.** This approach determines which states, if any, have an "interest" in having their law applied. This view may eventually predominate. Note that the interest analysis eliminates the substance-procedure distinction.

f. **Proof of facts.** Rules of evidence, competency, and credibility of witnesses are generally deemed procedural and thus are governed by the forum's law. [Restatement (Second) §135] But again, if such matters would have a material effect on the outcome of the case, the foreign law should control up to the point of inconvenience, etc.

g. **Privileged testimony.** The purpose of allowing privileged testimony is to protect the underlying relationship of the parties and to encourage their full and free communication. An interesting question arises when a communication is made in one state (*e.g.*, between husband and wife, attorney and client) and it is called into question in a suit brought in another state, and it appears that the communication would be privileged under one state's law but not the other's. [Restatement (Second) §139]

1) **The traditional approach.** Traditionally, privileged testimony was considered "procedural" and thus forum law controlled.

2) **The most significant relationship approach.**

a) **Testimony privileged under forum law.** The Restatement (Second) focuses on the law of the state that has the most significant relationship with the communication. If the communication is not privileged under that law, the forum should not treat it as privileged under its own law, unless introduction of the evidence would be contrary to the forum's strong public policy.

b) **Testimony privileged under foreign law.** In this case the law of the state having the most significant relationship with the communication protects the testimony. *Rationale*: Insofar as the parties govern their relationship according to the law of the place where they normally communicate, they may have relied on that law and their reliance deserves protection. Nevertheless, according to the Restatement (Second), the forum should admit the testimony (*i.e.*, apply its own law) "unless there is some special reason why the forum policy favoring admission should not be given effect" (*e.g.*, the forum's contacts with the parties are insignificant or the testimony is relatively immaterial).

3) The policy-oriented approaches. The policy-oriented approaches can be very useful here, since they cut behind verbiage to analyze the competing policies and interests.

4) Discovery of records confidential by statute--Samuelson v. Susen, 576 F.2d 546 (1978).

    a) Facts. Samuelson (P), a neurosurgeon and resident of Ohio, brought this defamation and interference with business relationship action against Ds, two doctors, alleging that Ds published defamatory statements to other doctors in Ohio and West Virginia. During discovery, P sought to depose doctors and administrators of two Ohio hospitals. The proposed deponents filed motions for protective orders, which the district court granted on the basis of an Ohio statute that provided that records and proceedings of review committees are confidential and not subject to discovery in actions against health care professionals or institutions. P appeals.

    b) Issue. Is the district court (located in Pennsylvania) required by conflict of law principles to apply Ohio law?

    c) Held. Yes.

        (1) Rule 501 of the Federal Rules of Evidence requires a district court exercising diversity jurisdiction to apply the law that would be applied by the courts of the state in which it sits. It does not state, as P contends, that the federal court must apply the law of the forum, whether or not the forum's state courts would apply their own law.

            P's interpretation would prevent the application of all of the forum state's law, including its choice of law rules, thereby defeating the primary purpose of Rule 501—to have federal courts apply the same rules of law that the states would apply. Therefore Pennsylvania's conflict of laws rules are applied to determine whether Ohio or Pennsylvania law should apply.

        (2) Pennsylvania has adopted the interests analysis approach to conflict of laws questions. Under this approach, the law of the predominantly concerned jurisdiction (the one with the most relevant contacts) is applied. Here the review committee proceedings were held in Ohio, they concerned an Ohio doctor's use of Ohio medical facilities, all the participants were Ohio residents, and the proceedings were for the protection of Ohio residents. Under these circumstances, the district court was justified in concluding that Ohio had the more significant relationship to the dispute and that Ohio law should apply.

h. Time limitations.

1) The traditional approach. Traditionally courts in the state-state context have applied their own statute of limitations (S/L), using the intrinsic test and labeling the matter "procedural." In the state-federal context, *see Guaranty Trust v. York* (*infra*), where the New York federal district court in a diversity case applied the state court S/L in the interest of "uniformity of outcome."

2) Two major qualifications to the common law rule.

   a) Statute of limitations in transaction state cuts off right and remedy. If it can be shown that the S/L in the state where the cause of action arose has the effect of cutting off both the "right" and the "remedy," then the forum state will normally apply that S/L. The interest advanced is the limitation on forum shopping. This is the position of the Restatement (Second) (*i.e.*, the only time the forum's S/L does not control is when the action is timely by forum standards but is barred in the state of the otherwise applicable law by a S/L that bars the right and not merely the remedy).

   b) The issue. What is the legislative purpose of the transaction state's statute of limitations? Issues important in answering this question include:

      (1) Does the S/L have the attributes of a "procedural" or "substantive" rule?

         (a) If the transaction state does not require that the defense be raised by a certain point in the trial, then the S/L appears to be a part of the "right."

         (b) If subsequent acknowledgment (of a debt, for example) will revive the cause of action, then the S/L appears to go only to the "remedy."

      (2) How does the foreign court classify its rule?

      (3) What is the language of the statute?

      (4) Is the S/L directed to a particular cause of action?

         (a) Typical case: Wrongful death statutes, where the S/L is part of the statute.

   c) Application of the traditional approach--Bournais v. Atlantic Maritime Co., Ltd., 220 F.2d 152 (2d Cir. 1955).

      (1) Facts. Bournais (P) brought suit under Panamanian law for back wages, earned as a seaman, claimed to be due from Atlantic Maritime (D) under the Panamanian Labor Code. Suit was brought in a United States federal court after the Panamanian statute of limitations had run, and D moved to dismiss the suit on that basis.

(2)   Issue. Did a general statute of limitations provision (which would prevent P from recovering if suit were brought in Panama) contained in the Labor Code, bar the "right" not just the "remedy?"

(3)   Held. No.

    (a)   The Panama statute of limitations was a general provision of the Labor Code, which did not specifically refer to the section of the Labor Code that gave P his right. Therefore the general statute of limitations goes to the "remedy" rather than the "right" and as such is a foreign procedural rule that can be ignored by the forum.

(4)   Comment. The underlying question is whether the statute of limitations goes to the "right" or just the "remedy." To decide this the court needed to look at broader criteria than it did—*e.g.*, does Panama itself see the statute of limitations as going to the right, etc.? If the statute goes to the right, the forum is bound to apply the foreign law as "substantive."

Heavner v.
Uniroyal, Inc.

d)   Limitations law "borrowed"--Heavner v. Uniroyal, Inc., 63 N.J. 130 (1973).

(1)   Facts. Heavner, a resident of North Carolina, was injured when his truck crashed into an abutment on a North Carolina highway. The crash was caused by a defective tire that blew out. The tire was manufactured by Uniroyal (D), a New Jersey corporation. Heavner purchased the tire from Pullman (D), a North Carolina retailer incorporated in Delaware. Heavner and his wife (Ps) brought this product liability action against Ds in New Jersey. Ds moved to dismiss on the ground that Ps' claim was barred by New Jersey's two-year statute of limitations. The motion was granted and the appellate division affirmed. Ps appeal.

(2)   Issue. Should the New Jersey statute of limitations apply?

(3)   Held. No, but judgment affirmed on an alternative holding.

    (a)   New Jersey has no substantial interest in the matter. The substantive law of North Carolina is applicable because the cause of action arose there and the parties were present in, and amenable to the jurisdiction of, that state. The North Carolina limitations statute is applicable and bars this action.

Cropp v.
Interstate
Distributor
Co.

e)   No choice of law analysis--Cropp v. Interstate Distributor Co., 129 Or. App. 510 (1994).

(1)   Facts. The Cropps (Ps), an Oregon couple, are self-employed truck drivers. Ps sustained injuries when a truck, owned by Interstate Distributor Co. (D), a Washington corporation, and operated by co-defendant Rust, collided with their parked truck in California. Ps appeal from a summary judgment that their action was barred by California's one-year statute of limitations.

(2)   Issue. Should the statute of limitations of California govern this action?

(3)   Held. Yes. Judgment affirmed.

(a) The Uniform Conflict of Laws-Limitations Act requires courts to apply the statute of limitations that corresponds to the substantive law forming the basis of Ps' claims.

(b) Ps allege that Rust was negligently operating his vehicle. Ps' allegations concern the parties' rights and responsibilities in operating motor vehicles on highways in California. Thus Ps' claims are substantively based on California law only.

(4) Dissent. Oregon contacts are more important. Where the parties live, or are deemed to live, and the economic impact of the litigation are Oregon contacts that create a substantive interest in Oregon.

f) **Borrowing statute applies to both residents and nonresidents--Trzecki v. Gruenewald,** 532 S.W.2d 209 (Mo. 1976).

(1) Facts. Trzecki (P), a Missouri resident, brought this action against two other Missouri residents (Ds) for injuries sustained in an Illinois automobile accident. P was a passenger in D1's disabled vehicle, which was being towed by D2. Under the Illinois guest statute a cause of action against a driver accrues to a guest only if his injuries are caused by willful and wanton misconduct of the driver. The Illinois statute of limitations is two years. A Missouri borrowing statute provides that "whenever a cause of action has been fully barred by the laws of the state . . . in which it originated, said bar shall be a complete defense to any action thereon, brought in any of the courts of this state." The trial court dismissed P's complaint, holding that P's action was barred by the Illinois statute of limitations. P appealed. The appellate court reversed and the case was ordered transferred. P contends that since he did not charge Ds with willful and wanton misconduct, no cause of action accrued to him under Illinois law and his claim for relief is therefore based on the common law of Missouri, which has a five-year statute of limitations.

(2) Issue. Should the Illinois statute of limitations apply?

(3) Held. Yes. Judgment of the trial court affirmed.

(a) The Missouri borrowing statute made the Illinois statute of limitations, in effect, a Missouri statute for the purpose of determining the timeliness of this action, notwithstanding that P did not charge Ds with willful and wanton misconduct.

(b) The borrowing statute applies in cases involving resident as well as nonresident parties.

(4) Comment. P relied in part on *Coan v. Cessna Aircraft*, 53 Ill.2d 526 (1973). The Illinois statute that tolled the running of the limitations statute while the defendant was out of state provided that it did not apply if neither plaintiff nor defendant were residents of Illinois at the time the action accrued. The state supreme court held the tolling exception for state residents required reading a like exception into the state borrowing statute so that a conflict would be avoided when an Illinois defendant, who was subject to suit in another state, was absent from Illinois during the period of limitations. The Illinois supreme court in *Haughton v. Haughton*, 76

Ill.2d 439, 394 N.E.2d 385 (1979), *cert. denied*, 444 U.S. 1102 (1980), held the nonresident exception in the Illinois tolling statute violated the Equal Protection Clause of the United States and Illinois constitutions.

Sun Oil Co.
v. Wortman

g) Modern approach to choosing a statute of limitations--Sun Oil Co. v. Wortman, 486 U.S. 717 (1988).

(1) **Facts.** The case involves an action in Kansas state courts to recover interest on royalties whose payment had been deferred. The royalties were from properties in Texas, Oklahoma, and Louisiana, and the statutes of limitations of each of those states barred the action. The Kansas courts applied the longer Kansas statute of limitations and imposed interest at a rate higher than the maximum specified by statutes in the other three states. The Supreme Court granted certiorari.

(2) **Issue.** Does the United States Constitution bar application of the forum state's statute of limitations to claims that in their substance are and must be governed by the law of a different state?

(3) **Held.** No. Judgment affirmed.

(a) Petitioner's (P's) argument that *M'Elmoyle v. Cohen* was wrongly decided cannot be sustained. The *M'Elmoyle* holding that a statute of limitations may be treated as procedural and thus may be governed by forum law even when another state's law must govern the substance of a claim rested on two premises. The first express premise was that this reflected the rule in international law at the time the Constitution was adopted and the second, an implied premise challenged by P, was that this rule could properly be applied in the interstate context without violating the Full Faith and Credit Clause.

(b) P's second argument is that a modern understanding of the Full Faith and Credit Clause should apply and that statutes of limitation are substantive under this application. We disagree. P argues that it is now agreed that the primary function of a statute of limitations is to "balance the competing substantive values of repose and vindication of the underlying right" and that this understanding should be applied here as we have applied it in the area of choice of law for federal diversity jurisdiction where we have held that statutes of limitation are substantive. [*See* Guaranty Trust Co. v. York, *infra*] However, *Guaranty Trust* rejects the notion that there is an equivalence of what is substantive under the *Erie* doctrine and what is substantive for conflicts of law purposes. Predictable outcome between cases tried in federal court and cases tried in courts of the state in which a federal court sits is the purpose of *Erie* jurisprudence. In the context of full faith and credit, the purpose of the substance-procedure dichotomy is to delimit spheres of state legislative competence. Further, we see no basis for "updating" our notion of what is sufficiently "substantive" to require full faith and credit. The words "substantive" and "procedural" do not appear in the Full Faith and Credit Clause and do not have a precise content. The purpose of their usage in the full faith and credit context is to give both the forum state and other interested states the legislative jurisdiction to which they are entitled. If states choose no longer to treat a particular issue as procedural for conflict of law purposes, those states can adopt a rule to that effect. It is not for this Court to make departures from established choice of law precedent and practice constitutionally mandatory.

(4) Concurrence (Brennan, Marshall, Blackmun, JJ.). The question here is whether a forum state can constitutionally apply its limitation period, which has mixed substantive and procedural aspects, where its contacts with the dispute stem only from its status as the forum. The forum state's contact with a claim creates a sufficient procedural interest to make application of its limitations period to wholly out-of-state claims consistent with the Full Faith and Credit Clause. Any slightly arguable inconsistency with current full faith and credit jurisprudence does not merit deviating from 150 years of precedent holding that choosing the forum state's limitations period over that of the claim state is constitutionally permissible. The Court asks the wrong questions and resorts to tradition rather than analysis to answer this question. It is a misperception to believe that this case cannot be resolved without conclusively labeling statutes of limitation as either procedural or substantive.

(5) Concurrence in part; dissent in part (O'Connor, Rehnquist, JJ.). The Kansas Supreme Court violated the Full Faith and Credit Clause when it concluded that the three states in question would apply the interest rates set forth in the regulations of the Federal Power Commission. The Court's decision was based on unsupported speculation. Insofar as the statute of limitations is concerned, the Court reached the proper conclusion.

i. **Determination of domicile as a matter of local law—not as part of the court's jurisdiction to act.**

1) **Forum decides--*In re* Annesley,** [1926] Ch. 692.

In re
Annesley

a) **Facts.** Decedent's personal property was located in England (this is the basis of the court's jurisdiction to administer the estate). At the time of her death, she resided in France (and had resided there for 58 years), but she had not taken the steps required by French law to acquire legal domicile in France. The internal law of England allowed decedent to dispose of *all* of the property by will. However, French local law allowed dispositions of only one-third. The action here was brought to determine the distribution of personal property in England. At issue is whether the property should be distributed according to the decedent's will, which depended on whether the will was valid.

b) **Issue.** What law should control the issue of whether decedent's will is valid?

c) **Held.** French law. The law of the domicile governs.

(1) Decedent's domicile was in France because decedent had her sole residence there and had intent to remain there, despite the

fact that in her will decedent had stated her intention to have her domicile remain in England.

    2)   **General rule.** The local law of the forum controls the meaning of words in a forum's own choice of law rules. [Restatement §7 (1934)]

j.   **Reference to the local law of the whole law of another jurisdiction.**

    1)   **Internal or local law.** This is the law that a forum would apply in litigation involving its own citizens.

    2)   **Whole law.** This is the internal law plus the forum's choice of law rules. *Example*: If reference is to the "whole law of France" it is to the internal law plus the choice of law rules of the French courts.

    3)   **Renvoi problem in** *Annesley*. Because the English court decided that the decedent's domicile was in France, it then referred the matter of disposition to French law.

        a)   **Problem.** Is the "internal" or the "whole law" of France to be applied? The judge indicated that precedent controlled and reference therefore had to be made to the whole law of France.

        b)   **The whole law of France.** A French court would have said that the law of the domicile governed if the decedent was a French citizen; if not, then the law of the decedent's nationality (English law) controlled. Thus a French court would have referred the matter back to English law. Is this reference back to the whole law of England? If so, then apparently an unresolvable circuity is established.

        c)   **Resolution.** The court solved this dilemma by saying that two French decisions had decided that if the law of England referred the issue back to French law, French internal law would then control. But query—in a case of first impression how is this "endless cycle" broken?

C.   CHOOSING THE RULE OF DECISION: THE THEORIES USED

1.   **Questions Raised.** Should local (forum) law or foreign (non-forum) law be applied? If the latter, which state should provide the law (and, of course, should it be the local or the whole law of the foreign jurisdiction)?

2.   **Traditional Mode of Analysis.**

    a.   **Introduction.** The traditional mode of analysis of conflict questions was based on the "vested rights" theory. This theory held that the law of the state where a right was created should apply. Thus, in tort cases the law of the "place of the wrong" (*i.e.*, the state where the last event took place necessary to make an actor liable for a tort) applied. In contract cases, the law of the state where the contract was made applied to questions of validity of the contract. The First Restatement supported the vested rights theory.

b. **Examples of the traditional analysis.**

    1) **Divorce.** In *Torlonia v. Torlonia,* 108 Conn. 292 (1928), the court stated that the law of the state of domicile applies, no matter where the commission of the offense creating a basis for divorce occurred.

    2) **Crimes--People v. Olah,** 300 N.Y. 96 (1949).

People v. Olah

        a) **Facts.** A New York statute provided that a defendant convicted of a felony must be punished as a second offender if previously convicted of a felony under the laws of another state. Olah (D) pled guilty to a theft which amounted to a misdemeanor in New Jersey but would have been a felony in New York. New York applied its second felony offender statute in sentencing D because his New Jersey conviction would have been a felony in New York. D appeals.

        b) **Issue.** Must the New York court apply the law of the state of the previous conviction (New Jersey) to determine whether D had previously been convicted of a felony?

        c) **Held.** Yes. Judgment reversed.

            (1) The New Jersey statute cited in the previous indictment created a misdemeanor and not a felony. New York cannot look to the underlying offense to determine whether it would have been a felony under New York law.

        d) **Comment.** This really is not a choice of law case since New York law clearly applies. The decision dealt with interpretation of the New York second offender statute.

c. **Procedural rules.** Under the First Restatement approach, the forum's "procedural" rules were applied, no matter which state's "substantive" law was applied.

d. **Well-established rules under the First Restatement approach.**

    1) **Torts cases.**

        a) **Application of the law where the injury occurred--Alabama Great Southern Railroad Co. v. Carroll,** 97 Ala. 126 (1892).

Alabama Great Southern Railroad Co. v. Carroll

            (1) **Facts.** Carroll (P) was injured in Mississippi as a result of the railroad's (D's) failure to inspect a railroad car in Alabama. P sued in Alabama under Alabama law. Mississippi law would not have recognized the cause of action.

            (2) **Issue.** Will torts be governed by the law where the injury occurred even when the alleged negligence took place in another jurisdiction?

(3) Held. Yes.

(a) The law of the place where the injury occurred (Mississippi) must govern, on the rationale that when there is a series of events that leads to liability, the cause of action arises where the last event that results in liability takes place (and the law of that state should control).

(4) Comment. This case illustrates a shift away from the strict application of the First Restatement approach for the following reasons:

(a) Focusing only upon the law of the place of the injury (*i.e.*, the wrong) often led to entirely fortuitous results—*e.g.*, when injuries were sustained in an accident in state A involving parties who both resided in state B and were merely passing through state A.

(b) The First Restatement rule frequently defeated the policies and laws of states having far more intimate contact with the parties and their injuries (*e.g.*, the state where the plaintiff is domiciled no doubt is far more concerned with his compensation than the state where the impact took place).

(c) There were many cases in which it was more appropriate to look to the place of the defendant's conduct to determine his liability (*e.g.*, if he claims a privilege), and in such cases inflexible reference to the place of injury resulted in cutting off a defense that the defendant otherwise might have asserted.

Victor v.
Sperry

b) Law of place of injury against public policy--Victor v. Sperry, 163 Cal. App. 2d 518 (1958).

(1) Facts. Victor (P), an automobile guest, brought this action against two automobile drivers and the owner of one of the vehicles (Ds) for injuries sustained in an automobile collision in Mexico. P and the drivers of both vehicles were and now are residents and citizens of California. The trial court calculated P's damages according to Mexican law. In addition, the trial court entered judgment in favor of the D owner of one car, finding that the Mexican statute that provides for owner liability without fault is in opposition to the public policy of California. P appeals.

(2) Issues.

(a) Should the court measure P's damages according to Mexican law?

(b) Should California apply Mexico's liability without fault statute?

(3) Held. (a) Yes. (b) No. Judgment affirmed.

(a) Since the accident occurred in Mexico, P's cause of action arose there and the character and measure of his damages are governed by the laws of Mexico. The measure of damages is inseparably connected to the cause of action and cannot be severed therefrom.

flict of Laws

The limitation upon the amount of damages imposed by the laws of Mexico is not contrary to the public policy of California or injurious to the welfare of the people thereof.

(c)   No right of action for damages for liability without fault under the circumstances set forth herein exists in California. This provision is contrary to California's public policy and in substantial conflict with California law.

c)   **Law of place of injury permits liability--Gordon v. Parker,** 83 F. Supp. 40 (D. Mass), *aff'd*, 178 F.2d 888 (1st Cir. 1949).

Gordon v. Parker

(1)   Facts. P and his wife are citizens and domiciliaries of Pennsylvania. P's wife came to Massachusetts, while P was serving in the armed forces in India, and met D, a Massachusetts citizen and domiciliary. P sued D in Massachusetts for alienation of affection. The parties have stipulated the alleged acts occurred in Massachusetts. On the basis of Pennsylvania statutes abolishing this cause of action, D moves for summary judgment.

(2)   Issue. Will the use of alienation of affection be governed by the law where the alleged acts took place?

(3)   Held. Yes. Motion denied.

(a)   This action having been brought in this court solely on the basis of diversity, we must apply the law of Massachusetts, including its conflict of law rule.

(b)   Pennsylvania has no law regulating the rights of that state's domiciliaries to bring actions in other states based on conduct outside Pennsylvania.

(c)   Both states have an interest, Pennsylvania as the place of matrimonial domicile and Massachusetts as the place where the alleged acts occurred and D resides.

(d)   Massachusetts holds a defendant liable for alienation of affections only if adultery or separation results, not when the results involve emotional upsets or decreased loyalty or affection in a domestic or foreign marriage.

(e)   Massachusetts interests are more fundamental here because the alleged conduct is stamped wrongful—so many people regard it as sinful and offensive to public morals and are likely to take the matter into their own hands in the absence of public tribunals.

(f)   Pennsylvania's policy of freeing its courts of this sordid type of controversy is not connected with the "purification of Massachusetts courts or the immunization of Massachusetts defendants who have been acting illicitly in Massachusetts."

2)   **Contract cases.**

a)   **In general.** Problems involving construction and enforcement of contracts are among the most frequently litigated in the choice of laws area. Although numerous theories and "rules" have been formulated, the courts have generally attempted to evolve principles that will give effect to the expectations of the contracting parties, except when clearly outweighed by the interests or public policies of a state having a direct and immediate relationship to the transaction.

b)   **Contractual designation of applicable law or the absence thereof.**

      (1)   **Effect of parties' express designation as to applicable law.** Often, contracting parties will expressly stipulate that the law of a particular state (or country) will govern all rights and obligations arising under the contract. What is the effect of such an agreement?

      (2)   **Early view.** Early decisions stressed the "vested rights rationale" (*supra*) and held that the parties were precluded from designating any different law. "If the contract was made in one state, it should not do the parties any good to wish they were in another."

      (3)   **Modern view.** This is clearly not the law today. Many modern courts allow the parties to incorporate foreign law into the contract as a "shorthand" alternative to including other provisions or interpreting those provisions already in their contract as long as the foreign law is not against public policy.

           (a)   Some courts allow the parties to designate a foreign law with which there are no "contacts" at all.

           (b)   However, the Restatement (Second) asserts that party choice will be upheld only if there is a "substantial relationship" with the law chosen, or some other "reasonable basis" for selecting that law. [Restatement (Second) §187(2)]

                1]   This is also the position of the Uniform Commercial Code: The parties to a contract may agree that the law of any state that has a "reasonable relation" to the transaction shall govern their rights and duties. [U.C.C. §1-105(1)]

                2]   However, party choice cannot evade or avoid fundamental interests or policies of the forum state. For example, if State A is the common domicile of a minor and a merchant, and State A law prohibits the minor from selling his property without his parents' consent, clearly the parties (minor and merchant) could not evade State A law by inserting a provision in the sales contract designating State B's law as controlling. [*See* Restatement (Second) §187(2)]

      (4)   **Exception—adhesion contracts.** The modern rule, recognizing the parties' right to designate which law will control their contractual rights and obligations, will not be applied when the parties were not in equal bargaining positions in choosing such law. Thus, if the designation is incorporated as a fine-print provision of an adhesion contract to which one party has no real bargaining power—*e.g.*, employment, insurance, suretyship, loan agreements—the courts are reluctant to uphold the designation, particularly if to do so would evade forum laws for the protection of that party.

c) **Effect of failure to designate applicable law.** In the absence of express designation by the parties as to which law is to govern their contract, the courts must make the determination. While there are various "approaches," as will be seen, the basic policy behind each is to obtain a result which is consistent with the presumed intention of the parties; *i.e.*, what they would have intended had they considered the particular problem.

(1) **Traditional vested rights approach.** Traditionally, courts applied a separate choice of law to "validity" problems, as distinguished from "performance" problems.

(a) **Validity problems—"place of making rule."** According to the traditional approach, all problems relating to the validity of a contract were to be determined by reference to the law of the place where the contract was "made." [Milliken v. Pratt, *infra*]

(b) **"Performance" problems—the "place of performance rule."** "Performance" problems, as distinguished from "validity" problems (above), were traditionally governed by the law of the place at which performance is called for in the contract. [Restatement (First) §358]

1] **Rationale.** Parties presumably intended to resolve performance disputes with respect to the laws of the place where the performance was to be rendered. Also, the place where the contract was to be performed created the rights and duties flowing therefrom—the "vested rights" rationale.

2] **What constitutes "performance" problems.** "Performance" problems include matters involving the sufficiency of performance; the manner of performance; any excuses for nonperformance; the existence and materiality of breach; all questions relating to damages (measure, amount, etc); and the right to rescind, when based on performance issues.

(c) **Criticisms.**

1] The characterization of issues as "validity" or "performance" problems was often difficult to make and frequently overlapped; *e.g.*, questions as to interpretation of the contract provisions relating to performance were classified as "validity" problems, without adequate explanation.

2] And, there was no reason to assume parties intended different states' laws to apply to "validity" vs. "performance" issues. In fact, it would be logical to assume they intended the same laws to apply to both: "performance being merely the other side of the obligation coin."

3] Finally, and most importantly, by relying on what may have been purely fortuitous "contacts," these rules sometimes led to arbitrary results. For instance, the mere fact that the parties happened to reach an agreement while passing through State A hardly justified applying State A's laws to interpretation of their agreement, when every other "contact" was in other states.

d) **Modern approaches.** Reacting to the shortcomings of the "vested rights" approach (above), most modern courts have abandoned the "validity" vs. "performance" characterization as unworkable and have adopted more policy-oriented approaches.

(1) **"Grouping contacts—center of gravity" approach.** A number of cases have utilized a quasi-mechanical approach of "grouping" the various "contacts" in the case, and applying the law of the "center of gravity." In *Auten v. Auten, infra,* the court applied the law of England as the "center of gravity" to sustain a support agreement between English nationals, even though the contract was made in New York and was to be performed (payments made) there.

(a) **Criticisms.**

1] First of all, the approach is too mechanical. The mere fact that more "contacts" occur in one state than another is not always reason enough to apply the former state's law. For example: in one case the court ended up invalidating a contract that would have been valid where entered into, simply because more "contacts" occurred in a different state. [Rubin v. Irving Trust Co., 305 N.Y. 288 (1953)—holding unenforceable an oral promise to make a will, even though the promise was enforceable under the law of the place where it had been made]

2] Also, the approach "breaks down" in cases without a preponderance of "contacts" in one state or the other. In such cases, the forum's determination of the "center" of gravity is often merely a legal conclusion disguising the real choice-influencing considerations.

(2) **"Most significant relationship" approach.** The Restatement (Second) approach is not as mechanical; it applies the law of the state having the "most significant relationship" to the transaction and the parties, with respect to the particular issue or kind of contract involved. The Uniform Commercial Code also adopts this approach. U.C.C. section 1-105 specifies that in transactions subject to the Code, reference is to be made to the law of the state with "appropriate relations" to the transaction, which is generally equated as similar to the Restatement (Second) approach.

(a) **Determinative factors.** In determining which state has the "most significant" relationship, the court will consider the competing policies together with the following specific "contacts" applicable to contracts problems generally: (i) place of contracting; (ii) place of negotiation; (iii) place of performance; (iv) location of subject matter of contract; and (v) domicile, residence, nationality, place of incorporation, and place of business of each of the parties to the contract. [Restatement (Second) §188(2)]

(b) **Exceptions as to "minor details of performance."** For "minor" details of performance of a contract, *e.g.*, time, manner, and place of performance not provided for in the contract, the Restatement (Second) retains the "place of performance" rule (above). [Restatement (Second) §206]

e) **Application of law where contract was made--Milliken v. Pratt,** 125 Mass. 374 (1878).

Milliken
v. Pratt

   (1) **Facts.** A Massachusetts wife (D) executed a guarantee of credit contract in Massachusetts, and sent it to business partners in Maine (Ps) so that her husband could obtain goods on credit in Maine. Ps sued D in Massachusetts to recover on the guarantee contract. Under the laws of Maine the contract would be valid. But under Massachusetts law, a wife had no capacity to contract. Judgment was entered for D, and Ps appeal.

   (2) **Issue.** Will issues of formation of a contract be governed by the law where the contract was made?

   (3) **Held.** Yes. Maine law applies. Judgment for Ps.

   (a) The guarantee contract was made when it was accepted in Maine, when Ps loaned money to D's husband. The fact that the forum's law would disallow the contract is of no consequence when the contract was formed in a foreign jurisdiction.

   (4) **Comment.** Note that the court properly applied its own law to determine where the contract was formed. Once that determination was made, then under the traditional approach, the forum was obligated to apply the law of that jurisdiction to resolve formation issues.

f) **Nature of dispute--Louis-Dreyfus v. Paterson Steamships, Ltd.,** 43 F.2d 824 (2d Cir. 1930).

Louis-Dreyfus
v. Paterson
Steamships,
Ltd.

   (1) **Facts.** Louis-Dreyfus and another business (Ps) shipped wheat with Paterson Steamships (D) from Iowa to Montreal, transshipment occurring at a point in Canada. The ship ran aground in Canada before it reached its destination and Ps' wheat was destroyed. Under United States law, D was liable for the loss; under Canadian law, D was excused if it could show that it had used due care in choosing a crew and seeing that the ship was seaworthy. Ps sued in federal district court in New York. The cause of action was dismissed, and Ps appeal.

   (2) **Issue.** Will a dispute involving obligations created by contract be governed by the law of the place where the contract was made?

   (3) **Held.** No. Canadian law applies. Decree reversed and remanded on a related issue.

   (a) Canada was the place of performance so its law governs. Although the contractual rights and obligations are determined by the law of the place where the contract was made (Minnesota), this dispute concerns performance rather than contractual rights and obligations.

(4) Comment. The court could easily have decided that the issue was a matter of contractual obligations to be governed by the law where the contract was made. It is impossible to distinguish between matters of performance and matters running to the obligation between parties (presumably governed by a different law).

Pritchard v. Norton

g) Policy to obtain a result consistent with presumed intention--Pritchard v. Norton, 106 U.S. 124 (1882).

(1) Facts. Pritchard (P) was surety on an appeal bond in Louisiana. P executed and delivered a contract in New York whereby Norton (D) was to indemnify P on the appeal bond in Louisiana. New York law would not recognize the indemnity contract, and D defended on that basis when P was called on to perform on the bond. The lower court decided that New York law governed. P appeals.

(2) Issue. Should New York law govern the validity of contract to be performed in Louisiana?

(3) Held. No. Louisiana law will apply. Judgment reversed.

(a) It is reasonable to assume that the parties contracted with reference to the law that would uphold the contract. The parties cannot be presumed to have contemplated a law that would defeat their promises. Since the contract was to be fulfilled in Louisiana, which would uphold the contract, Louisiana law will apply.

(4) Comment. The decisions tend to apply whichever law would uphold the sufficiency of consideration, provided the parties could reasonably be assumed to have contracted with reference to that law.

Seeman v. Philadelphia Warehouse Co.

h) Lawful application of the most liberal law--Seeman v. Philadelphia Warehouse Co., 274 U.S. 403 (1927).

(1) Facts. Philadelphia Warehouse (P) brought suit in New York to recover for the conversion of canned salmon pledged as security for a loan. The pledgor fraudulently regained possession of the collateral and subsequently sold it to Seeman (D). D claims that the original debt was usurious under New York law, where D conducted his business and allegedly where the salmon was pledged as collateral. Usury rates were higher in Pennsylvania and the loan would not have been usurious under Pennsylvania law, where the contract was executed. The jury was instructed under New York law, and ruled for D. The ruling was reversed on appeal, and D appeals.

(2) Issue. Will the court apply the law of the jurisdiction that will uphold the contract?

(3) Held. Yes. Pennsylvania's rate applies. Judgment affirmed.

(a) If the rate of interest allowed at the place of contract (Pennsylvania) is higher than at the place of performance (New York), the parties may lawfully contract for the higher rate. This is in keeping with the policy of upholding contractual obligations assumed in good faith.

i) **Higher interest rates that do not violate the forum's policy--Kinney Loan & Finance Co. v. Sumner,** 159 Neb. 57 (1954).

    (1) Facts. Kinney (P), a Colorado corporation, sued Sumner (D), a Nebraska resident, to replevy a trailer coach. P loaned money to D in Colorado in return for a promissory note secured by a chattel mortgage on D's trailer coach. The interest rate on the loan was usurious under Nebraska law, but not under Colorado law. D defaulted and P sued in Nebraska to replevy the trailer to secure repayment of the loan. The trial court entered judgment for D. P appeals the application of Nebraska law.

    (2) Issue. Will the forum enforce repayment of a foreign loan that bears a usurious interest rate under the forum's law?

    (3) Held. Yes. Judgment reversed and remanded.

        (a) Colorado has a similar statute as Nebraska, although the allowable interest in this case is higher in Colorado than Nebraska. Under Nebraska's statute, its "installment loans" provisions apply to foreign made loans only when the foreign jurisdiction does not have a similar loan statute. Such loans ought to be enforced because residents of the state frequently are involved in business transactions in other states.

j) **Contractual designation of applicable law upheld--Siegelman v. Cunard White Star, Ltd.,** 221 F.2d 189 (2d Cir. 1955).

    (1) Facts. Siegelman's (P's) wife purchased a "contract ticket" from Cunard (D), a British steamship company, for a voyage from New York to England. The terms of the contract provided that suit for loss of life or injury must be brought within one year, any alteration of the contract must be in writing, and English law would govern all contractual issues. P's wife was injured on the vessel. D's claim agent indicated to her lawyer that a suit would not be necessary to protect her rights. D made a settlement offer, which it retracted when Mrs. Siegelman died. P as administrator of her estate, brought suit to recover for the injury. The trial court dismissed P's complaint on the grounds that it was not brought within one year, as the contract required. P appeals, claiming that the representations of D's agent waived the limitation.

    (2) Issue. Will the court apply English law as designated in the contract to the issues of validity, so long as it bears a reasonable relationship to the contract?

    (3) Held. Yes. Judgment affirmed.

        (a) This case raises contract rather than tort issues and therefore the court will attempt to enforce the contractual intent of the parties. Parties may always make reference to particular bodies of law relative to issues of "interpretation," since parties are free to contract and such reference amounts to definition of contract terms. However, questions of validity of the contract cannot be governed by the designated body of law unless that body of law is reasonably related to the contract—*i.e.*, represents the place the contract was made or to be performed. Since the issue of the potential waiver is more closely related to issues of "interpretation" rather than "validity," English law, which would not recognize the waiver, applies.

(4) **Dissent.** This adhesion contract must be most strongly construed against D. The contract provision is ambiguous in regard to post-injury conduct. New York law should apply because New York was the place the contract was made, for a journey beginning in New York.

Sinclair v.
Sinclair

k) **Law of the situs of real property applied--Sinclair v. Sinclair,** 99 N.H. 316 (1954).

(1) **Facts.** Epps Sinclair died domiciled in Vermont, leaving no surviving issue. He was survived by his widow, the appellee, and by his brother, appellant. Decedent owned real estate in New Hampshire. Appellee was appointed administratrix of his estate by decree of the probate court in Vermont. Appellant was appointed administrator in New Hampshire. Appellee filed in New Hampshire waiver of dower and homestead and claim of her distributive share in decedent's real estate. The probate court entered this order. Appellant appeals.

(2) **Issue.** Should New Hampshire law be applied to determine what share of New Hampshire real estate would be awarded to the surviving spouse of a Vermont domiciliary?

(3) **Held.** Yes.

(a) The descent of real property is governed by the law of the state where the property is located; the domicile of the intestate is irrelevant.

(b) The inconvenience of searching for title and the impossibility of determining the validity of title if foreign judgments are considered as directly affecting the title to land are persuasive reasons why the law of the situs applies.

Toledo Society for Crippled Children v. Hickok

l) **Testamentary gift valid--Toledo Society for Crippled Children v. Hickok,** 152 Tex. 578 (1953).

(1) **Facts.** Hickok died domiciled in Ohio, survived by a wife and two children. In his will, executed less than a year before his death, he established a trust, the income to be paid to his widow and children for 20 years and then the corpus to be divided among 20 charities. The charities (Ps) sought to establish their rights under the will to certain land and mineral interests in Texas. The trustees were given the power to sell the mineral interests owned individually by Hickok and reinvest the proceeds. The most valuable interest was owned by Hickok in a partnership. Prior to his death, Hickok had contracted with his partner to form a corporation and convey the assets of the partnership to the corporation in exchange for stock. Under Ohio law, the testamentary gifts to the charities were invalid. In prior litigation, the Ohio courts applied Ohio law invalidating the gifts. In Texas, the district court, on motion for summary judgment, held the gifts valid to some of the Texas property and invalid to the rest. The Texas appeals court denied Ps any relief, stating Ps' interest was contingent rather than vested. Ps appeal.

(2)   Issue. Should Texas law govern the validity of the gifts to the extent of all of the lands and mineral interests in Texas?

(3)   Held. Yes. Judgment reversed.

   (a)   The "fiction of equitable conversion from realty to personalty or vice versa" has no place in conflict of laws. This doctrine may not even exist in some jurisdictions and to apply it would produce unnecessary confusion. Further, as to the mineral interests, there is insufficient ground on which to claim equitable conversion.

   (b)   A contingent interest in land is an interest in land, if it is anything at all, and as such its validity is as much a matter of the law of the situs, here Texas, as is any other interest in immovables.

e.   **The traditional approach today.** The "vested rights" rationale has become increasingly discredited. The notion that a right is "created" by the law of some particular jurisdiction implies that there is some overriding body of law that delineates which jurisdiction can "create" specific rights and duties and compels the courts of every other state to recognize rights so "created." But there is no such superlaw, and the courts have increasingly come to realize that their reference to foreign law is a matter of their own choice and discretion. Therefore, although a minority of courts still adhere to the traditional approach, the majority has abandoned it in favor of one of the modern approaches (*see* below).

f.   **Devices to escape mechanical application of conflict rules.**

1)   **Introduction.** More perceptive courts saw that blind application of conflict rules could lead to unreasonable results. Thus, while still stating adherence to the rules, they found ways to get around them.

2)   **Characterization.** One obvious way was to "characterize" a problem in a manner so as to apply the law the court desired to apply. One characterization device was to label a matter "substance" or "procedure," and thus be able to apply the law desired. [*See* Noe v. United States Fidelity & Guaranty Co., *supra*] By calling an action a "contracts" case, or a "torts" case, etc., courts were able to apply the law they thought should apply.

   a)   **Substance vs. procedure.**

      (1)   **No new cause of action--Grant v. McAuliffe,** 41 Cal. 2d 859 (1953).   Grant v. McAuliffe

         (a)   **Facts.** Pullen died shortly after an Arizona auto accident in which his alleged negligence caused injury to Ps. All parties were California residents. Ps sued Pullen's administrator (D) in California. Under Arizona law, tort actions do not survive the death of the tortfeasor; under California law they do. The lower court applied Arizona law.

         (b)   **Issue.** Will the issue of "survivability" be viewed as "substantive" such that Arizona law will apply?

(c) Held. No. California law will apply.

    1] Although courts differ on whether laws that go to the survival of causes of action are "procedural" or "substantive," we think they are procedural because they do not create a new cause of action. They only provide for the continuation of an existing cause of action.

(d) Comment. The court avoided the rigid "place of the wrong" rule by characterizing the issue of survivability as a problem in the administration of decedent's estates, rather than a torts problem, and thus governed by the law of the place where the decedent's estate is being administered. The court indicated that the question was really one related to the administration of the decedent's estate, a purely "local" proceeding. Since the estate was in the forum state, the parties were residents there, and the state's courts were administering the estate, then California law should control. This is really an unarticulated "weighing of the contacts" approach.

b) Nature of the action.

Haumschild
v. Continental
Casualty Co.

(1) Recharacterizing auto accidents--Haumschild v. Continental Casualty Co., 7 Wis. 2d 130 (1959).

(a) Facts. Mrs. Haumschild (P) sued her husband in Wisconsin for negligence arising out of a California car accident. The couple was domiciled in Wisconsin. Under California law P had no cause of action against her husband, but Wisconsin would allow the suit. The trial court dismissed P's action based on California law. P appeals.

(b) Issue. May Wisconsin apply its own law although the injury occurred in California?

(c) Held. Yes. Judgment reversed and remanded. Wisconsin law, that of the domicile, applies.

    1] This case is a "family law" problem, not a torts case. The purpose of California's immunity statute is to preserve marriages and prevent collusion suits. California, however, has no legitimate interest in protecting the marital harmony of Wisconsin domiciliaries or of preventing collusive suits in Wisconsin courts.

(d) Comment. To avoid an unfavorable law at the place of injury ("wrong"), courts often characterize the basic problem as something other than a "tort." The question of interspousal immunity has been characterized as a "family law" problem in this case rather than a "torts" problem so as to justify reference to the law of the spouses' domicile rather than the place of injury. In effect, the court adopted a "weighing of interests" approach.

Garza v.
Greyhound
Lines, Inc.

(2) Alternative claims--Garza v. Greyhound Lines, Inc., 418 S.W.2d 595 (Tx. 1967).

(a) Facts. Garza (P), a resident of Texas, brought this action against Greyhound (D), a Texas corporation, for personal injuries sustained by him while he was a passenger on a bus in Mexico on a trip arranged by D. P's basis of recovery was negligence, or alternatively, breach of an implied contract. The trial court sustained D's plea to the "jurisdiction" and dismissed P's suit on the ground of dissimilarity between Texas law and that of Mexico. P appeals.

(b) Issues.

1] May P's tort claim be dismissed because of the dissimilarity of Texas law with that of Mexico?

2] May P avoid Mexican law by characterizing the claim as one based on contract?

(c) Held. 1] Yes. 2] Yes. Reversed and remanded.

1] The law of the place of the tort must be looked at to determine the rights of the parties. Here, however, no proper proof of foreign substantive law was made.

2] The law of Texas, the place of contract, governs P's action based on D's breach of its implied contractual duty to carry its passengers safely.

(d) Comment. In *Slater v. Mexican National Railroad Co.*, *supra*, Justice Holmes dismissed a Texas action under the "dissimilarity" doctrine.

(3) Recharacterizing to avoid harsh results. In *Levy v. Daniels' U-Drive Auto Renting Co.*, 108 Conn. 333 (1928), Daniels' U-Drive Auto Renting Co. (D), a Connecticut automobile leasing company, rented a car in Connecticut to a Connecticut lessee. A passenger in that car (P) was injured in Massachusetts. A Connecticut statute subjected D to liability for any injuries arising out of the use and operation of its leased vehicles. Massachusetts had no such statute, and under the tort choice of law rule, the place of injury governs all issues. Thus, under Massachusetts law, P could not maintain an action against D, even though the statute was designed to regulate leasing companies. The issue was whether the court would apply the law of the state where the injury occurred. The Connecticut court held for P, by characterizing the case as one in contract and thereby employing the contract choice of law rule (contractual liability is determined by the place of contracting); the statute became a part of the leasing contract and P was entitled to sue as a third party beneficiary.

g. Renvoi.

1) The problem—reference to the "whole" law of foreign state. When the choice of law rules of the forum refer a matter to a foreign law for decision, is the reference to the whole body of the foreign law, including its choice of law rules; or is the reference to the purely internal rules of the foreign systems—those which would be applied to purely local litigation involving no outside contacts? If the forum decides to apply the whole law of the other state, the other state's choice of law rules may differ from those of the forum, and thus may refer the court back to its own law or perhaps that of a third jurisdiction ("renvoi"). However, if the forum decides to apply only the local law of the other state, the renvoi problem does not arise.

2) **Example.** A person domiciled in State B dies leaving stock certificates located in State A. The corporation in which the stock is held is located in State C. In inheritance litigation brought in State A (the forum), the court decides that this particular type of problem should be determined according to the law of decedent's domicile (State B). But to which law of State B is the reference to be made? (i) That which State B would apply if the litigation was purely local in nature and there were no factors involved outside of State B? Or (ii) State B's own choice of law rule as to this particular type of inheritance problem, which, for example, might refer the matter or decision to the law of the place where the certificates are located (State A) or to the law of the place where the corporation is located (State C)?

3) **A conflict of choice of law rules.** Renvoi, then, is a "conflict of choice of law rules." It is said to be a remission when the other state's choice of law rules refer the forum back to its own law (State A's choice of law rule looks to the law of State B and State B's choice of law rule looks back at State A's law). On the other hand, if the choice of law rules of the other state refer the forum to the law of a third state, transmission has occurred (State A's choice of law rule looks to the law of State B and State B's choice of law rule looks to the law of State C).

4) **Three positions have been taken on the renvoi problem.**

   a) **Reject the renvoi (majority view).** The forum (State A) should reject the "renvoi" or reference back (or reference to a third jurisdiction's law) from the foreign conflict of laws rule; *i.e.*, the forum should look only to the internal law of State B, and not to B's choice of law rules. This is the position taken by both the First and Second Restatements, subject to certain exceptions in which the Restatements adopt the "whole renvoi" position (below). Also, the "policy-oriented" approaches uniformly reject the renvoi.

   b) **Partial renvoi.** The forum should accept the "renvoi" or reference back from the foreign conflict of laws rule, but hold that the foreign reference is purely to local internal law—*i.e.*, following its local choice of law rule, the State A forum looks to State B's "whole law" (including B's choice of law rules). Assume it is then determined that State B courts would decide the problem by reference to State A's law (or law of some third state). The State A forum will hold that B's reference to State A's law (or to third state's law) is to A's internal law only, not to its choice of law rule (which would bounce it back to B, etc.).

   c) **Whole renvoi.** The forum should approach the choice of law problem as the foreign court would. If the foreign court refers back to the forum law (including its choice of law rules), which would then refer it back to them, the forum should accept this "final bounce back," but only to the extent of the foreign state's internal law.

5) **Limited form of renvoi adopted--American Motorists Insurance Co. v. ARTRA Group, Inc., 338 Md. 560 (1995).**

a) **Facts.** ARTRA (D) sold property located in Maryland to Sherwin-Williams. The Maryland environmental department ordered Sherwin-Williams to clean up hazardous waste contamination at the site. Sherwin-Williams sued D to recover the clean-up costs. D was insured by American Motorists (P) under a general liability policy. D requested that P defend and indemnify D in the suit. P refused and sued for a determination that the policy did not cover D's liability to Sherwin-Williams. P's refusal was based on a pollution exclusion contained in the policy. P and D were both headquartered in Illinois and the policy was countersigned on behalf of P in Illinois. Under Illinois law, the exclusion was ambiguous and the ambiguity would be construed in favor of D. Under Maryland law, the exclusion was not ambiguous and did not cover D's liability to Sherwin-Williams. The trial court applied Maryland law and granted P's motion for summary judgment. The court of special appeals reversed on the ground that under Maryland choice of law rules, the law of Illinois as the lex loci contractus governed and that it was irrelevant that an Illinois court would apply Maryland law. P appeals.

b) **Issue.** Should Maryland courts apply Illinois substantive law?

c) **Held.** No. Judgment reversed.

(1) Under a limited renvoi exception to lex loci contractus, Maryland was to apply Maryland substantive law if the law of Illinois (the place where the contract was entered into and the law which Maryland would ordinarily apply under the lex loci rule) would not apply its own substantive law but would look to Maryland law.

d) **Comment.** In *University of Chicago v. Dater*, 277 Mich. 658 (1936), the court accepted renvoi, while the dissent took the majority view and rejected renvoi. Price and his wife lived in Michigan and owned property with D in Illinois. The University made a loan to D, secured by the property. The documents were drafted in Illinois with a Chicago company acting as trustee. The notes were payable in Illinois and the papers were signed in Michigan. A check was paid to D and Price in Illinois and cashed there. Price died; his wife (who had signed on the loan) inherited his interest in the property, which was foreclosed. In an action in Michigan, P sought a deficiency judgment. (In Michigan a wife lacked capacity to sign and therefore P would have no action against Mrs. Price. In Illinois, married women could contract and P could bring an action against Mrs. Price.) Acknowledging that "capacity to contract" issues are resolved by reference to the state where the contract was made, the court determined that the contract was made in Illinois and under Illinois law "capacity to contract" issues would be resolved under the law where Mrs. Price signed on the loan (Michigan). Michigan, therefore, applied the whole law of Illinois, which refers to Michigan "capacity-to-contract" law, and P had no cause of action against Mrs. Price. The dissent argued that the law where the contract was entered into should govern "capacity to contract" issues. The final act in the making of the loan was the payment of money in Chicago and, therefore, the dissent argued, the contract was made in Illinois and Illinois' "capacity" law should apply.

6) Public policy.

    a) Introduction. Courts attempting to avoid the unreasoning application of hard-and-fast conflict rules also came up with the argument that although the normal rule would be to apply the law of another state, the "public policy" of the forum state would not permit the other state's law to apply.

Kilberg v. Northeast Airlines, Inc.

    b) Recovery limits--Kilberg v. Northeast Airlines, Inc., 9 N.Y.2d 34 (1961).

        (1) Facts. Kilberg, a New York domiciliary, purchased a ticket in New York from Northeast Airlines (D), a Massachusetts corporation, for a flight from New York to Massachusetts. He was killed in a crash in Massachusetts. The New York Constitution forbade limits on recovery, but Massachusetts law would limit D's liability for wrongful death to $15,000. Kilberg's administrator (P) sued for wrongful death under Massachusetts law and an additional $150,000 for breach of a contract for safe passage. The appellate division dismissed the "contract" cause of action because, "however labeled, it was in tort for wrongful death and was subject to the Massachusetts limitation."

        (2) Issue. If the Massachusetts recovery limitation violates the forum's public policy, may the forum apply its own policy?

        (3) Held. Yes. Dismissal of the "contract" action affirmed, but the wrongful death action is not subject to the $15,000 Massachusetts limit.

            (a) In air travel cases the place of injury may be entirely fortuitous and a forum court ought to provide protection for its citizens. Since both New York and Massachusetts have wrongful death statutes, the amount of recovery is the only controversy. The Massachusetts limitation violates "strong, clear, and old" policies of the New York constitution. Although P must sue under the Massachusetts' wrongful death statute, the damage provision will not be enforced.

        (4) Comment. The concurring opinion of Judge Froessel points out that under this decision different law may apply to each passenger in the crash, depending on the passenger's state of domicile.

    h. Conclusion. The application of these devices to temper the results of the traditional, rigid choice of law principles indicates the general dissatisfaction with that approach. Courts have become increasingly willing to sacrifice certainty, simplicity, and uniformity in search of different "conflicts" standards that are more compatible with general notions of justice. As a result, conflicts decisions among the various jurisdictions are often inconsistent. You should not attempt to "square" all the cases, but rather to understand the forces that operate on each decision.

3. **Transitional Approaches to Conflicts Questions.**

   a. **Introduction.** The feeling by many courts that the transitional mode of analysis represented "mechanical jurisprudence" led to gropings for new approaches.

   b. **Early rationales.**

      1) **Place of the wrong--Schmidt v. Driscoll Hotel, Inc.,** 249 Minn. 376 (1957).

         Schmidt v. Driscoll Hotel, Inc.

         a) **Facts.** Minnesota had a dramshop act, imposing liability on saloonkeepers who sell liquor for injury caused by their intoxicated customers. Driscoll Hotel (D), a Minnesota saloonkeeper, sold liquor to a Minnesota driver who injured Schmidt (P), a passenger, when he crashed the car in Wisconsin. Wisconsin had no dramshop act and would not hold the saloonkeeper liable. The trial court granted Ds motion to dismiss. P appeals.

         b) **Issue.** May the forum refuse to apply the law of the state where the injury occurred?

         c) **Held.** Yes. Judgment reversed.

         d) **Comments.** The court rejected the law of Wisconsin (the place of the injury) and applied the Minnesota statute since the "wrong" (the sale of the liquor) occurred in Minnesota. This is a designation of the conduct (rather than the injury as in the traditional rule) as the "wrong" involved.

            If the state in which a defendant acts has established special controls over the kind of activities in which the defendant is engaged, plaintiff should be accorded the benefit of the special conduct and financial protection of those sanctions. This is true even though plaintiff has no special relationship to defendant and even though the state of injury has imposed no such controls or sanctions.

      2) **Center of gravity--Auten v. Auten,** 308 N.Y. 155 (1954).

         Auten v. Auten

         a) **Facts.** Mr. and Mrs. Auten were married and lived in England for 14 years. He deserted her, came to the United States, got a Mexican divorce, and remarried. Mrs. Auten came to New York where she and Mr. Auten signed a separation agreement under which he promised support payments and she promised not to bring any legal action relating to their separation. Mr. Auten discontinued his payments; Mrs. Auten sued in England for divorce and alimony and then sued in New York several years later for back support payments. Mr. Auten defended on the basis that by bringing the suit in England, Mrs. Auten had repudiated the separation agreement. The trial court dismissed the complaint and the appellate division affirmed. Mrs. Auten appeals.

b) **Issue.** Will the New York court choose the law to apply by "grouping" the various contacts and selecting the law where the "center of gravity" is located?

c) **Held.** Yes. Judgment reversed.

(1) English law applies.

(2) Under the "grouping contacts" or "center of gravity" test, England has the most significant contacts and the "most interest" in the problem. Its law should therefore be applied to determine the effect to be given to institution of suit by Mrs. Auten (*i.e.*, is it a breach of the agreement?).

(3) Distribution of the contacts:

(a) *England:* Husband and Wife were English subjects; they married and lived there 14 years; Wife and the children continued to live there; English law would govern the separation in the absence of an agreement between the parties; and Wife's performance of the separation agreement was to be performed there in part (*i.e.*, no suits were to be brought there).

(b) *New York:* The contract was made there; Husband's performance was there (to pay money); the trustee was there (to receive payments); Wife's performance was there (no suits); and Husband may have been domiciled there.

d) **Comment.** This approach is criticized as too mechanical. The mere fact that more "contacts" occur in one state than another is not always reason enough to apply the former state's law. For example, in one case the court invalidated a contract, which would have been valid where entered, because more "contacts" occurred in a different state. The approach also breaks down in cases when the contacts do not preponderate to any particular state.

c. **The "most significant relationship" doctrine.**

1) **Introduction.** Since about 1960 the basic approach of the Restatement has been to apply the law of the state having the "most significant relationship" to the matter under consideration.

2) **Query.** Was the court in *Auten* applying a preponderance of contacts theory (simply counting the contacts) or weighing the relative interests of the jurisdictions involved?

a) **The modern modes of contacts analysis.** The modern modes of contacts analysis emphasizes two methods: (i) the "massing of contacts" approach, which determines which elements of the transaction occurred where and then applies the law of the place that is the "center of gravity"; and (ii) the "state of interest" approach, which consists of a qualitative analysis of the contacts.

b) **Overlap.** These approaches do tend to overlap. The Restatement adopts the "most significant place" rule, which suggests both a counting and a qualitative weighing of contacts.

   (1) The rights and duties of the parties with respect to an issue in a contract case are determined by the local law of the state that, as to that issue, has the most significant relationship to the transaction and the parties.

   (2) In the absence of an effective choice of law by the parties, the contacts to be taken into account to determine the law applicable to an issue include:

       (i) The place of contracting;

       (ii) The place of negotiation of the contract;

       (iii) The place of performance;

       (iv) The location of the subject matter of the contract;

       (v) The domicile, residence, nationality, place of incorporation, and place of business of the parties; and

       (vi) The place under whose local law the contract will be most effective.

       These contacts are to be evaluated according to their relative importance with respect to the particular issue.

   (3) If the place of negotiating the contract and the place of performance are in the same state, the local law of this state will usually be applied.

d. **Other modern approaches.** The following are additional modes of analysis suggested by modern scholars in the conflicts field.

1) **Cheatham and Reese.** These authors suggested the following policies be used in conflict cases:

   a) **Needs of the interstate and international legal systems.** Courts should consider the broader framework of the interstate and international legal systems when determining which law to apply.

   b) **Local law theory.** In the absence of any other controlling factors, the court should apply its own law.

    c)   **Uniformity of result in all forums.** Forum shopping is thought to be undesirable. Choice of law rules should therefore strive to achieve uniformity of results wherever a suit is brought.

    d)   **Expectations of the parties.** One goal of the law should be to give effect to the legitimate expectations of the parties. "Expectations" arguments generally apply to consensual transactions, *e.g.*, contract cases, rather than torts.

    e)   **Dominant state interests.** One theory is that the state having the greatest interest should apply its law.

    f)   **Ease in determination of the applicable law; the convenience of the court.** The easier choice of law rules are to understand, the better. The easiest rule of all would be that the local forum always applies its own law. While this rule probably should not be paramount, nevertheless, it is deserving of consideration.

    g)   **The fundamental policy underlying the law.** Courts should consider not only the local law invoked by the parties, but also the fundamental policy of the broader field. For example, usury laws are to protect the borrower, and may restrict the validity of contracts; on the other hand, the broad field involved is contract law, and the policy that a contract demands the performance of its promises may override the usury policy. Thus, the courts should apply the law that would uphold or give effect to the fundamental principles of the law.

    h)   **Justice in the individual case.** Courts should look at the facts of each individual case and apply the law that will achieve the best result.

2)   **The state interest analysis (the Currie approach).**

    a)   **The basic theory.**

        (1)   Look at the policies of the laws and into the circumstances in which it is reasonable for the states to assert an interest in the application of those policies.

        (2)   If one state has an interest in the application of its policy and the others do not, apply the law of the interested state. This is a "false conflict" case (since in reality no true conflict of interests exists).

        (3)   If there is a conflict, however (*i.e.*, more than one state has an interest, a true conflict), then reconsider the interests involved.

        (4)   If there is still a conflict, then apply the local law of the forum.

        (5)   If the forum is disinterested, but there is a conflict between the interests of two other states, then apply the law of the forum if its law is the same as one of the two states. If not, decide the case acting as a supreme court, attempting to decide which interest should be upheld.

    b)   **Application of the interest analysis.** Compare the results of two cases studied previously with this newer "interests analysis" approach.

(1) False conflicts case. In *Alabama Great Southern Railroad Co. v. Carroll, supra*, recall that there was a difference in the Alabama and Mississippi fellow-servant laws.

    (a) Alabama's interest. The contract of employment was in Alabama; the plaintiff was domiciled there; the railroad was in Alabama; the negligence occurred there. It is reasonable to conclude that Alabama does have an interest in applying its law to this cause of action.

    (b) Mississippi's interest. The plaintiff was injured in Mississippi. Mississippi had the common law fellow-servant rule. The underlying policies of the common law rule were as follows:

        (i)   No liability without fault—the employer should be liable only when negligent in hiring, training, or retaining employees.

        (ii)   The old capitalist economics—it aids infant industries by reducing potential liability.

        (iii)   The fear of collusion between employees against the employer.

    Mississippi probably does not have an interest in applying its fellow-servant rule in this case.

    (c) Result. This is possibly a "false conflict" case. Even if it were not, once it is determined that Alabama had an interest it would apply its own law since it was the forum state.

(2) A true conflicts case. *Milliken v. Pratt,* (discussed *supra*) dealt with a conflict between Massachusetts and Maine law. In Massachusetts married women lacked capacity to contract. In Maine, they did not. Massachusetts therefore seems to have had an interest since the purpose of the rule was to protect the state's women, of which D was one.

    (a) True conflict. Since Maine also had an interest (*i.e.*, that of protecting Maine businesses), this seems to be a true conflicts case. If the Massachusetts and Maine policies are extended beyond the territorial limits of their respective states, then under the Currie analysis if the suit is brought in Massachusetts D will win; if the suit is brought in Maine, however, P wins.

    (b) Reconsideration when a true conflict exists. As of what time are the "interests" ascertained? At the time of the transaction or at the time of suit? Here by the time the suit was brought, Massachusetts had changed its statute; possibly, therefore, Massachusetts had no interest at the time of the suit.

c) Problems with the interest analysis.

(1) How provincial are we to assume that a state's policy is? A problem underlying the Currie analysis is in determining who a state's law is trying to protect. For example, in *Milliken*, who was the Massachusetts law trying to protect? Massachusetts women? All women? On the other hand, does Maine have an interest here? Would it apply its policy to the advantage of Massachusetts businesses as well as to its own? Note that the more narrow the scope of coverage intended by the state legislation, the more "false conflicts" cases arise. The less provincial a state legislature is, or is assumed to be, the more "true conflicts" cases will arise.

(2) **What kind of an "interest?"** A second problem is in determining what Currie means when he says "interest." Is it limited to a state's "pocket-book" interest? If so, this probably raises constitutional problems (equal protection).

3) **Lex fori and "true rules"—Ehrenzweig.** Most conflict solutions are found by interpreting forum rules. Whether a foreign contact should result in foreign law being applied is determined by looking at the territorial scope of the local law of the forum. Foreign policies are relevant only if deemed so by a super-law (such as constitutional law) or by the law of the forum, which is rarely the case. Thus, the law of the local forum is normally applied.

4) **Choice-influencing considerations—Leflar.** Leflar indicates that there are no hard and fast rules to be applied, only "choice influencing" factors:

(i) Predictability of results;

(ii) Maintenance of interstate and international order;

(iii) Simplification of the judicial task;

(iv) Advancement of the forum's governmental interests; and

(v) Application of the better rule of law.

This is akin to a "common law" of conflicts, to be applied by the court using good sense. Courts recently seem to have been strongly influenced by Leflar's thinking.

5) **The functional analysis—VonMehren and Trautman.** This is a more involved application of the "interests analysis."

6) **Principles of preference—Cavers.** This approach is similar to that of Leflar—the courts should reach principled decisions, and various factors need to be considered in arriving at a reasoned answer to the choice of law question.

7) **Restatement (Second) section 6.**

a) **Introduction.** The methodology of the Second Restatement—which focuses upon identifying the state with the most significant relationship to the particular issue involved—directs the forum court to consider the relative importance of specific contacts, which vary with each subject matter—*e.g.*, torts, contracts—and is listed in separate sections of the Restatement in light of the general choice of law principles set out in section 6.

b) **The choice of law principles.**

(1) **The needs of the interstate and international systems.** It is desirable to further harmonious relations and commercial intercourse between states and nations.

(2) **The relevant policies of the forum.** The forum should evaluate the purpose of its own law to determine whether that purpose would be furthered by application of its law in the instant case.

(3) **The policies of other involved states and their interests in having their policies applied.** The forum should also analyze the purposes of the laws of the other interested states to ascertain whether those purposes would be furthered by the application of their laws.

(4) **Protection of justified expectations.** In contract cases and other planned transactions, the forum should examine the parties' expectations as to what law would govern their affairs. (*Note*: This factor is not considered in tort cases.)

(5) **The basic policies underlying the particular field of law.** A choice of law decision should also reflect the basic policies underlying the particular field of law. For instance, one basic policy in the area of contract law relates to the validation of contracts wherever possible. Thus, in a contract case, the forum should consider how that policy could be furthered.

(6) **Certainty, predictability, and uniformity of result.** Such objectives are preferred over, *e.g.*, forum shopping.

(7) **Ease in determination and application of law to be applied.** This is purely a matter of convenience and should not be allowed to outweigh the goal of attaining a desirable result. However, in a particular case, it may discourage application of esoteric laws (especially those of foreign nations).

c) **Specific contacts for each kind of problem.** The Second Restatement also establishes specific contacts—which vary according to the substantive area of the law involved—to be used in applying the general principles (above) for the purpose of identifying the state with the most significant relationship to the particular issue in question (discussed *infra,* under the specific subject matter areas). Thus, the state with the "most significant relationship" will vary with the type of problem presented.

4. **Application of Modern Doctrines.**

a. **"Most significant relationship" approach.** Recognizing the shortcomings of the rigid "place of wrong" rule, a number of authorities in recent years have adopted the "most significant relationship" approach (*supra*). Under this approach, the forum is directed to consider the "contacts" and interests of each state involved and apply the law of the state having the most significant relationship with the particular issue before the court. [Restatement (Second) §145]

1) **The "significant" contacts.** According to the Second Restatement, the significant "contacts" to be isolated in a torts case are: (i) place of injury; (ii) place of conduct; (iii) place of each party's residence and/or business; and (iv) place where the relationship, if any, between the parties is centered.

   a) These contacts are to be evaluated according to their relative importance as to the particular issue involved in the case, together with the various general factors and policies enumerated, *supra*.

   b) Note, however, that the Second Restatement retains the basic preference for the law of the place of injury, unless other factors establish a "more significant" relationship. [Restatement (Second) §§146, 147]

Babcock v. Jackson

2) **Departure from traditional doctrine--Babcock v. Jackson,** 12 N.Y.2d 473 (1963).

   a) **Facts.** Babcock (P) and Jackson (D), New York domiciliaries, left New York in D's car for a weekend trip to Ontario, Canada. Due to D's negligence they had an accident there and P was injured. The Ontario guest statute provided that there should be no recovery; New York law allowed recovery. P brought suit in New York. The lower court granted D's motion to dismiss the complaint based on Canadian law. The appellate division affirmed. P appeals.

   b) **Issue.** Under the "most significant relationship" test, must the New York court apply the law of the place where the injury occurred?

   c) **Held.** No. New York law governs. Judgment reversed.

      (1) This court will apply the "grouping" or "center of gravity" test of *Auten (supra)* and compare the "contacts" and the "interests" of Ontario and New York. Under this analysis, New York clearly has the "greatest concern" with the issue. The only contact with Ontario was the fortuitous occurrence of the accident there, and since the Ontario guest statute was meant to prevent the assertion of fraudulent claims in its courts, Ontario really had no interest in this suit (since it was brought in New York and a New York defendant and a New York insurance company are involved).

   d) **Comment.** This case also illustrates a "false conflict" case under the "governmental interest approach." The forum's policy is one of permitting injured persons, including guests, to be made whole by recovery of damages from the host. The forum has an interest in the application of its policy because both host and guest are residents of the forum. Ontario has a contrary policy (that of limiting the host's liability to protect him against an ungrateful guest, or perhaps to prevent collusive suits against the host's insurance company), but in this case Ontario has no contrary interest in the assertion of its policy—because neither the host nor his insurance company are residents of or doing business in Ontario.

Thus, there are conflicting policies but no conflicting interests. This is a false conflict case; the forum should apply its own law as that of the only interested state. If the suit had been brought in Ontario, it too should follow the same analysis to reach the same result: application of the law of the common domicile of the host and guest.

3) Application of foreign guest statute when injured party is a foreign resident--Neumeier v. Kuehner, 31 N.Y.2d 121 (1972).

Neumeier v. Kuehner

   a) Facts. Neumeier, a Canadian, was killed when the auto in which he was riding, owned and driven by a New York resident (D), collided with a train in Ontario. Neumeier's wife (P) sued D for wrongful death in New York. Ontario's guest statute would preclude recovery. The trial court applied Ontario's law, but the appellate court reversed. D appeals.

   b) Issue. If the defendant-host and the plaintiff-guest are domiciled in different jurisdictions, will the court apply the law of the place where the injury occurred?

   c) Held. Yes. Judgment reversed and the trial court's holding is reinstated.

      (1) When the driver's conduct occurs in the state of his domicile and that state does not cast him in liability for that conduct, he should not be held liable by reason of the fact that liability would be imposed upon him under tort law of the state of the victim's domicile; conversely, when the guest is injured in the state of his own domicile, which permits recovery, the driver who has come into that state should not be permitted to interpose the law of the driver's state as a defense, absent special circumstances. However, if the passenger and driver are domiciled in different states, as here, the law of the state where the accident occurred will normally apply, unless it is shown that displacing the normally applicable rule will advance the relevant substantive law purposes without impairing the smooth working of the multistate system or producing great uncertainty for litigants.

   d) Comment. The *Neumeier* decision has been criticized by several commentators as a retreat to the "place of injury" rule. But even in New York, courts may refuse to apply a guest statute in effect at the place of injury if both host and guest are from different states, neither of which has a guest statute.

4) Lex loci rules no longer apply--Duncan v. Cessna Aircraft Co., 665 S.W.2d 414 (Tex. 1984).

Duncan v. Cessna Aircraft Co.

   a) Facts. Parker, a Texas resident, was killed in a plane crash in New Mexico. Duncan (P), Parker's widow, brought a wrongful death action against Air Plains West, Inc., the owner of the plane. P settled with Air Plains. P executed a release discharging Air Plains and "any other corporations or persons" responsible for Parker's death. Subsequently, P instituted a wrongful death action against Cessna (D), the manufacturer of the plane. D contended that its liability was discharged by the release. D argues that in determining the effect of the release on D's liability, the court should apply New Mexico law. Under New Mexico law, D would be discharged by the release; under Texas law, D would not be released.

The trial court rendered judgment non obstante verdicto for D. P appealed. The appeals court reversed and remanded for a partial new trial.

b) **Issue.** Should Texas law control the construction of the release?

c) **Held.** Yes. Reversed; judgment rendered for P on the jury verdict.

   (1) The law of the state with the most significant relationship to the particular substantive issue will be applied to resolve conflicts problems.

   (2) Here, Texas has the most significant relationship. New Mexico has no governmental interest. D is a Kansas corporation seeking the benefit of a release executed in Texas by an injured Texas resident as part of a settlement of a suit filed in Texas. Texas has an interest in protecting P's reasonable contractual expectations since it is reasonable for P to have expected the laws of Texas would govern, and in avoiding unfairly depriving injured Texas residents of their full satisfaction.

Rudow v.
Fogel

5) **Situs law does not apply in property transaction--Rudow v. Fogel,** 12 Mass. App. Ct. 430 (1981).

a) **Facts.** Marvin and Florence Rudow lived in New York and owned summer property in Massachusetts. After the couple separated, Florence domiciled in New York with their son, William (P), and Marvin domiciled in Massachusetts. Later, Marvin conveyed the Massachusetts property to Florence as a gift. Florence conveyed the property to her brother (D), without consideration. D orally agreed to hold such property for the benefit of P. Marvin brought this action on behalf of P to obtain judgment that D held the property in interest for P. The trial court applied Massachusetts law and found that there was no constructive trust. The court found that D promised to hold the property for P and awarded P the value of the property less expenses. D appeals.

b) **Issue.** Should the court look to New York law in determining whether D holds the property in constructive trust for P?

c) **Held.** Yes. Remanded.

   (1) The trial judge looked to the law of the situs to resolve the constructive trust issue. The law of the situs is not the only criterion for resolving that issue. The trial court should examine the interests of the concerned jurisdictions and the interests of the interstate system before deciding what law is appropriate to apply.

   (2) Here, New York had dominant contacts and superior claims for application of its law notwithstanding that the situs of the property in question is Massachusetts. Florence, P, and D resided in New York at the time of the transaction; Florence was not yet divorced and transferred the property to prevent her husband from having any interest, and she had a legitimate expectation, enforceable under New York law, that D would hold the property for P.

b. **The court's new approach.** The states that have abandoned the vested rights theory of the First Restatement have not formulated new rules but, instead, apply one of the modern approaches.

1) **Applying the law of parties' common domicile--Schultz v. Boy Scouts of America, Inc.,** 65 N.Y.2d 189 (1985).

Schultz v. Boy Scouts of America, Inc.

a) **Facts.** In 1978, Ps' sons attended a school owned and operated by the Roman Catholic Archdiocese of Newark. Brothers of the Poor of St. Francis (D), incorporated in Ohio, supplied teachers for the school. One Brother, Coakeley, served as scoutmaster for a Boy Scout troop sponsored by Boy Scouts of America (D). Coakeley took the boys to camp in upstate New York, sexually molested them there and later at school, and threatened to harm them if they revealed what had happened. Ps claimed that the boys suffered severe psychological, emotional, and mental pain and suffering and that as the result of Coakeley's acts, one boy committed suicide. Ps charged Ds with negligence in assigning Coakeley to positions of trust where he could molest young boys and in failing to dismiss him despite actual or constructive notice that Coakeley had previously been dismissed from another Boy Scout camp for similar improper conduct. Ps lived in New Jersey; Boy Scouts of America originally maintained its headquarters in New Jersey, but moved to Texas in 1979. Ds moved for summary judgment, claiming that Ps' claims were barred by New Jersey's charitable immunity statute. Special Term granted Ds' motions; the Appellate Division affirmed. Ps appeal.

b) **Issues.**

(1) Should New York apply its law in an action involving codomiciliaries of New Jersey when tortious acts were committed in New York?

(2) Should the law of the place of the tort apply when the parties' different domiciles have conflicting charitable immunity rules?

c) **Held.** (1) No. (2) Yes. Judgment affirmed.

(1) New York employs interest analysis in its analytical approach to choice of law actions. Thus, the significant contacts are the parties' domiciles and the locus of the tort; the relative interests of these two jurisdictions in having their laws apply will depend on the particular tort issue in conflict. Therefore, when the conflicting rules involve standards of conduct, the laws of the place of the tort will usually apply; when they relate to allocating losses that result from admittedly tortious conduct, as they do here, the state's admonitory interest and party reliance are less important. Then, the locus jurisdiction has at best minimal interest in determining the right of recovery or the extent of the remedy in an action by a foreign domiciliary for injuries resulting from the conduct of a codomiciliary that was tortious under the laws of both jurisdictions. Analysis then favors the common domicile because of its interest in enforcing the decisions of both parties to accept both the benefits and burdens of identify-

ing with that jurisdiction and to submit themselves to its authority.

    (2)   In this case, both Ps and Ds have identified themselves in the most concrete form possible, domicile, with a jurisdiction that retains the defense of charitable immunity. None of the reasons most often urged in support of applying the law of the forum-locus are persuasive here, but there are persuasive reasons for consistently applying the law of the parties' common domicile: (i) forum shopping is reduced because the common domicile and locus jurisdiction will apply the same law; (ii) the charges that the forum-locus is biased in favor of its own laws and in favor of rules permitting discovery are rebutted; and (iii) mutuality and reciprocity support consistent application of the common-domicile law. In any given case, one person could be either plaintiff or defendant and one state could be either the parties' common domicile or the locus, and yet the applicable law would not change depending on their status.

    (3)   Insofar as Franciscan Brothers are concerned, Ps and D are domiciled in different jurisdictions with conflicting loss-distribution rules and the locus of the tort is New York. Here, the law of the place of the tort will normally apply unless displacing it will advance the substantive law purposes without impairing the smooth working of the multi-state system or producing great uncertainty for the litigants. For the same reasons stated above in regard to applying New Jersey law in Ps' action against Boy Scouts, applying New Jersey law against Franciscan Brothers would further that state's interest in enforcing the decision of its domiciliaries to accept the burdens as well as the benefits of that state's loss distribution tort rules and its interest in promoting the continuation and expansion of D's charitable activities in that state. Also, New York has no significant interest in applying its law to this dispute, since the parties had only isolated and infrequent contacts as a result of Coakeley's position as scout leader.

    (4)   There are no sufficient contacts between New York, the parties, and the transactions involved to implicate New York's public policy against charitable immunity.

    d)   **Dissent.** The majority does not adequately explain why the law of New York ought not govern this case. Neither corporate D is a resident of New Jersey presently, and it cannot be disputed that New Jersey's interest in protecting resident charities cannot in actuality be relied upon. D's contacts with the foreign state are insignificant for the purposes of interest analysis while the parties' contacts with New York are clear and direct and the resulting interests of this state so strong.

Cooney v. Osgood Machinery, Inc.

2)   **Protection of reasonable expectations--Cooney v. Osgood Machinery, Inc., 81 N.Y.2d 66 (1993).**

    a)   **Facts.** Cooney (P), an employee of Mueller Co., was injured by a machine he was operating at Mueller's Missouri plant. P received worker's compensation. Under Missouri law, an employer providing such benefits is released from all other liability whatsoever, whether to the employee or any other person. Thus, P was prohibited from bringing a suit against Mueller. P did, however, bring a product liability action against the machine's New York distributor, Osgood Machinery (D). D, in turn, sued Mueller for contribution. Mueller moved for summary judgment, arguing that the Missouri worker's compensation statute released the company from all other liability. The trial court denied Mueller's motion and Mueller appealed. The appellate division reversed and dismissed the complaint against Mueller. D appeals.

b) **Issue.** Should a Missouri statute barring contribution claims against an employer be given effect in a third-party action, even though it conflicts with New York law permitting such claims?

c) **Held.** Yes. Judgment affirmed.

(1) If the local law of each litigant's domicile favors that party, and the action is pending in one of those jurisdictions, the place of injury governs. Thus, Missouri law governs.

3) **Place-of-wrong rule not applied--Trailways, Inc. v. Clark,** 794 S.W.2d 479 (Tx. 1990).

Trailways, Inc. v. Clark

a) **Facts.** The decedents, Mayorga and Trejo, while traveling on a bus in Mexico, were killed when the bus left the highway and overturned. Their survivors and the representatives of their estates (Ps) brought this wrongful death action against Transportes Del Norte (TDN), the Mexican bus line on which decedents were traveling, and Trailways, operating out of Texas (Ds). The decedents, Texas residents, purchased the bus tickets from a subsidiary of Ds in Texas. Trailways had an "interlining" agreement with TDN, whereby Trailways would issue tickets to destinations in Mexico and TDN would honor the tickets from the border to the destination in Mexico. The trial court entered judgment for Ps. Ds appeal.

b) **Issue.** Should Texas law apply?

c) **Held.** Yes. Judgment affirmed as to TDN and reversed as to Trailways.

(1) Generally, wrongful death damages will be determined according to the law of the place of injury. However, when additional considerations favor one state or the other, the place of injury is no longer the controlling factor. The next task is to determine the relative significance of the states' interests in the particular case and issues.

(2) Here, Texas has the most significant contacts for choice of law purposes. Ps and decedents were Texas residents; the tickets were purchased in Texas; the parties had an interlining agreement. TDN solicited business in Texas through the interlining agreement.

4) **Expectation of the parties--Bernkrant v. Fowler,** 55 Cal. 2d 588 (1961).

Bernkrant v. Fowler

a) **Facts.** Granrud sold Nevada land to Bernkrant and other Nevada domiciliaries (Ps), then made an oral promise to Ps (in Nevada) that if they would refinance their obligation to Granrud and make a substantial payment immediately, then he would make a provision in his will that if the indebtedness for the land was not paid off by the time he died it would be canceled. Ps made the payment; Granrud died in California without including such a provision in his will. Ps sue Granrud's executor (D) in California. Nevada law enforces such oral promises; California's Statute of Frauds, which the trial court applied, made such contracts unenforceable. P appeals.

b) **Issue.** Do the facts that the parties were domiciled in Nevada when the contract was made and that the contract was made there require California to apply Nevada law?

c) **Held.** Yes. Judgment reversed. Nevada law governs. The case must be decided on either of two hypotheses (the record did not show which one was correct):

(1) Granrud was domiciled in Nevada when the contract was made. Here the expectation of the parties would be that Nevada law would govern, since they would all be Nevada residents at the time the Nevada contract was made.

(2) Granrud was domiciled in California when the contract was made. The court indicated that in this event the plaintiffs should not have been required to take into consideration California law when entering the transaction since Granrud might have moved out of California at a later time and the plaintiffs could not possibly know where he would go and thus would have no idea of what law might govern. In addition, the court said that California had no interest in applying its law.

d) **Comments.**

(1) This is poor reasoning. If Granrud had been domiciled in California it seems only reasonable that the parties would have to refer to both Nevada and California law to see that their contract was valid. Also—California seems to have a clear interest in protecting the estates of its decedents from such oral contracts, not to mention the interest of its forum in not entertaining suits on such oral agreements.

(2) The modern trend treats the question of formalities as one of "substance," particularly if necessary to uphold a contract. The courts thus apply the statute in effect in the state that has the most significant "interest" in or "relationship" to the formalities issue. Many courts have reached this result by interpreting the forum's statute of frauds as not applicable to contracts having their principal "contacts" outside the forum or by adopting new choice of law rules allowing reference to whichever law will uphold the contract.

5) **Note.** The Restatement (Second) provides that validity questions are determined according to the same choice of law rationale as in other contract cases, and then notes that formalities meeting the requirements of the place where the parties executed the contract are normally sufficient to make a valid contract.

6) **Choice of law contract provision does not apply--Peugeot Motors of America, Inc. v. Eastern Auto Distributors, Inc.** 892 F.2d 355 (4th Cir. 1989).

a) **Facts.** Eastern Auto (D), a Virginia corporation, entered into a distributor agreement with Peugeot (P), a Delaware corporation. The agreement contained a nonrenewal provision and a choice of law provision. The choice of law clause provided that the agreement would be governed by New York law. D did not conduct any business in New York. Later, P sent D a notice of nonrenewal. P then sued D for declaratory judgment. D counterclaimed, alleging violations of New York law. The court granted D summary judgment on P's declaratory judgment claim. P appeals.

b) **Issue.** Do the New York regulatory statutes apply?

c) **Held.** No. Judgment reversed in part, affirmed in part, and remanded.

   (1) A federal court sitting in diversity must apply the choice of law rules of the forum state. This action was filed in Virginia; thus, Virginia's choice of law rules apply. Under Virginia law, the choice of law provision is valid.

   (2) The New York statutes regulating automobile franchise renewals only apply to distributors doing business in the state of New York. Here, D never conducted business in New York; thus, the statutes are not applicable and New York common law controls. There is nothing in New York law to indicate that P did not act properly.

d) **Concurrence and dissent in part.** The choice of law provision should be interpreted to include an agreement to be bound by the New York statutes. The majority's refusal to apply the statutes, based on explicit geographical limitations in the definition section of that state's code, is the result of a strained statutory construction and of a failure to focus on the intent of the contracting parties.

7) **Applicable law in a diversity case--Bledsoe v. Crowley,** 849 F.2d 639 (D.C. Cir. 1988).

a) **Facts.** Bledsoe (P) sued Crowley and Friedman (Ds), claiming negligence in their failure to diagnose his brain tumor during the 12 years they treated him for psychiatric disorders. P first consulted Crowley in 1969. In 1984, after P had discontinued therapy, a CAT scan revealed a brain tumor that had been growing for many years. P's condition improved after removal of the tumor, but P allegedly suffered permanent brain damage and loss of vision, which prevented him from pursuing his radiology practice. P lived in Maryland when he began seeing Crowley, but moved to Washington, D.C., sometime later and was a D.C. resident when suit was filed; he always maintained his radiology practice in Maryland. Ds lived and practiced in Maryland, where P's therapy sessions took place, although Ds were also licensed in D.C. Maryland law provides that P's malpractice claim must initially be submitted to an arbitration panel. Although the panel's award may be rejected, it is admissible in a subsequent action as presumptively correct, and the party rejecting the award bears the burden of rebutting the presumption. The district court applied Maryland law. P appeals.

b) **Issues.**

    (1)   Should the law of the District of Columbia apply?

    (2)   If Maryland law applies, should the arbitration provisions apply?

c) **Held.** (1) No. (2) Yes. Judgment affirmed on the merits; case remanded for a stay pending arbitration.

    (1)   The federal court must follow the choice of law rules of the forum to determine applicable law in a diversity case. Applying the rules of D.C., we must apply a government interest analysis here. P contends that the district court erred in failing to inquire into the law that a court in the foreign jurisdiction would apply; *i.e.*, if Maryland's choice of law rules would apply D.C. law here, then Maryland's interests, when weighed against D.C.'s, would be much diminished. We agree that this type of inquiry does apply, but we disagree that Maryland would apply D.C. law. We believe that Maryland adheres to the general principle that the applicable law is the place where the "wrong" occurred, and that was Maryland.

    (2)   P also contends that D.C.'s silence on the question of malpractice reform does not indicate, as the district court thought, a lack of interest. This argument is speculative, and in any event, Maryland is the state with the stronger interest.

    (3)   P's argument that the Maryland statute was not intended to have extraterritorial application because it is procedural and for choice of law purposes, not part of Maryland's substantive law, fails both under the application of the *Erie* doctrine and the application of Maryland's choice of law principles. The argument that the Maryland provision is procedural and one that a federal court could not apply was rejected in *Davison v. Sinai Hospital*, where the court found that the Maryland arbitration requirement should be treated as substantive so that (i) the character or result of litigation would not differ materially because suit was brought in federal court, and (ii) incentives to forum shopping would be avoided. Under Maryland's choice of law principles, according to which the law of the forum is applied to "procedural" matters, P's argument fails also. P claims that the Maryland legislature, in defining the statute as procedural, intended to deny it extraterritorial application. Thus, a federal court sitting in Maryland might apply the arbitration statute, but a federal court in another state could not do so. This is incorrect. Once a court has determined that Maryland law governs, a D.C. federal court would apply Maryland law no differently than would a Maryland federal court.

d) **Concurrence.** The Restatement (Second) of Conflict of Laws lists "the needs of the interstate . . . system" as the first relevant "factor" in interest analysis. This suggests that states have shared, nonparochial interests. In reference to medical malpractice, there are interests in states being able to develop coherent policies governing malpractice liability and in individuals being able to seek medical services outside their home states. The law of the jurisdiction where the services are provided seems to best accommodate the systemic values. Medical associations can readily communicate with members as to liability hazards, and patients are inherently on notice that traveling to new jurisdictions may expose them to new rules.

c.   New problems.

1)   **Moving away from tradition.** As courts have moved away from the traditional territorial choice of law rules, problems of unfairness and inequity have diminished, but new problems have arisen.

2)   **Predictability.** The application of modern approaches lessened the predictability and reasonable certainty that accompanied the traditional choice of law rules. Different courts reached different results by "weighing" contacts differently.

   a)   **Temporary residence in a state--Dym v. Gordon,** 16 N.Y.2d 120 (1965).

Dym v. Gordon

   (1)   **Facts.** Dym (P) and Gordon (D), New York domiciliaries, were attending summer school in Colorado. While riding in D's car, on a trip between points in Colorado, an accident occurred with another car and P was injured due to D's negligence. Colorado's guest statute denies recovery absent wanton or willful conduct. New York allows P recovery. The New York court ruled that ordinary negligence was not a sufficient basis for recovery under Colorado's guest statute.

   (2)   **Issue.** Will New York apply the law of the place where the injury occurred when the parties were temporarily residing in that state?

   (3)   **Held.** Yes. Judgment affirmed. Colorado law applies.

      (a)   The policy of Colorado law is to protect Colorado drivers and insurance carriers and to insure the injured parties in other cars priority to defendant's assets. Thus Colorado has an interest in having its law applied. Colorado also has the most significant contacts. The parties were temporarily residing in Colorado—the state has an interest in regulating the conduct of such residents. The relationship between the parties was formed in Colorado and the accident was not a fortuitous occurrence there—it grew out of Colorado-based activity.

   (4)   **Dissent.** This case is not significantly different from *Babcock v. Jackson* (*supra*). Colorado has no conceivable interest in denying a remedy to a New York guest against his New York host for injuries suffered in Colorado by reason of conduct that was tortious under Colorado law.

   (5)   **Comment.** One of the primary criticisms of the "most significant relationship" approach is that different courts weigh the contacts differently. The extreme unpredictability of the rule is illustrated by the fact that the New York court, which decided the *Babcock* case, reached the opposite result in the *Dym* case, where the only factual difference was that the guest and driver were students in Colorado.

Conflict of Laws - 149

DeSantis v.
Wackenhut
Corp.

b)   Multiple jurisdictions--DeSantis v. Wackenhut Corp., 793 S.W.2d 670 (Tx. 1990).

   (1)   Facts. Wackenhut (P), a Florida corporation, employed DeSantis (D) as a manager in Texas. At the inception of his employment, D executed a noncompetition agreement. The agreement was executed in Texas but contained a provision that the contract would be governed by Florida law. After three years, D resigned and went into business for himself. P sued D and his company to enjoin them from violating the noncompetition agreement. The trial court applied the law of Florida and held the agreement valid but overly broad as to geographical area. D's claims for damages were denied. The appeals court affirmed. P appeals.

   (2)   Issue. Should Florida law govern the noncompetition agreement?

   (3)   Held. No. Judgment reversed.

      (a)   Parties to a contract who reside in different jurisdictions may express in their agreement which state law governs. However, this choice is not unlimited. They cannot choose a jurisdiction that has no relation to them or their agreement.

      (b)   Here, the relationship of the transaction and parties to Texas was clearly more significant than their relationship to Florida. Texas has a materially greater interest than Florida in deciding whether the noncompetition agreement should be enforced. The application of the law of a state other than Texas to determine the enforceability of the agreement would be contrary to the fundamental policy of Texas.

      (c)   P hired D in Texas. The agreement was executed in Texas. The place of performance for both P and D was Texas. These factors are more significant than those that occurred in Florida, *e.g.*, P's corporate offices are in Florida; P and D negotiated in Florida; P supervised D from Florida.

      (d)   The core of the agreement was the performance of personal services in Texas.

      (e)   The law governing the enforcement of noncompetition agreements is fundamental policy in Texas. [Restatement §187(2)(b)]

3)   Clashes in states' policies. When the policies of states clash, some states hold a preference for the application of the forum's law.

Lilienthal
v. Kaufman

a)   A contract in which two states have a significant interest--Lilienthal v. Kaufman, 239 Or. 1 (1964).

   (1)   Facts. Kaufman (D), an Oregon domiciliary, was declared a spendthrift by an Oregon court, which also appointed a guardian for D and deprived D of his capacity to contract. D went to California where he convinced Lilienthal (P), who was unaware of D's incapacity, to loan him money for a business venture. P sought to collect on the loan, but D's guardian defended on the basis of D's incapacity to contract. California law does not recognize the disability of spendthrifts. The trial court held for D. P appeals.

(2) Issue. If the forum and a sister state both have strong policy in favor of application of their law, will the forum's law apply?

(3) Held. Yes. Judgment affirmed.

    (a) Oregon law controlled. There can be no recovery on the contract. The strong Oregon public policy on spendthrifts outweighs other policy considerations (*e.g.*, validation of contracts made in good faith, protection of innocent persons from fraud, the encouragement of those in other states to do business with Oregon citizens).

(4) Concurrence. There is no reason to believe that the Oregon legislature intended to protect California creditors to a greater extent than our own.

(5) Dissent. Both states have general policies to uphold the validity of contracts. The majority improperly balanced the interests of the states.

(6) Comment. Most courts applying the "interest" analysis would have applied California law. So long as there is a good reason for applying the forum's law, the strength of the foreign state's interest may not be carefully weighed.

b) A cause of action available only under foreign law--Casey v. Manson Construction and Engineering Co., 247 Or. 274 (1967).

Casey v. Manson Construction and Engineering Co.

(1) Facts. Casey, an Oregon resident, was working in Washington on a project for a Washington construction company (D). D was negligent and Casey was injured. His wife (P) sued in Oregon for loss of consortium, an action recognized by Oregon but not by Washington. The trial court applied Washington law and P appeals.

(2) Issue. Under the "most significant relationship" test, does Washington law apply?

(3) Held. Yes. Judgment affirmed.

    (a) The Restatement rule applies ("most significant relationship"), and although both states have an interest, Washington's interest is the greatest (D is a Washington resident, the action arose there, the parties had expectations that their liability would be governed by Washington law). The judgment could have been different if the place of injury was a mere happenstance, but in this case the accident could only have occurred in Washington.

(4) Concurrence. Applying Washington law is most practical. Otherwise, citizens of that state carrying on activities there could theoretically be subjected to 49 different levels of responsibility.

(5) Comment. Compare this "torts" case with the "contracts" case (*Lilienthal*) above. The rationale here appears to be in direct conflict with the rationale applied by the same court in *Lilienthal*.

Bernhard v.
Harrah's Club

c) Vicarious liability applied to a foreign defendant--Bernhard v. Harrah's Club, 16 Cal. 3d 313 (1976).

(1) Facts. Two Californians patronized Harrah's Club (D), a Nevada corporation, where they became intoxicated. While driving back to California and after entering California, they collided with a motorcycle operated by Bernhard (P), also a California resident, who then brought an action for damages for personal injuries against D. The trial court sustained D's demurrer on the grounds that Nevada law placed no liability on the innkeeper. P appeals.

(2) Issue. Under the "state interest" analysis, should Nevada law apply?

(3) Held. No. Judgment reversed.

(a) Since this case involves a California plaintiff injured in California by a driver intoxicated in Nevada, each state has an interest. Therefore, the "comparative impairment" approach applied: the state's interest that would be more impaired if its policy were subordinated to the policy of the other state, will govern. California's interest, "to prevent tavern keepers from selling alcoholic beverages to obviously intoxicated persons who are likely to act in California in an intoxicated state," would be significantly impaired if its policies were not applied to D, who solicits much of its business in California. Nevada's interest in protecting its tavern keepers who solicit business in California would be less impaired because the increased liability is foreseeable and "coverable" as a business expense.

d) The "comparative impairment" approach applied to true conflicts. In *Offshore Rental Co. v. Continental Oil Co.*, 22 Cal. 3d 157 (1978), Offshore Rental Co. (P), sued Continental Oil Co. (D) for the loss of services of a "key" employee whom D negligently injured. P, a California corporation, sent the employee, Kaylor, to Louisiana to obtain contracts to lease oil drilling equipment to Louisiana drillers. While in Louisiana, Kaylor was injured on D's property due to D's negligence. P sued in California for $5 million occasioned by the loss of Kaylor's services. The trial court, using the most significant contacts theory, decided that Louisiana's law applied, which precluded P's cause of action. Under California law, P probably could maintain the action. P appealed the choice of law. The appeals court, applying "government interest" analysis, affirmed the dismissal. Although the trial court applied the wrong analysis, the government interest approach led to the same result. There was a "true conflict" since both California and Louisiana had an interest: Louisiana in protecting resident tortfeasors from excessive legal liability and California in protecting California employers from economic harm caused by the temporary loss of key employees. The court found that the "comparative impairment" approach, which seeks to determine which state's interest would be more impaired if its policies were subordinated, should be applied. Under this approach, the court should consider the history and current status of the state's laws (whether they are little respected relics of past thought or current, progressive law), the function and purpose of the laws, and whether the same policy could be satisfied by some other means (*e.g.*, private insurance). Since California's law was unusual, outmoded, and less strongly held than Louisiana's, and P could most reasonably have anticipated insurance needs based on Louisiana law, Louisiana law was properly applied.

e) **Three competing interests--Reich v. Purcell,** 67 Cal. 2d 551 (1967).

Reich v. Purcell

(1) **Facts.** This case involves a wrongful death action arising out of a collision in Missouri in which Mrs. Reich and her son Jay were killed. The Reichs were residents of Ohio, and Purcell, the defendant-driver, was a resident of California. A statute limiting the amount of damages in a wrongful death action was in effect in Missouri (the place of the wrong) but no such statute was in effect in California or Ohio. Mr. Reich (P) moved to California following the accident and sued there. The trial court limited recovery to $25,000 according to Missouri law, the place of the injury. P appeals.

(2) **Issue.** Under "state interest analysis," should the forum recognize a limit on the amount of damages under the law of the place of death?

(3) **Held.** No. Judgment modified for full recovery.

   (a) It is the forum's duty to consider all the "interests" involved to determine the applicable rule. Missouri had no conceivable interest in having its limitation on damages applied, since neither plaintiff nor defendant resided there. Defendant had no basis to rely on a rule limiting damages, since the law in effect in his domicile (California) allowed unlimited damages. Consequently, the law of the decedents' domicile (Ohio) will apply because of its paramount interest in the distribution of decedents' estates and compensation to beneficiaries thereof.

(4) **Comment.** If the forum finds that it has no interest in applying its own law, but that two other states do have competing policies, the problem of the "disinterested third state" is presented. If the ostensible conflict between the other two states is "false" (only one of them has an interest in having its law applied), then the forum will simply apply the law of the only interested state. This type of case does not present any real difficulties.

f) **Effect of post-accident changes.** Several courts have held that the plaintiff's change of domicile after the cause of action arose is irrelevant. [Reich v. Purcell, *supra*]

(1) **Rationale.** To apply a different rule because a party moves his residence might encourage forum shopping, or possibly subject defendant to liabilities he could not have foreseen when he acted.

(2) **Consider changes.** But other authorities assert that post-accident changes or events (such as change of domicile of either party) should be considered insofar as they affect a state interests analysis.

(3) Defendant's change of domicile--Miller v. Miller, 22 N.Y.2d 12 (1968).

    (a) Facts. Earl Miller, a New York resident, went to Maine, where he was killed in a car accident while riding with his brother and sister-in-law (Ds). Following the accident, Ds moved to New York, where Earl's wife (P) filed a wrongful death action. Ds claim that the New York court should apply Maine's $20,000 limitation on damages.

    (b) Issues.

        1] May the forum refuse to apply the limitation on recovery in effect in the foreign state where death occurred?

        2] Should the post-accident change of domicile be considered in applying the "state interest" analysis?

    (c) Held. 1] Yes. 2] Yes. New York law applies.

        1] Courts should be disposed to apply their own law, unless there is a strong reason for applying foreign law (such as most significant interest). Here there are no such countervailing considerations—Maine law does not purport to regulate conduct; the parties could not have had expectations based on it, they did not insure with its limits in mind, etc. Furthermore, the liability insurer, the real party in interest, must have expected that accidents occurring outside of Maine would be governed by other state laws having higher limits.

        2] The application of New York law will not unduly interfere with the legitimate interest of a sister state. The defendants have moved to New York and are no longer residents of Maine.

4) Fairness. Factors other than state interests affect the fairness of the outcome.

a) Wrongful death damages limitation--Rosenthal v. Warren, 475 F.2d 438 (2d Cir. 1973).

    (1) Facts. Rosenthal (decedent) and his wife (P), New York residents, went to Boston to obtain health care for the decedent. When he died, P sued the hospital and Dr. Warren (D) in New York for malpractice. D asserted the Massachusetts wrongful death damages limitation (not less than $5,000 nor more than $50,000). New York law allowed unlimited recovery. The trial court applied New York law and D appeals.

    (2) Issue. Does the forum's interest in providing full recovery for its citizens outweigh the foreign state's interest in limiting recovery against its citizens?

    (3) Held. Yes. Judgment affirmed.

(a) Strong New York public policy against damage limitations predominates, particularly in wrongful death actions where the prohibition against damage limitations is written into the New York constitution.

(4) Dissent. The "interest analysis" should lead to the application of Massachusetts law where malpractice insurance premiums are low, relying on the application of the Massachusetts limitation.

(5) Comment. This case illustrates the difficulty and potential inconsistency of the "interest" approach. The Restatement (Second) applies a similar test to tort cases; the law of the place of the injury controls unless another state has a "more significant relationship" to the parties or the occurrences.

5) **"No interest."** Sometimes the law of the plaintiff's state favors the defendant, while the law of the defendant's state favors the plaintiff.

a) **State's interest in protecting consumers--Reyno v. Piper Aircraft Co.,** 630 F.2d 149 (3d Cir. 1980).

(1) Facts. This wrongful death action was brought after a plane manufactured by Piper Aircraft (D), a Pennsylvania corporation, crashed in Scotland. The owner, passengers, and crew of the plane were all residents of Scotland. The action was originally brought in California and was then transferred to Pennsylvania under 28 U.S.C. section 1404(a). (The court of appeals held that California choice of law rules should be applied and then addressed the following issue.)

(2) Issue. Under California choice of law rules should Pennsylvania strict liability or Scottish negligence law be applied?

(3) Held. Pennsylvania law.

(a) A California court would apply Pennsylvania's strict liability analysis. Scotland has an interest in encouraging industry by protecting manufacturers and making it more difficult for consumers to recover. Pennsylvania's strict liability law furthers the state's interest in regulating manufacturers and protecting consumers from defective products. Applying Pennsylvania law would serve the state's interest and it would not impair Scotland's interest in encouraging industry within its borders since D has no industrial operations in Scotland.

(4) Comment. This case was reversed by the Supreme Court in *Piper Aircraft v. Reyno*, 454 U.S. 235 (1981), on the ground of forum non conveniens.

6) **Multistate injuries in a defamation case--Dale System, Inc. v. Time, Inc.,** 116 F. Supp. 527 (D. Conn. 1953).

a) **Facts.** Dale System (P) is a Connecticut corporation; Time (D) is a New York corporation. P sued in Connecticut federal district court for an alleged libelous article published in *Life*, republished in *Reader's Digest,* and broadcast on a radio station that covered the East Coast.

b)   Issues.

   (1)   How many causes of action does P have?

   (2)   What law should be applied?

c)   Held. (1) Three. (2) Connecticut conflict rules apply.

   (1)   *Single publication rule:* A number of states have adopted the Uniform Single Publication Act, which provides that only a single cause of action for defamation is created by a defamatory publication, no matter where the damages take place. A judgment on the merits in any jurisdiction that has adopted the act bars suit elsewhere.

   (2)   *Causes of action:* There are, therefore, only three causes of action—one for the *Life* article, one for the *Reader's Digest* article, and one for the radio broadcast.

   (3)   *Single conflicts rule:* A single conflicts rule applies in each instance; the law of the plaintiff's domicile controls when the libel has been communicated there as well as elsewhere. *Rationale*: A single rule is needed to prevent forum shopping, to provide certainty, and to aid ease of publication.

d)   Comments.

   (1)   Probably the court first should have decided what law was to be applied and then determined whether according to that law the single publication rule applied.

   (2)   The Restatement purports to apply the law of the state having the "most significant relationship" with the occurrence and the parties. However, it does state that this is normally the state of the defamed person's domicile if the matter was published in that state.

d.   Depecage.

1)   The nature of depecage. In determining which law to apply, the traditional approach to choice of laws directs the forum to analyze cases as a whole and apply a single state's law to all the issues presented, whereas all the modern approaches direct the forum to focus on each specific issue separately. Thus, under the modern approaches, the laws of different states may govern the resolution of the different issues presented in the case; this is known as "depecage."

2) **Applications.**

a) **Statutes of limitations conflict--Lillegraven v. Tengs,** 375 P.2d 139 (Alaska 1962).

(1) **Facts.** Plaintiff (P) shared expenses on an auto trip from Seattle to Alaska and was injured when the nonowner-driven car had an accident in British Columbia on October 8, 1958. P sued D on September 26, 1960, within Alaska's two-year statute of limitations, but beyond British Columbia's one-year statute. P relied on the British Columbia statute, which imposed liability on the consenting owner, as the basis of the suit. Suit was brought in Alaska. The trial court applied the British Columbia statute of limitations, thus barring the suit. P appeals.

(2) **Issue.** Should the statute of limitations of the forum govern?

(3) **Held.** Yes. Judgment reversed.

(a) The purpose of the British Columbia statute is to encourage promptness in prosecution of actions and to avoid injustice that would result if claims were asserted after evidence has been lost, memories have faded, and witnesses have disappeared. The minimum period of time that would best effect this purpose is a matter of policy of government. We see no good reason why this state's policy should give way to a foreign state's policy.

b) **Situations where the complete law of either jurisdiction would preclude the action--Marie v. Garrison,** 13 Abb. N.C. 210 (N.Y. 1883).

(1) **Facts.** Marie (P) brought suit in New York state court based on a Missouri transaction (an oral promise given pursuant to an earlier written agreement). D moves to exclude evidence of the oral promise as a violation of the Statute of Frauds.

(2) **Issue.** If the contract violated both New York's and Missouri's Statutes of Frauds, may the court still recognize the cause of action?

(3) **Held.** Yes.

(a) Neither state's Statute of Frauds is applicable. The language of the New York statute is that "agreements" in contravention of its provisions are void and is thus "substantive" since it voided the contract and did not merely go to the remedy. Therefore, it can not be applied since Missouri substantive law governs. The Missouri statute ("No cause of action can be brought") also can not apply since it is "procedural" and the procedural law of New York applies.

D. WORKERS' COMPENSATION

1. **Introduction.** Early cases characterized these cases as either "contract" or "tort" and decided them accordingly. Modern courts treat them as distinct and the basic rationale of most decisions is to see that the most favorable recovery possible is given. Thus, the choice of law rules are reasoned with this objective in mind.

2. **Jurisdiction.** Statutes govern workers' compensation actions. These statutes normally allow actions to be brought for injuries occurring outside the state; thus, jurisdiction normally is proper wherever the employer is subject to jurisdiction.

3. **Choice of Law.** Most of these cases have contacts with more than one state—*i.e.*, one state may be the place of employee's residence; another the place of injury; another the place of hiring, etc. Thus, most compensation boards apply their own law to the case. This is constitutional as long as the forum has some reasonable interest (contact) in regulating the employment relationship.

Wilson v.
Faull

4. **Policy of workers' compensation--Wilson v. Faull,** 27 N.J. 105 (1958).

   a. **Facts.** Faull (D), a New Jersey general contractor, was sued for the personal injuries of a subcontractor's employee, Wilson (P). D entered a contract in Pennsylvania to repair a building there. In New Jersey, D subcontracted part of the repairs to Tragle and agreed to erect a scaffold from which they would work. Tragle hired P in New Jersey. P subsequently fell from the scaffold in Pennsylvania. P obtained workers' compensation in New Jersey from Tragle and now seeks a common law negligence recovery from D. Under New Jersey law P's recovery of workers' compensation from a subcontractor would not preclude a negligence action against the general contractor, but the action would be precluded under Pennsylvania law. The trial court in New Jersey granted D summary judgment on the ground that the law of the place of injury (Pennsylvania) controlled tort actions. The appellate division reversed, claiming the "preponderance of contacts" were with New Jersey. D appeals.

   b. **Issue.** May New Jersey enforce the general policy underlying workers' compensation to provide a rapid, but exclusive remedy?

   c. **Held.** Yes. Judgment reversed.

      1) Workers' compensation schemes are designed to aid both the employee and the employer. They generally protect the employer against common law actions while they provide the employee with predictable compensation and rapid recovery without proof of fault. Although strictly speaking New Jersey law would not preclude this common law action, there is an almost universally accepted principle that the forum will recognize the law of a sister state that grants immunity to the employer, and this is in keeping with the general policy that workers' compensation is an exclusive remedy.

d. **Concurrence.** The cause of action arose in Pennsylvania and therefore its law, which would grant workers' compensation, as an exclusive remedy, should apply.

e. **Comment.** The court is applying a government interest analysis and is basically concluding that there is a false conflict—that the policies of the two states do not differ.

E. CHANGING CHOICE OF LAW PRINCIPLES: AN INTERNATIONAL LAW

1. **Introduction.** The area of choice of law relates to whether, and to what extent, the forum will recognize and apply foreign law to resolve a case that has "contacts" with more than one jurisdiction. The subject of choice of laws is broad enough to cover those cases where the laws of other states of the union ("interstate") may be concerned, as well as those wherein the laws of foreign nations ("international") may be involved.

2. **International Choice of Law Problems.** Although generally international cases have been considered in the same framework as interstate cases, additional considerations must be taken into account:

    a. **Diplomacy.** Since foreign interests are involved, "diplomacy"—*i.e.*, the necessity of maintaining international order and goodwill—may require a more delicate approach. [Leflar, American Conflicts Law §6]

        1) **Note.** Different results may be had depending on the particular nation involved—considering the similarities and dissimilarities between the procedural and substantive laws of the other nation and those of the forum.

    b. **Proof of law.** Moreover, if the law to be applied by the American forum is that of a foreign nation, rather than a sister state, whose legal system is not drawn from English sources and whose language is other than English, discovering the content of that law may prove to be a more difficult task. As a result, the forum court may be inclined to reject the foreign law and, instead, apply its own law.

    c. **Forum non conveniens.** Further application of forum non conveniens is less likely if the dismissal of the action would remit the suit to a foreign court rather than a sister state court.

        1) **Comment.** Because dismissal is unlikely, one scholar has suggested that choice of foreign rule "may be required in order to avoid unfair application of the forum rule." [Ehrenzweig, Private International Law 21 (1967)]

    d. **Foreign treaties.** Finally, under the Constitution, foreign treaties are recognized as "the law of the land," governing those fact situations covered by them. However, to date, few private lawsuits have arisen under such treaties.

1) **Note—Full Faith and Credit Clause not applicable.** It should be noted here that the Full Faith and Credit Clause of the Constitution does not apply to foreign acts, records, or judgments.

e. **Comment.** It has been suggested that the framework established for choice of law cases within the federal system is inadequate to treat international cases, due to the different considerations involved. [Ehrenzweig, Private International Law 21 (1967)]

3. **Applications.**

a. **Foreign law applied to a contract made in New York--Lauritzen v. Larsen,** 345 U.S. 571 (1952).

1) **Facts.** Larsen (P), a Danish citizen temporarily in New York, signed a contract joining the crew of a Danish ship owned by Lauritzen (D), a Danish citizen. The contract provided that crewmen disputes would be governed under Danish law. Due to D's negligence, P was injured while on the ship in Havana and in the course of his employment. P brought suit in New York federal district court under an American statute, the Jones Act. The Jones Act would allow recovery even though under Danish law P had received all the compensation to which he was entitled. The district court ruled that American law applied. The court of appeals affirmed. The Supreme Court granted certiorari.

2) **Issue.** Will the United States court apply United States law to a contract made in the United States between Danish domiciliaries who stipulated that Danish law should apply?

3) **Held.** No. Judgment reversed. Danish law applies.

a) We will weigh the significance of the connecting factors between the shipping transaction and the national interest severed by the assertion of authority (application of the forum's law). The following contacts must be considered:

(1) The place of the wrongful act (Cuba);

(2) The law of the flag;

(3) The law of the domicile of the injured party;

(4) The law of the shipowner;

(5) The place of contract (New York); and

(6) The law of the forum.

b) We are hesitant to accept P's idea of applying the law of the place of contract. The stipulation was for Danish law, the local contract was an entirely fortuitous one, and there is a disposition in international conflict cases to give greater weight to the claim of territorial sovereignty than in interstate situations. Also there are practical considerations of international policies. There are good reasons for not accepting an unfettered seizure on "contacts" to justify the application of the forum's law:

(1) Mutual forbearance and reciprocity are the most important concepts in these cases.

(2) The contacts should be weighed to achieve uniformity of results, to avoid forum shopping, to achieve certainty and predictability, and to avoid races to judgment.

F. ASSIGNMENT AND ARBITRATION

1. **Introduction.** The choice of law rules vary with the kind of problem involved. In determining the basic rights of a third-party assignee, the courts generally look to the law of the place where the assignment takes place. [Restatement (Second) §209] But questions as to the assignability of the underlying contract should be determined by the law that otherwise governs the "validity" of the contract. [Restatement (Second) §208] In determining priority among successive assignees of the same debt, reference should generally be made to the place where the performance is due (*e.g.*, where the assigned debt is to be paid). [Restatement (Second) §211]

2. **Impact of the Uniform Commercial Code.** The U.C.C. establishes choice of law principles which, to a large degree, have eliminated the problems in this area.

3. **Arbitration Clauses.**

   a. **Introduction.** In contracts with arbitration clauses, the issues are not the normal contracts issues (validity, etc.); the issues are whether one side can compel arbitration (as called for) and which state's law will determine this issue.

   b. **Early view.** Early courts did not look favorably on arbitration clauses, since they purported to oust courts from their jurisdiction.

   1) **Foreign award--Parsons & Whittemore Overseas Co., Inc. v. Societe Generale de L'Industrie Du Papier (RAKTA),** 508 F.2d 969 (1974).

      a) **Facts.** Overseas (P) appeals from the entry of summary judgment confirming a foreign arbitral award holding P liable to RAKTA (D) for breach of contract. In 1962, P and D entered into a contract under which P agreed to construct and manage a paperboard mill in Egypt. The contract contained an arbitration clause and a "force majeure" clause excusing delays in P's performance due to causes beyond its control. In May 1967, most of P's work crew left Egypt because of the Arab-Israeli Six Day War and Egyptian hostility to Americans. In June, Egypt broke diplomatic ties with the United States and ordered all Americans expelled except for those who qualified for a special visa. P notified D that it regarded the contract as excused by the force majeure clause. D disagreed and sued for breach of contract, and when P refused to settle, D invoked the arbitration clause. The arbitration tribunal issued a preliminary award, limiting P's force majeure defense to the period from May 28 to June 30. In its appeal, P claims that enforcement of the award would violate the public policy of the United States and that the award represents an arbitration of matters not appropriately decided by arbitration.

    b)   **Issue.** Should the foreign arbitration award be enforced?

    c)   **Held.** Yes. Judgment affirmed.

       (1)   The issues raised by P on appeal are derived from the language of the United States Convention on the Recognition and Enforcement of Foreign Arbitral Awards. The Convention allows a court in which enforcement is sought to refuse enforcement if this would be contrary to the public policy of the forum country. Because of the pro-enforcement bias of the Convention and considerations of reciprocity, the public policy defense should be narrowly construed. We conclude that enforcement will be denied on public policy grounds only if enforcement would violate the forum state's most basic notions of morality and justice. Here it would not.

       (2)   The Convention also authorizes a court to deny enforcement when the subject matter is not capable of settlement by arbitration under the law of the forum country. P claims that United States foreign policy was at issue and that, because the foreign arbitrators were charged with the execution of no public trust and had loyalties to foreign interests, the matter was nonarbitrable. We hold that the mere fact that an issue of national interest may incidentally enter in the resolution of the breach of contract claim does not make the dispute nonarbitrable. The fact that acts of the United States might be implicated in the case does not lead to the conclusion that the United States is vitally interested in the outcome. Thus, the foreign award against P dealt with a subject arbitrable under United States law.

   2)   **Modern view.** More recent courts have been more favorably disposed to arbitration provisions. An agreement that any dispute arising under the contract shall be settled in arbitration in accordance with the statutes of state X has been supported and interpreted as an agreement to submit to the jurisdiction of the courts in state X, if necessary for enforcement of the arbitration board's award.

G. NEGOTIABLE INSTRUMENTS

   1.   **Introduction.** The Restatement (Second) covers certain types of negotiable instruments such as checks, notes, and certificates of deposit and does not cover certain others. Most states have enacted the Uniform Commercial Code ("U.C.C."), which covers bills of exchange, including checks, notes, and certificates of deposits (Article 3) and bills of lading and warehouse receipts (Article 7). Before the adoption of the U.C.C., many states had passed the Uniform Negotiable Instrument Law, so not many conflict problems have arisen in this area; when they did, the validity and rights created by each obligation were determined by the law applicable to that obligation. That is, for any given negotiable instrument, the laws of several states may apply in determining all of the rights involved.

a. **Section 214.** For example, section 214 of the Restatement covers the rights of makers and acceptors and indicates that normally the law of the state designated in the instrument as the place of payment applies. If no place of payment is designated, then the law of the state where the instrument is delivered by the maker is applied (presumptively that state where the instrument is dated).

b. **Section 215.** Section 215 indicates that obligations of indorsers and drawers are determined by the law of the state where the obligor delivers the instrument (presumptively the state where the paper was dated is the state of delivery; the place of payment is the source of law as to where presentment may be made).

c. **Section 216.** Section 216 provides that the law of the state where the negotiable instrument actually was when transferred determines whether the transferee holds the instrument in due course and has title.

d. **Section 217.** Section 217 indicates that details of presentment, payment, protest, and dishonor are determined by the law of the state where these actions occur.

2. **Restatement Concepts Applied to International Transfers--Koechlin et Cie. v. Kestenbaum Brothers,** 1 K.B. 889 (1927).

a. **Facts.** Koechlin (P) was the indorsee of a bill of exchange in France. The bill of exchange was payable by Kestenbaum Brothers (D) of London. D refused to pay the bill of exchange on the grounds that under English law, the indorsement was improper. P claims that French law should apply since the indorsement occurred in France. The English trial court applied English law and P appeals.

b. **Issue.** Should the indorsement be governed by the law of the place where the indorsement occurred?

c. **Held.** Yes. Judgment reversed.

1) The validity of a transfer of movable chattels must be governed by the law of the country where the transfer occurs. The same rule applies to the indorsements of negotiable instruments. Questions of validity (form requirements) are governed by the law where the bill was issued. But questions as to the validity of transfers will be governed by the law where the transfer occurred.

d. **Comment.** The various sections of the Restatement essentially adopt these traditional "vested rights" rules on the basis that they secure the interests of the jurisdiction with the most significant contacts.

3. **Usury Cases.**

a. **Introduction.** In determining the legality of a contract, the courts consider the nature of the grounds on which the illegality is asserted. If the claimed illegality consists of an alleged violation of statutes in the forum or elsewhere that are principally aimed at regulation of business transactions, then the courts generally will apply whatever reasonably applicable law would uphold the validity of the contract.

b. **General rule.** In the interest area, a number of decisions have involved contracts claimed to be usurious. The courts have tended to apply whichever law would hold the contract to be valid, provided there is a reasonable relationship with the transaction and the parties were in equal bargaining positions.

H. CONFLICT BETWEEN FEDERAL AND STATE LAW

1. **Introduction.** Assuming that the case is one in which there is concurrent federal and state court jurisdiction, certain questions must be considered: If the action is filed in a state court, to what extent, if any, is the state court bound to apply federal law? And conversely, if filed in a federal court, will it apply the laws (including the choice of law rules) of the state in which it is located, or will it apply some separate and different "federal" rules? The answer depends upon the nature of the issue involved.

2. **If No Federal Right Is Involved.** If the claims or defenses involved in the lawsuit do not turn on any issue of federal law, the Supremacy Clause is not applicable, and the question becomes whether the plaintiff can expect more favorable treatment in a state or federal court—*e.g.*, in the typical diversity of citizenship lawsuit, can the plaintiff expect the federal court to apply some different, and perhaps better, rules of law than would be applied if she filed her action in the local state court?

a. **Background.**

1) **Judiciary Act.** In 1789, Congress enacted the Judiciary Act, which required the federal courts to apply "the laws of the several states" as "rules of decision" in common law actions in federal courts.

2) *Swift v. Tyson.* However, the Supreme Court at first construed the Act as applicable only to state statutes and not to state case law, meaning that on all matters not specifically regulated by local statutes, federal courts were free to adopt and apply "general principles of federal common law." [Swift v. Tyson, 41 U.S. 1 (1842)]

a) **Effect.** In major areas of litigation not generally regulated by local statute (commercial law, torts, etc.), there were two separate systems of law: state and federal. This led to "forum shopping"—plaintiff would file her action in whichever court had the more advantageous rules of law for her particular case.

3) Destruction of the federal substantive common law created by *Swift v. Tyson*--Erie Railroad Co. v. Tompkins, 304 U.S. 64 (1938).

    a)   Facts. Tompkins (P), a citizen of Pennsylvania, was injured in Pennsylvania by a New York railroad. P sued the railroad in the federal district court in New York. Everyone assumed that if state law applied, then P's rights would be governed by Pennsylvania law, because in 1938 the "place of injury rule" governed tort cases. The lower court applied a general federal common law under the *Swift v. Tyson* opinion (which made reference to state law mandatory only when state statutes were involved) on the rationale that federal courts were applying the "true rules" of the common law.

    b)   Issue. Should federal courts recognize a federal substantive common law rather than apply the substantive law of the forum state?

    c)   Held. No. Judgment reversed.

        (1)   There is no general federal common law, no "transcendental body of law outside of any particular state" or governmental unit; law is the command of the sovereign and therefore when federal courts create law it must be federal law. *Swift* is therefore unconstitutional because it violates the Tenth Amendment; *i.e.*, federal courts are making law in areas that Congress has no constitutional authority to do so.

        (2)   The 1789 Judiciary Act was merely declarative of the constitutional obligation of federal courts to apply state substantive law on nonfederal questions; *i.e.*, the Act applies both to state statutory and case law.

    d)   Comment. The purpose of the decision was to eliminate the uncontrolled forum shopping between state and federal courts—to compel federal courts to reach the same result on nonfederal questions as state courts would have reached.

b.   Scope of *Erie* doctrine. The gist of the decision in *Erie* is that, while federal courts are free to apply their own rules of "procedure," any issue of "substantive" law (other than a "federal question," below) must be determined according to the laws of the state in which the federal court sits.

    1)   Characterization as "substance" or "procedure." Obviously, the difficulty in applying the *Erie* doctrine is determining whether a particular matter or issue is "substantive" (and hence to be governed by state law) or merely "procedural" (so that the federal court is free to apply its own rules).

        a)   Former "outcome determinative test."

            (1)   Introduction. For many years, the Court held that whatever might have a material effect on the outcome of the case (*i.e.*, who wins and who loses) was "substantive," and hence subject to state law. Anything else was "procedural" and governed by federal rules.

(2) Outcome-determinative test--Guaranty Trust Co. v. York, 326 U.S. 99 (1945).

(a) Facts. In 1942, York (P) filed a class action in federal district court (diversity jurisdiction) against Guaranty Trust Co. (D) for breach of trust occurring in 1931. D was granted summary judgment on the ground that New York law time-barred the suit. The court of appeals reversed, ruling that in equity cases the court was not bound to apply the New York statute of limitations.

(b) Issue. Should a federal court acting under diversity jurisdiction apply rules that achieve the same outcome as would have been obtained in state court?

(c) Held. Yes. Summary judgment in favor of D sustained.

1] Generally the federal courts may apply their own rules of "procedure," but in diversity cases, under *Erie*, the federal district court is just like another state court and therefore the guiding principle is not whether a rule could be classified as "procedural" or "substantive." It should be classified in the federal court so that the outcome reached there would be identical with that reached by a state court had it heard the cause of action.

(d) Rationale. To achieve uniformity of decisions within a state between the decisions of the state courts and the federal courts sitting therein, anything that might endanger such uniformity because it would have material effect on the outcome of the case is classified as "substantive" and will be governed by state law.

(e) Comment. Since in many cases procedural matters may be outcome determinative, a number of decisions have subordinated the Federal Rules of Procedure and made reference to state law when the two were in conflict.

(3) Conflict with FRCP. It soon became clear, however, that many matters that otherwise would be controlled by the Federal Rules of Civil Procedure were "outcome determinative," and federal courts, accordingly, found themselves forced to apply state procedural rules, rather than the FRCP to such matters.

b) Modern test. The modern position of the Court appears to restrict the "outcome determinative" test.

(1) Federal law controls characterization. First of all, it is clear that the characterization of an issue as "substantive" or "procedural" is itself a federal question; and hence state determinations as to what is "procedure" or "substance" are immaterial. [Hanna v. Plumer, *infra*]

(2) Other federal policies may outweigh.

(a) **Introduction.** The Court has indicated that other constitutional doctrines or federal policies may occasionally prevail over the *Erie* doctrine in determining whether state or federal law will be applied.

(b) **Basic federal rights--Byrd v. Blue Ridge Rural Electric Cooperative, Inc.,** 356 U.S. 525 (1958).

1] **Facts.** Byrd (P) was injured in South Carolina while working there for a firm that had a contract with Blue Ridge Rural Electric Cooperative (D). P brought a negligence action in the federal district court in South Carolina. D said P was a "statutory employee" (under a South Carolina statute) and therefore could recover only statutory damages; furthermore, this issue was to be decided by the judge since in a previous state decision it had been so decided. The trial court submitted the issue to the jury, which decided in favor of P. D appealed. The court of appeals reversed. The United States Supreme Court granted certiorari.

2] **Issue.** If the application of substantive state law would violate federal policy, must the federal court in diversity cases apply state law?

3] **Held.** No. The federal district court does not have to apply the state court rule. (But the case is reversed and remanded on other grounds).

    a] In these kinds of cases, state courts are merely reviewing an administrative body, so the judge naturally determined jurisdictional questions rather than the jury. There is no indication, however, that the state-created "right" has included in it the provision for a judge as opposed to a jury determination of this question.

    b] Furthermore, "outcome" is not the only consideration in *Erie* situations:

        1/ A "countervailing consideration" is that the federal system is an independent one. An essential feature of this system is the way in which judge and jury functions are distributed.

        2/ The "outcome" test is not always determinative when state rules are not bound up with state-created rights and obligations.

4] **Rationale.** The Seventh Amendment guarantees a jury trial in federal court, and this provision is "essential to the integrity of the federal judiciary."

5] **Comment.** The meaning of this case for the "outcome" test is not clear. The Court noted, for example, that there was no certainty even in *Byrd* that the outcome would be different even if the jury had decided the issue in the federal district court. So perhaps the Supreme Court did not depart from the outcome test. Of course, even under *York* and the outcome test, the Supreme Court did make some distinction between "procedural" and "substantive" matters. With regard to the former, the federal district courts could apply their own rules. But the dividing line between the two was shifted to widen the scope of substantive matters—this in the interest of uniformity of outcome. *Byrd* may have realigned somewhat the "procedural-substantive" dividing line of *York*.

Even given the *Byrd* decision, it is doubtful that federal policy that is *not* "essential to the integrity of the federal judiciary" will be sufficient to deny the application of substantive state law.

(3) FRCP prevails.

(a) Introduction. The Court has held that in any conflict between the Federal Rules of Civil Procedure and state law, the FRCP control; *i.e.*, all such matters are presumptively "procedural" so that they need not yield to state law under *Erie*.

Hanna v.
Plumer

(b) Service of process--Hanna v. Plumer, 380 U.S. 460 (1965).

1] Facts. Hanna (P) filed a negligence action against Plumer (D) in federal district court in Massachusetts under diversity jurisdiction. Personal jurisdiction over D was acquired by leaving the summons with D's wife. Federal rules recognized such service of process, but state law required that D be served personally. The trial court granted summary judgment in favor of D for lack of service. P appeals, claiming the federal rules applied. D defends on the ground that service rules are "outcome determinative" in this case and therefore, under the *Erie* doctrine, require the application of state law.

2] Issue. Will the Federal Rules of Civil Procedure be applied in federal court even in situations where their application may determine the outcome?

3] Held. Yes. Judgment reversed.

a] Such service is permissible even though the outcome of the litigation if held in a state court would have been different. Article III of the Constitution granted Congress the power to formulate the Federal Rules of Civil Procedure, and by the Supremacy Clause these can be applied to *Erie* type cases.

4] Concurrence (Harlan, J.). The proper line of approach in determining whether to apply a state or federal rule, whether "substantive" or "procedural," is to stay close to basic principles by inquiring if the choice of rule would substantially affect those primary decisions respecting human conduct which our constitutional system leaves to state regulation.

5] Comment. Although the 1789 Judiciary Act compels reference to state law (*supra*), the 1934 Rules Enabling Act authorizes the adoption of procedural rules for federal courts. This latter Act is said to "amend" the former, thereby establishing the supremacy of the FRCP over state law, whenever they conflict.

c. The *Erie* doctrine's effect on choice of law.

1) **Introduction.** A federal district court must, in effect, sit as a trial court of the state in which it is located, in deciding whatever problems are classified as "substantive" for *Erie* purposes. Accordingly, it must adopt that state's body of choice of law rules and apply it as its own. There are no federal choice of law rules apart from state law. Thus, a federal court located in State A must apply whatever choice of law rules the courts of State A would apply: If the courts of State A would look to the law of State B, then the federal court in State A will apply State B's law.

2) **Applications.**

a) **Federal court application of state conflict rules--Klaxon Co. v. Stentor Electric Manufacturing Co.,** 313 U.S. 487 (1941).

Klaxon Co. v. Stentor Electric Manufacturing Co.

(1) **Facts.** Stentor Electric (P), a New York corporation, sold its corporate assets to Klaxon Co. (D), a Delaware corporation. The sale was executed in New York. P filed this diversity action in the federal district court in Delaware. P alleged that the New York statute, awarding interest from the time suit is filed until judgment is entered, was applicable. D argued that Delaware law applied, which would not give interest. The lower court applied New York law. D appeals.

(2) **Issue.** Must a federal court in diversity citizenship cases apply the conflict of laws rules that apply in the state where the court sits?

(3) **Held.** Yes. Judgment reversed and remanded.

(a) Conflict of laws rules applied by the federal court in Delaware must conform to those prevailing in Delaware state courts. Otherwise, the accident of diversity of citizenship would constantly disturb equal administration of justice in coordinate state and federal courts sitting in Delaware. Delaware is free to determine whether a given matter is to be governed by the law of the forum or some other law, subject only to federal question review. Delaware could label the interest issue as "substantive" and governed by the law where the contract was made or as "procedural" and governed by forum law. The federal court should determine what Delaware law is, and not what it ought to be. Full faith and credit would not require Delaware to apply New York law that offends its local public policy.

(4) **Comment.** This case attempts to prevent forum shopping by requiring the federal court to apply the conflicts principles of the state where the federal court sits. However, this concept may increase forum shopping since the state may label certain outcome determinative issues as procedural and therefore uniformly apply its own law. Note the pervasive problem that the federal court must divine state law.

b) **Transferor court's law applies--Ferens v. John Deere Co.,** 494 U.S. 516 (1990).

(1) **Facts.** Ferens (P) lost his hand when it allegedly became caught in a combine manufactured by John Deere (D), a Delaware corporation. The accident occurred in Pennsylvania. P's tort claim was barred by that state's two-year statute of limitations. P filed a diversity suit against D in the district court in Mississippi because P knew that the federal court would have to apply Mississippi's six-year statute of limitations. P then moved to transfer the action to federal court in Pennsylvania on the ground that Pennsylvania was a more convenient forum. The case was transferred, but the court then applied Pennsylvania's limitations period. P appealed and the court of appeals affirmed on the grounds that the Mississippi limitations would violate due process because Mississippi had no legitimate interest in the case. P petitioned for certiorari. The Supreme Court vacated and remanded. On remand, the court of appeals affirmed. The Supreme Court granted certiorari.

(2) **Issue.** Should the Mississippi limitations period continue to govern the suit?

(3) **Held.** Yes. Judgment reversed and remanded.

(a) The transferee forum was required to apply the law of the transferor court.

(b) The legislature did not intend 28 U.S.C. section 1404(a) to deprive parties of state law advantages that exist absent diversity jurisdiction.

(c) To discourage plaintiff-initiated transfers by applying the transferee law might encourage states to enact laws that would bring in out-of-state business that would not be moved at a plaintiff's insistence.

(d) Convenience is also a consideration, not only for the plaintiff, but for the witnesses and the court.

(4) **Dissent** (Scalia, Brennan, Marshall, Blackmun, JJ.). Congress did not intend to provide P with a vehicle by which to appropriate the law of a distant inconvenient forum in which he does not intend to litigate, and to carry that "prize" back to the state in which he wishes to try the case. The application of the transferor court's law in this context would encourage forum shopping between federal and state courts in the same jurisdiction on the basis of different substantive law.

c) **State created privileges and the meaning of "state law"--Samuelson v. Susen,** 576 F.2d 546 (3d Cir. 1978).

(1) **Facts.** *See* same case, *supra.*

(2) **Interpretation of "state law."** (Only a portion of the opinion appears here.) *Erie*, prior to the enactment of Rule 501, determined that state-created privileges conferred substantive rights beyond regulation by federal procedural rules. Congress sought, in drafting Rule 501, to recognize this position for the following reasons: (i) privilege rules are substantive for *Erie* purposes; (ii) they are outcome determinative; (iii) when state law provides the rules of decision, state privilege laws should apply because there is no federal interest substantial enough to justify departure from state policy; and (iv) state policy regarding privilege, if thwarted merely because of diversity, would encourage forum shopping. A federal court's application of the forum state's laws of privilege is consistent with Congress's goals.

Plaintiff's interpretation of "state law" would prevent the application of all of a forum state's law, including its choice-of-law rules. This would be antithetical to one of the primary goals of Rule 501, *i.e.*, the recognition that when states have created rights, the federal courts should apply the same rules of law to those rights as the states themselves would apply.

d) **State characterization of a foreign statute as penal--Doggrell v. Southern Box Co.**, 208 F.2d 310 (6th Cir. 1953).

Doggrell v. Southern Box Co.

(1) **Facts.** Two Arkansas and one Tennessee residents formed an Arkansas corporation. The Arkansas shareholders failed to file the articles as required by state law, making the three personally liable (under Arkansas law) as partners for goods purchased in the corporation's name. A creditor brought suit in Tennessee federal district court. The defendant argued that the Arkansas statute was "penal"; the court rejected this. While a petition for rehearing was pending, the Tennessee Supreme Court held in another case that the Arkansas statute was penal and could not be enforced by the Tennessee state courts.

(2) **Issue.** Must the federal court recognize the forum state's characterization of a foreign state's law?

(3) **Held.** Yes. Judgment reversed.

(a) The federal court must recognize the Tennessee Supreme Court decision that the Arkansas statute was penal and therefore not enforceable in Tennessee. Thus, the shareholders will be protected by the existence of a "de facto" corporation.

e) **State exclusionary policies followed by the federal district court--Angel v. Bullington**, 330 U.S. 183 (1947).

Angel v. Bullington

(1) **Facts.** Bullington (P), a Virginia citizen, sold land in Virginia to Angel (D), a citizen of North Carolina. D defaulted on his promissory note. P had the land sold and then sought a deficiency judgment in a North Carolina state court. The North Carolina Supreme Court relied on a state statute (no deficiency judgments) to dismiss on the grounds of no jurisdiction, even though P argued that the Full Faith and Credit Clause required the court to hear his cause of action. P then brought the same action in the federal district court in North Carolina. D argued that the prior state court

judgment barred the action. The district court found for P and the court of appeals affirmed. The United States Supreme Court granted certiorari.

    (2) Issue. Can P maintain the cause of action in the federal district court when he could not in the state court?

    (3) Held. No. Judgment reversed. If the state court has a policy against entertaining a cause of action arising in another state, and that policy is constitutional, then the federal district court sitting in that state must follow the same policy.

    (4) Dissent (Reed, J.). Since the state court ruled that the anti-deficiency judgment statute was remedial rather than substantive, the federal court ought to be free to apply its own rule.

    (5) Dissent (Rutledge, J.). The majority mistakenly applies the *Erie* doctrine to allow state courts to determine the jurisdictional scope of the federal court, something which ought to be determined only by Congress or the Constitution.

3.   **When a Federal Right Is Involved.** If the litigation involves any claim or defense arising under the United States Constitution, statutes, or treaties, there is no choice of law problem. It makes no difference whether the action is tried in federal or state court, as federal law alone will be applied to that issue. This follows from the Supremacy Clause of the United States Constitution (Article VI), which provides, "This Constitution, and the Laws of the United States which shall be made in Pursuance thereof . . . shall be the supreme Law of the Land; and the Judges in every State shall be bound thereby."

    a.   **Effect.** Federal law alone is applied to any issue arising in the fields in which federal power is "exclusive" (*e.g.*, admiralty, foreign commerce, national banking, etc.); or which Congress has "preempted" (*e.g.*, most of interstate commerce). Conflicting state rules are of no importance, even if the case is being litigated in state courts.

        1)   In spheres of national power, of course, Congress may specify the rules of decision, entirely supplanting any state rules and thereby eradicating choice of law problems. The Federal Employers' Liability Act is an example of this.

        2)   Congress in some instances may legislate directly on the conflicts problem. For example, the Federal Tort Claims Act makes the federal government liable in certain instances "in accordance with the law of the place where the act occurred."

        3)   Congress may choose to incorporate state definitions of legal rights by using terms and referring to subjects as to which the states alone have well developed bodies of law. In each case not ruled entirely by

federal law, a federal court must decide first whether it is bound to apply state law or whether it is free to apply rules from whatever source (*i.e.*, federal law). If the court chooses the federal source, then it may still have to look to state law to give content or meaning to some terms of the federal law.

b. **"Federal law" defined.** The "federal law" that is to be applied to any federally created right includes not only the Constitution and all statutes and administrative orders or regulations pursuant thereto but also the decisions of federal courts ultimately required to interpret, implement, and enforce the same so-called federal common law. [*See* Bank of America National Trust & Savings Association v. Parnell, *infra*]

c. **State "procedural" rules.** If the suit is brought in a state court, that state's procedural rules will normally apply—subject to the limitation that novel rules of pleading and practice cannot be invoked to defeat a claimant's rights under federal law.

d. **Applications.**

1) **"Federal question" cases in state courts--D'Oench, Duhme & Co. v. Federal Deposit Insurance Corp.,** 315 U.S. 447 (1942).

    D'Oench, Duhme & Co. v. Federal Deposit Insurance Corp.

a) **Facts.** The Federal Deposit Insurance Co. (P) sued D, a Missouri company, on a demand note which P gave to an Illinois bank and which P took as collateral when it insured the bank. Suit was in the federal district court in Missouri. The note was given pursuant to a side agreement that it would not be collected—it was purely for the purpose of influencing bank examiners so that the bank could get insurance. D set up this agreement as a defense. The district court applied Illinois law and rejected the defense. The circuit court affirmed. The Supreme Court granted certiorari.

b) **Issue.** Must the federal court apply federal law to effectuate the purposes of the Federal Reserve Act?

c) **Held.** Yes. Judgment affirmed.

(1) This is not a diversity of citizenship case, but one brought under a federal statute (Federal Reserve Act), and the federal courts must have the power to formulate rules of decision to effectuate the purposes of the federal act where Congress has "occupied the field."

d) **Concurrence** (Jackson, J.). There is a body of federal common law that we should call upon in this case. That a particular state happened to have the greatest connection, in the conflict of laws sense, with the making of the note involved or that the subsequent conduct happened to be chiefly centered there is not enough to make us subservient to the legislative policy or the judicial views of that state.

2) **State law incorporated as the federal rule of decision--United States v. Kimbell Foods, Inc.,** 440 U.S. 715 (1979).

   a) **Facts and issue.** No detailed facts are given. Two decisions, which applied state law to the issue of whether contractual liens arising from certain federal loan programs take precedence over private liens in the absence of controlling federal statutes, were being reviewed.

   b) **Held.** Although federal law governs questions involving the rights of the United States arising under federal programs, the Court chooses to incorporate state commercial law as the federal rule of decision. In deciding whether to fashion a federal uniform commercial law or to adopt the commercial law of the various states, the Court considered: (i) the need for a national, uniform body of law; (ii) whether the application of state law would frustrate the purposes of the federal program; and (iii) the extent to which the application of a federal rule would disrupt commercial relationships predicated on state law. Because the application of state law to determine priority has worked in the past, the application of state law would preserve the expectations of creditors relying on state law, and there are no concrete reasons for adopting a federal rule, state law is adopted as the federal rule of decision.

Bank of
America
National Trust
& Savings
Association
v. Parnell

3) **Issues controlled by state law--Bank of America National Trust & Savings Association v. Parnell,** 352 U.S. 29 (1956).

   a) **Facts.** Bank of America (P) had owned bearer bonds of the Home Owner's Loan Corporation, a federal corporation, that were guaranteed by the federal government. They were stolen and later cashed when presented by an individual. Suit was filed in district court against Parnell, who presented the check, and First National Bank of Indiana, which cashed it (Ds). After P showed that the bonds had been stolen, the court applied Illinois law to place the burden of proof on Ds to show that they innocently acquired the bonds. The jury ruled against Ds, but the court of appeals reversed, holding that federal common law rules of burden of proof should apply to commercial paper insured by the federal government. Federal common law would place the burden of proof on P to show that Ds acted in bad faith. Since Ds did not have notice that the bonds were stolen, the court of appeals directed a verdict for Ds. P appeals.

   b) **Issue.** Will federal common law be applied to transfers of federal commercial paper exclusively between private parties?

   c) **Held.** No. Judgment reversed and remanded.

      (1) Although federal commercial paper is involved, federal law does not govern since the suit is one exclusively between private parties (the United States government is not a party and has no "interest" in the litigation). The mere fact that the cause of action involves United States commercial paper does not make it a "federal question" case, *i.e.*, not all issues are controlled by federal law.

   d) **Dissent** (Black, Douglas, JJ.). The purpose of a uniform law governing bonds, notes, and other paper issued by the United States is to provide a certain and definite guide to the rights of all parties rather than subjecting them to the vagaries of the law of many states.

I. INTERNATIONAL CONFLICTS OF LAW

1. **Introduction.** International cases have been considered in the same framework as interstate cases except in chapter V.E., which dealt with changing choice of law principles in the international setting. You should refer to that section to help understand the material here. International cases discussed earlier in this outline that may be helpful include *In re Annesley, Matter of Schneider, Hilton v. Guyot, Holzer v. Deutsche Reichsbahn Gesellschaft, Slater v. Mexican Railway Co., Walton v. Arabian American Oil Co., Babcock v. Jackson,* and *Home Insurance Co. v. Dick*.

   This section deals primarily with the need for a simple, uniform voice in dealing with cases that have contacts with foreign countries. It focuses on the limitations of applying state law in the international setting where the federal government is the accepted officiator. Note particularly the effect of treaties, common law, and federal preemption on international conflicts issues.

2. **Applications.**

   a. **State probate law which interferes with international affairs-- Zschernig v. Miller,** 389 U.S. 429 (1968).

      1) **Facts.** An Oregon resident died leaving his estate (personal and real property) to residents of East Germany, including Zschernig (P). An Oregon law allowed such bequests only if the foreign country would reciprocate and recognize bequests to United States residents and would not confiscate the United States bequests. The probate court invalidated the will under the Oregon statute but enforced it as to the proceeds from the real property as provided for in a treaty between the United States and East Germany. The Oregon Supreme Court upheld the decision. Miller (D), an Oregon Commissioner, appealed because the property would otherwise escheat to the state.

      2) **Issue.** Does the Oregon statute sufficiently interfere with international relations to render it unconstitutional?

      3) **Held.** Yes. Judgment reversed.

         a) Although former decisions have upheld state probate statutes, the application of which required the mere reading of foreign law, this statute goes too far. It requires hypothetical application of foreign law against the backdrop of varied foreign political systems. The Oregon statute is therefore unconstitutional because it extends too far into foreign affairs, a domain controlled by the federal government.

b.   **International contracts that stipulate to the application of a particular body of law--Dougherty v. Equitable Life Assurance Society, 266 N.Y. 71 (1934).**

   1)   Facts. Equitable Life (D), a New York corporation, obtained a business license in Russia before the Russian revolution. Russia required that insurance policies contain provisions that Russian law govern all disputes, that the Russian government could cancel D's license and require D to settle with policyholders under Russian law, that D deposit assets with the Russian government sufficient to exceed the liability of its policies, and that all D's property serve as security on the policies. After the revolution, the Soviet government required all insurance companies to liquidate their policies and confiscated D's assets in Russia. Dougherty (P), who left Russia, sued to recover the value of his Russian policy. D defended on the grounds that the new regime would not allow P to recover.

   2)   Issue. In light of the establishment of a new regime, will the New York court enforce the contract provision that Russian law would apply?

   3)   Held. Yes. Recovery denied.

       a)   It is not against public policy to hold a Russian national to the terms of a contract executed in Russia. Since the Soviet decree extinguished D's liability on the policies, and the Soviet government is recognized as the Russian government, D has no obligation. Assuming that the policy was enforceable, it was payable in rubles only, which are valueless outside Russia.

   4)   Concurrence. P's claim involved an intangible chose in action which had as its situs the residence of the debtor, as evidenced by D's pledge of its assets everywhere to fulfill its obligations. Therefore P should recover for D's refusal to pay (which constituted a repudiation or breach). But payment is required in worthless rubles and therefore of no consequence.

c.   **International insurance contracts that apply the law of the insured's domicile--Johansen v. Confederation Life Association, 447 F.2d 175 (1971).**

   1)   Facts. Turull and Johansen (Ps) were United States citizens who purchased insurance policies from a Canadian company while Ps lived and were doing business in Cuba. The policies were payable in Havana with United States dollars, which at the time were equivalent in value and directly interchangeable for pesos. When Castro came to power, possession of dollars in Cuba became illegal and D notified Ps that the policies would be paid in pesos. Ps returned to the United States, where the value of the peso had significantly declined relative to the dollar. Ps sought to have D pay in dollars. D defended claiming that Cuban law, which now required payment in pesos, should apply.

   2)   Issue. Will the court apply the law of the place where the insureds lived when they obtained the policies?

   3)   Held. Yes. Cuban law applies.

       a)   Since Ps entered the insurance contracts while living in Cuba, Cuba's law, which now requires payment in pesos despite the terms of the contract, will govern. This is an equitable result because D invested funds in Cuba to pay the policies and the pesos generated by the investments are now relatively worthless for other purposes.

4)   Dissent. D's promise to pay in United States dollars is unmistakably clear and the court violates D's selling practices and the insureds' expectations when it rules against enforcement. The Restatement rule, that the law of the insured's domicile at the time the insured applied for the policy, is not ironclad, especially in international situations.

d.   The act of state doctrine--Banco Nacional de Cuba v. Sabbatino, 376 U.S. 398 (1964).

Banco Nacional de Cuba v. Sabbatino

1)   Facts. The Cuban government expropriated a shipload of sugar (owned by American business interests) in retaliation for America's reduction in Cuba's sugar quota. An instrumentality of the Cuban government (P) sued an American commodity broker (D) for conversion of the bills of lading covering the sugar. D asserted that the expropriation should not be recognized because it violated international law. P claimed the expropriation must be recognized under the "act of state" doctrine. The district court granted summary judgment against P. The court of appeals affirmed. The United States Supreme Court granted certiorari.

2)   Issue. May the judicial branch of the United States government examine the validity of the expropriations of a foreign government?

3)   Held. No. Judgment reversed and remanded.

    a)   The Constitution does not require the act of state doctrine; it does not remove from the judiciary the capacity to review the validity of foreign acts of state. Nevertheless, the doctrine does have "constitutional underpinnings." It arises out of the basic relationships between the branches of government in a system of separation of powers. It is based on the idea that passing on the validity of foreign acts of state by the judiciary may hinder the pursuit of this country's goals in international relations.

    b)   The entire matter of the act of state doctrine is one to be governed by federal law.

    c)   The judicial branch will not examine the validity of a taking of property within its own territory by a foreign sovereign government, extant and recognized by this country at the time of suit, in the absence of a treaty or other unambiguous agreement regarding controlling legal principles, even if the complaint alleges that the taking violates customary international law.

4)   Comment. Had there been no "act of state" involved, but just a transaction occurring in Cuba, under most traditional conflicts analyses Cuban law would govern the transaction (most significant contacts, law of the situs of the property, etc.). Perhaps under Currie's interest analysis, however, New York (the forum state) would apply its own law.

a) **Query.** Should the idea of "territorial sovereignty" be given greater weight in international conflict cases (in deciding jurisdiction, conflicts, and other questions) than in interstate cases (where the idea has been abandoned)?

b) **Query.** Assuming Cuban law applies, could the New York court refuse to hear the case on the grounds of public policy?

(1) Since the Full Faith and Credit and Privileges and Immunities Clauses do not apply in the international context, the forum ought to be able to dismiss—there are no constitutional limitations.

(2) Note, however, that when the act of state doctrine applies, the state (according to *Sabbatino*) cannot dismiss on this ground. But suppose that a Cuban corporation is owned exclusively by Cubans and one of the Cubans escapes to the United States with its assets. This is a pure X-F case. Can the court dismiss here? In *Sabbatino*, the argument was that the defendant should look to a different arm of government to get redress. But in this hypothetical situation, no Americans are involved. If the thrust of the act of state doctrine is that it applies only when it is appropriate to transfer negotiations to another arm of government (the executive), then the court should be able to dismiss.

e. Limitations on the act of state doctrine.

1) *Sabbatino*. *Sabbatino* seemed to say that the act of state doctrine was applicable only when the act takes place in the foreign government's own territory.

2) Hickenlooper amendment.

a) After the *Sabbatino* case, the Hickenlooper amendment was enacted which provides, "no court in the United States shall decline on the ground of the federal act of state doctrine to make a determination on the merits giving effect to the principles of international law in a case in which a claim of title or other right to property is asserted by any party including a foreign state . . . [unless] the President determines that application of the act of state doctrine is required in that particular case by the foreign policy interests of the United States." [22 U.S.C.A. §2370(e)(2)] Upon remand of the *Sabbatino* case, the federal district court held that the *Sabbatino* case itself came under the scope of this amendment and that accordingly the complaint should be dismissed. [383 F.2d 166 (2d Cir. 1967)]

b) Note that this exception to the act of state doctrine applies only to expropriation cases.

f. The impact of *Sabbatino* on choice of law in international conflicts. The concept of territorial sovereignty is to be given more weight in the international context than in the interstate one. There is a notion of obligation to respect sovereign acts within its territory. United States foreign policy interests must be considered in any case having any international contacts.

3.   **Treaties.** International cases are often guided as to choice of law by conventions or treaties. Although the United States participates only in a few of these conventions, it has ratified the Hague Convention on the service of documents abroad, on the taking of evidence abroad, and on the civil aspects of international child abduction. In *Societe Nationale Industrielle Aerospatiale v. United States District Court for the Southern District of Iowa*, 482 U.S. 522 (1987), the defendant in a personal injury action against a French airplane manufacturer sought a protective order following a number of discovery requests under the Federal Rules of Civil Procedure. The defendant cited a French "blocking statute" prohibiting production of documents located in France pursuant to foreign judicial order and argued that the Hague Convention provided the exclusive procedure under which documents could be obtained. The Supreme Court held that the Convention provided optional means but was not exclusive; the "blocking statute" was relevant only insofar as it provided insight into the nature of the sovereign interests in nondisclosure. Justice Blackmun in a dissenting opinion favored adopting a rule that would require resorting first to convention procedures unless there were "strong indications . . . no evidence would be forthcoming."

a.   **Comity defense rejected--Hartford Fire Insurance Co. v. California,** 509 U.S. 764 (1993).

Hartford Fire
Insurance Co.
v. California

1)   **Facts.** Nineteen states and numerous private parties brought antitrust suits against domestic insurers, domestic and foreign reinsurers, and insurance brokers who agreed to boycott general liability insurers that used nonconforming forms. The United States defendants asserted a defense under the McCarran-Ferguson Act, which exempted from Sherman Act liability a defendant engaged in acts of "boycott, coercion, or intimidation." The London-based defendants contended that "international comity" prevented application of the Sherman Act to them. The district court dismissed the suits and appeals were taken. The court of appeals reversed and remanded. The Supreme Court granted certiorari.

2)   **Issues.**

a)   Did domestic insurers lose their McCarran-Ferguson Act immunity?

b)   Should the claims against the London-based defendants be dismissed as improper applications of the Sherman Act to foreign conduct?

3)   **Held.** a) No. b) No.

a)   Domestic insurers did not lose their exemption from regulation by the federal government simply because they agree or act with foreign reinsurers allegedly not subject to regulation by state law.

b)   The Sherman Act applies to foreign conduct that is meant to produce and does in fact produce some substantial effect in the United States.

c) The London-based defendants contend that applying the Act to their conduct would conflict significantly with British law, which permits such conduct. However, the fact that conduct is lawful in the state in which it took place will not, of itself, bar application of the United States antitrust laws, even if the foreign state has a strong policy to permit or encourage such conduct.

d) No conflict exists between the laws of the United States and a foreign state for purposes of principles of international comity if a person subject to regulation by both states can comply with the laws of both.

J. PROPERTY

1. **Introduction.** The initial conflicts question relative to property issues is characterization. Characterization is a double problem in property cases. First, the court must decide whether the case presents a property problem. Then, it must determine whether the interest involved is a "movable" or an "immovable."

   a. **Test for distinguishing between "movables" and "immovables."** How closely is the particular interest involved connected with land? If it is at all closely related to land, then it is classified as an "immovable" and the law of the situs of the land is applied.

      1) **Rationale.** The situs of land has traditionally been the most important and prevailing "contact" with problems involving land or related thereto, and there is a very strong public policy favoring the application of that law to all such problems; that state is most interested in the marketability and transferability of titles and the accuracy of its own records regarding property within its jurisdiction.

      2) **Application.** Using the above test, the following interests may be classified as "immovables": (i) a leasehold; (ii) proceeds from sale or rents of land; (iii) right to income and profits therefrom; and (iv) perhaps even a fence on the land, since there is little use for a fence apart from the land itself.

   b. **Forum vs. situs law as controlling characterization.** According to the general view, the forum characterizes an interest as "movable" or "immovable" according to its own law, without reference to any foreign law. The Restatement, however, asserts that the law of the situs of the interest should control even the characterization of the problem as "movable" or "immovable"—since the drafters felt so strongly with respect to this choice of law rule. [Restatement (Second) §208]

2. **Immovables.**

a. Approaches used for characterizing.

1) Old rationale. Courts using the vested rights theory applied the law of the situs to determine all claims involving land. Normally courts would apply the whole law of the situs, including its conflicts rules.

2) Restatement. The Restatement (Second) applies the law of the state having the "most significant relationship" with the parties and the transaction. In most instances, this will be the law of the situs of the property.

3) Interest analysis. This approach may result in states other than the situs applying their law; however, in most cases the state having the greatest interest will be the situs state.

b. Succession on death.

1) Inheritance of land. Normally, all questions as to testate or intestate succession to land are determined by reference to the law of the situs. This is, indeed, the strongest choice of law rule in existence. It is based on the very strong policies and interests of a sovereign to control the disposition of local land.

2) Will of land. The validity and effect of a will of an interest in land are determined by the law of the state where the land is located.

    a) Governs all aspects of will. For example, it is this law that determines the capacity of a person to make a will or to accept a devise, the form of the will, the validity of a particular provision in the will, and the nature of the estate created.

    b) Applications.

        (1) Disposition of real property by will--*In re* Estate of Barrie, 240 Iowa 431 (1949). *In re* Estate of Barrie

            (a) Facts. Barrie died in Illinois, where she was domiciled and where her personal property was located. Barrie had made a will that disposed of her personal property and of her real property, which was located in Iowa. The Illinois court declared the will revoked—the word "void" was written across the face of the will. The beneficiary under the will took it to Iowa for probate, but those who would take the property by intestate succession claim that the Illinois judgment deserves full faith and credit in Iowa, even as it applies to the disposition of real property in Iowa. Iowa law would not have revoked the will, but Iowa had a statute that stated that the validity of a will was to be determined by the law of the place where executed or the testator's domicile.

(b) Issue. Must the forum court recognize a foreign revocation of a will that disposes of real property in the forum?

(c) Held. No.

1] The Illinois judgment that the will was revoked will not be recognized as it applies to real property in Iowa. Iowa law will determine the issue of revocation as it applies to Iowa real property. The statute (which said that a will shall be valid if it would be valid by the law of the place where it was executed or of the testator's former domicile) referred only to the question of the formalities of execution of the will and did not deal with the question of revocation, so that the law of the situs controls the question raised.

(d) Dissent. The statute should be read as applying equally to the issues of the validity of execution and revocation.

(e) Comments.

1] The case demonstrates that issues as to the validity of wills are handled according to the conflicts principles that apply to real property when real property is involved.

2] In *Clarke v. Clarke*, 178 U.S. 186 (1900), the testator was domiciled in South Carolina. The court held that her will worked a conversion of all of her real property, including that located in Connecticut, into personal property. Testator's husband sought to have this judgment upheld in a Connecticut court, but the Connecticut court refused. The Supreme Court held that the South Carolina court's determination had no effect on Connecticut land—the law of situs controls the passage of land by will or intestacy.

In re
Schneider's
Estate

(2) Real property: Applying the law of the situs--*In re* Schneider's Estate, 96 N.Y.S.2d 652 (1950).

(a) Facts. The decedent (Schneider) was born in Switzerland, lived in the United States, and was domiciled in New York at the time of his death. He attempted by will to dispose of real estate he owned located in Switzerland. Swiss law would not allow real estate to be disposed of by will, but gave the heirs a fractional interest. The New York court is administering the personal property of the decedent, which was derived from the sale of the real property located in Switzerland. The court says that it will apply the law of the situs (Switzerland) of the property.

(b) Issue. Should the whole law or the internal law of the situs be applied?

(c) Held. Apply the whole law.

1] The whole law of Switzerland referred back to the internal law of New York (however, the opinion does not make clear what law of New York, internal or whole). Thus the will controls.

c. **Inter vivos transactions.**

1) **Traditional rule.** Under the traditional rule, the validity of a disposition of real property depends on the law of the state where the property is located. But this rule is merely the result of a long historical development; many commentators feel that it lacks a conclusive modern rationale. Therefore there is some pressure in the cases to yield such determinations to more flexible, policy-oriented modes of analysis (the interest analysis, for example).

2) **Characterization.** Note that the principal question in all of the problems that arise is the characterization problem referred to above—*i.e.*, whether the problem is even a "property" problem at all. If the problem is very closely tied in with the land, then it probably will be held to be a property problem; on the other hand, if the problem is less significantly tied in with the property, then it may be classified as some other type of problem (for example, a contracts problem).

3) **Security transactions.**

   a) **Mortgages.** The general rule is that the law of the situs determines whether a mortgage is valid and whether a party entering a mortgage has the capacity to do so, as well as other questions relating to the mortgage. Note that here again the question of property vs. contracts is raised since mortgages have similarities to contracts. Property rules govern these questions, however, since they are deemed ones of "title" to land.

   b) **Applications.**

      (1) **A security interest in land--Swank v. Hufnagle,** 111 Ind. 453 (1887).

      Swank v. Hufnagle

         (a) **Facts.** While in Ohio, Hufnagle (D), to act as a surety for her husband, executed a mortgage on land she owned in Indiana. Such a mortgage was invalid under Indiana law. P brought suit in Indiana and contended that Ohio law, which allows such mortgages, applies. The trial court invalidated the mortgage under Indiana law. P appeals.

         (b) **Issue.** Should the validity of a mortgage executed outside the situs state be governed by the law of the situs state?

         (c) **Held.** Yes. Judgment affirmed.

            1] The validity of the mortgage is determined by the law of the situs, *i.e.*, Indiana.

         (d) **Comment.** The courts have split as to whether a mortgagee's right to a deficiency judgment against the mortgagor is a "contracts" or "property" problem—*i.e.*, whether it is more closely related to a mortgagor's contractual undertakings or the security transaction involving the property.

4) Conveyances and contracts.

    a) Conveyances. The validity and effect of conveyances is determined strictly according to the laws of the situs. Thus, a conveyance made in F1 as to land located in F2 must be in the form required by F2, and its effect will be determined by F2 laws. Likewise, the capacity of the grantor to convey, and of the grantee to take title, must be determined by F2 law.

    b) Contracts to convey, executory land sale contracts, etc. Most courts treat these as "contracts" problems, and reference is thus made to appropriate contracts choice of law rules. The importance of the contractual undertakings is deemed to outweigh the property factors involved—even in cases when the contract operates as a conveyance of equitable title.

    c) Applications.

        (1) Property vs. contractual questions. There are many situations where land is involved in the transaction but the principal question is not a property question but one involving contracts. For example, the question may not concern the capacity of the parties to sell and receive land but may concern the rights and liabilities of each of them under the contract.

        (2) Contractual capacity of married women--Polson v. Stewart, 167 Mass. 211 (1897).

            (a) Facts. A married woman residing in North Carolina entered a contract with her husband that she would not divorce him if he would release his marital interest in her property. Her property included land in Massachusetts. Under Massachusetts law, married women did not have the capacity to contract and therefore the contract would be void. However, under the law where the contract was made (North Carolina), women had such capacity. Upon the wife's death, her administrator sued to quiet title in the Massachusetts property.

            (b) Issue. Is this a property question to be governed by the law of the situs?

            (c) Held. No. Demurrer overruled.

                1] The Massachusetts court will determine the validity of the contract according to the law of the couple's domicile, North Carolina. The result would have been different had the contract operated as a conveyance of real property rather than a release of rights.

            (d) Comment. In general, issues as to dower, community property, or other marital rights in land are determined by reference to the law of the situs of the land. But again, that reference is to the "whole" law of the situs (*supra*)—so that in determining marital rights, the situs law may refer to the law of the spouses'

Polson v.
Stewart

domicile at time of acquisition. [Restatement (Second) §233]

(3) Tortious conveyance of property--Irving Trust Co. v. Maryland Casualty Co., 83 F.2d 168 (2d Cir. 1936).

(a) Facts. A corporation on the verge of insolvency transferred its property to certain of its creditors (including Maryland Casualty). Some of the property was located in New York, the state where the transfer occurred. The corporation subsequently went bankrupt and Irving Trust Co., its trustee, (P) brought suit in federal court in New York to compel the transferee creditors to reconvey the land on the ground that a New York statute made the conveyance and acceptance of title tortious and illegal in the circumstances in which they occurred (*e.g.*, the Missouri land transfer could not be set aside by Missouri law).

(b) Issue. Will conveyances that are tortious where made be governed by the law of that state rather than the law of the situs?

(c) Held. Yes.

1] If the violation of the statute could be proven, then the defendants could be compelled to reconvey not only the land in New York but also the land in other states by whose law the defendants had secured perfect titles. Because the acceptance of title is a tort, "any court may compel the tortfeasor to restore the property, whatever the law of the situs."

(d) Comment. Most courts would have considered the question one of "title to land" (a property problem) and held that whether the conveyances could be set aside should be governed by the law of the situs. [*See* James v. Powell, *supra*] This shows that a court may use the characterization device to avoid the situs if it thinks this is required to reach a fair result. This is, of course, the objective of the "interests" analysis approach.

3. Movables.

a. In general.

1) **The old view—vested rights.** The old view was that the law of the owner's domicile controlled questions relating to tangible movables. The idea was that the movables have no situs but follow the owner. Until fairly recently, there was little occasion for conflict between domiciliary law and the law of the situs since persons traveled little

and thus the chattels of a person were usually in the state of his domicile anyway.

2) **The modern view.** The modern view is that the law of the situs of tangible chattels controls. The rationale is simply that many individuals (as well as businesses) have property in several or many states and since the property is located therein, that state's laws should control it; the technical domicile of a corporation, for example, may have nothing to do with its property located elsewhere.

3) **"Most significant relationship" approach.** The Restatement (Second) has reframed the choice of law rules above to indicate that domicile is usually the "most significant" contact or relationship as to succession and marital property questions, and situs is the "most significant" contact or relationship as to inter vivos transactions involving movables. [Restatement (Second) §§244, 260]

4) **The Uniform Commercial Code.** The U.C.C. now covers all sales and secured transactions in movables. It makes reference to the law of the state bearing "an appropriate relation" to the transaction, and this is interpreted as being similar to the "most significant relationship" approach of the Restatement.

b. **Succession on death.**

1) **Intestate succession to movables.**

a) The Restatement and the majority position is that questions of intestate succession to interests in chattels or in rights embodied in a document are determined by the law of the state where the decedent was domiciled at the time of her death. Questions of intestate succession to rights not embodied in a document are also determined by the law of the state where the decedent was domiciled at the time of her death.

b) Some states have modified the majority rule to provide that the law of the situs controls.

2) **Will of movables.**

a) **Majority position.** The majority position is that the validity and effect of a will, insofar as it affects interests in chattels or in rights embodied in a document, are determined by the law of the state where the testator was domiciled at the time of her death.

b) **Minority positions.**

(1) Some cases say that in matters of construction the law of the testator's domicile at the time she executed the will should control.

(2) Some states also hold that a will is valid as to its formal requirements (proper signature, witnesses, etc.) if it was executed

according to the law of the place of execution or the law of the testator's domicile at the time of execution.

c. **Inter vivos transactions.**

1) **Contract and conveyance.** The general rule is that the law of the state in which the property is located at the time of the transaction in question determines questions regarding the creation and transfer of interests in tangible chattels.

    a) **Note.** The same distinction that was made with regard to contracts and conveyances relating to immovables must be made with movables. So, for example, if an executory contract is made for the creation and then sale of a product, the agreement creates no interest in a thing and thus the rights of the parties to the contract are determined by contract law and conflict rules relating to contracts apply. This relationship between the contract aspects and the title aspects in a sale of movables can be a very close one and the distinction difficult to make.

2) **Applications.**

    a) **Contracts for the sale of movables--Youssoupoff v. Widener,** 246 N.Y. 174 (1927).

Youssoupoff
v. Widener

        (1) **Facts.** Youssoupoff (P) sold two Rembrandt portraits to Widener (D) on a contract that included a provision that P could repurchase the paintings "only if he finds himself in a position again to keep and personally enjoy" them. D, a Pennsylvania resident, wrote the contract and mailed it to his agent in London, where negotiations took place and P entered the contract and delivered the paintings with proceeds from a note with another party, which was to be secured by the paintings. D refused on the grounds that P had not complied with the buy-back provision. Pennsylvania law would not allow the repurchase, but English law would. The trial court applied English law.

        (2) **Issue.** Will the transfer of personal property located in the jurisdiction where the contract was made be governed by the law of that jurisdiction?

        (3) **Held.** Yes. Affirmed. The law of England applies.

            (a) The construction and legal effect of a contract for the transfer of, or the creation of a lien upon, property situated in the jurisdiction where the contract was made is governed by the law of that jurisdiction. The fact that D intended to remove the paintings to his home in Pennsylvania, and subsequently did, is of no consequence.

        (4) **Comment.** This case could easily have been characterized as purely "contract." Performance issues, as are present here, are generally governed by the law of the place of performance.

Since the option to repurchase would have to be exercised in Pennsylvania, it could have been argued that Pennsylvania law governed.

Cammell v. Sewell

b) **Third-party transactions following removal from the initial situs-- Cammell v. Sewell,** 5 Hurl. & N. 728 (1860).

 (1) **Facts.** Cammell (P), an English insurer, insured lumber traveling from Russia to England in a Prussian vessel. The ship was damaged on the Norwegian coast and the shipmaster subsequently sold the lumber in Norway to Clausen. Clausen sold it to Sewell (D), an English merchant. P, who as the insurer paid full value to the firm to which the shipment was to be delivered, now seeks to force D to turn the cargo over to P, on the grounds that English law would not recognize the shipmaster's sale. The trial court applied Norwegian law, which validated the sale and denied P recovery.

 (2) **Issue.** Does the law of the jurisdiction where the chattels are located when transferred govern the validity of the transfer?

 (3) **Held.** Yes. Affirmed. The shipmaster's power should be determined by reference to the law of the situs of the chattel (Norway) at the time of the transaction.

 (4) **Dissent.** The law of Norway is at variance with general maritime law and should not be given comity in England.

 (5) **Comment.** Again note the potential for a different result if traditional contract principles had been applied.

3) **Note the Restatement Second.**

 a) Section 244 states that the validity and effect of a conveyance of an interest in a chattel as between the parties to the conveyance are determined by the local law of the state which, with respect to the particular issue, has the most significant relationship to the parties, the chattel, and the conveyance.

 b) Section 245 indicates that the effect of a conveyance on a preexisting interest in a chattel of a person who was not a party to the conveyance will usually be determined by the law that would be applied by the courts of the state where the chattel was located at the time of the conveyance.

d. **Security transactions.**

1) **Validity.**

 a) **Introduction.** Generally, the validity of a security interest in a chattel (*i.e.*, a conditional sales contract or a chattel mortgage, etc.) depends on the law of the situs of the chattel. This means the situs at the time of the mortgage, sale, etc., which is the place of the delivery of the chattel because it is there that the transaction is finally legally complete. This is the "vested rights" approach—*i.e.*, rights and powers created in the situs state will control all future transactions involving the chattel.

b) **Law of the situs of the chattel--Green v. Van Buskirk,** 72 U.S. (5 Wall.) 307 (1866); 74 U.S. (7 Wall.) 139 (1868).

Green v. Van Buskirk

    (1) **Facts.** A New York resident executed and delivered a chattel mortgage on certain iron safes located in Chicago to Van Buskirk (P), also a New York resident. Green (D), without knowledge of the chattel mortgage, levied on the safes in order to satisfy a judgment. P sued D in New York to recover the proceeds of the sale of the safes. Under Illinois law (the situs), the mortgage was not enforceable until recorded and acknowledged. But the New York court applied its own law and rendered judgment in favor of P. D appeals.

    (2) **Issue.** Will the enforceability of a chattel mortgage be governed by the law of the situs of the chattel rather than the law of the owner's domicile?

    (3) **Held.** Yes.

        (a) Since P was not a party to the proceeding in Illinois, he is not bound by it. But the forum must give effect to the laws of Illinois, the situs of the chattel. It remains to be decided what effect Illinois law would have between the parties.

    (4) **Comment.** In another opinion by the Supreme Court, it was decided that the attachment sale would prevail over the New York mortgage.

2) **Foreclosure.**

a) **Introduction.** Generally, the power to foreclose or redeem a mortgage, pledge, or lien depends on the law of the state where the chattel was (situs) at the time of the mortgage, pledge, or lien. However, many states now apply the "most significant contacts" approach.

b) **Application of the "most significant contacts" approach--John J. Shanahan v. George B. Landers Construction Co.,** 266 F.2d 400 (1st Cir. 1959).

John J. Shanahan v. George B. Landers Construction Co.

    (1) **Facts.** A machine was delivered to the buyer, Landers Construction (P), in Vermont by a Massachusetts company, Shanahan Inc. (D). The conditional sales contract and promissory notes were signed by the buyer in New Hampshire. The contract was later signed by the seller in Massachusetts, where the contract was thus technically made. It was contemplated that the machine would ultimately be moved to New Hampshire, the buyer's headquarters. The seller repossessed the machine in New Hampshire and resold it in Massachusetts (such resale was lawful in Massachusetts; in New Hampshire, it was a conversion). P sued for conversion in Massachusetts, which applied New Hampshire law. D appeals.

(2) **Issue.** Must the court apply the law of Massachusetts, where the property was when the alleged conversion occurred?

(3) **Held.** No. Judgment affirmed but remanded to determine the proper amount of the award.

    (a) New Hampshire law controlled, so that there was a cause of action for conversion. The law of New Hampshire is the relevant law since the buyer executed the contract there, had its corporate headquarters there, the machine was kept there most of the time, and the conversion grew out of repossession there.

3) Priorities.

a) Introduction. Section 9-103 of the Uniform Commercial Code governs the question of whether the interests of the secured creditor or the third person (purchaser or attaching creditor) should be preferred.

b) Reliance on law--Gordon v. Clifford Metal Sales Co., 602 A.2d 535 (1992).

(1) **Facts.** Fleet loaned money to Clifford, a Rhode Island company, and perfected a security interest in all of Clifford's assets, then owned or thereafter acquired, by filing a financing statement with the Rhode Island secretary of state. Maksteel, a Canadian corporation, sold steel to Clifford. Each bill of lading stated that the steel remains the property of Maksteel until full payment is received. Maksteel was never paid for the steel and Clifford was placed in receivership. Maksteel petitioned to reclaim the steel. Under Canadian law, Maksteel would be entitled to reclaim the steel or its proceeds. The superior court denied the petition and Maksteel appeals.

(2) **Issue.** Should Maksteel be allowed to reclaim the steel under Canadian law?

(3) **Held.** No. Judgment affirmed.

    (a) The most important function of choice of law rules is to make the interstate and international systems work well. Here, Fleet and the receiver relied upon Rhode Island law in seeking to protect their interests; a uniform and consistent international system can only be served by the application of Rhode Island law. Otherwise, third parties from in or out of the United States would be without the ability to verify the existence or nonexistence of other interests in a corporation's assets.

e. Future interests and trusts.

1) Introduction. There has been a tendency by the courts to depart from ordinary choice of law rules when dealing with trusts of movables. The underlying approach is to give effect to the trust and uphold its validity, as well as the exercise of any power under the trust, if at all possible. [Restatement (Second) §268] Courts will refer to the law of whatever state would hold it valid, provided there are sufficient contacts with that state. Thus, in identical fact situations, a court may refer to the law of the situs, the place of administration, or the domicile of the trustor, whichever would uphold the trust. The same rule is applicable to transfers of future interests in movables.

2) **Applications.**

a) **Validity of an inter vivos trust--Hutchinson v. Ross,** 262 N.Y. 381 (1933).

Hutchinson v. Ross

   (1) **Facts.** Under an antenuptial agreement executed in Quebec between Quebec residents, Roth (D) agreed to leave his future wife $125,000, by will or trust. Following their marriage, D inherited $10 million. D set up a trust in New York that provided that his wife would receive $1 million in lieu of the $125,000. D subsequently lost his fortune. When D discovered that antenuptial agreements could not be modified under Quebec law, D attempted to have the trust set aside. Upon D's involuntary bankruptcy, his trustee in bankruptcy and a creditor sought to invalidate the trust under Quebec law. The trial court invalidated the trust but the appellate division reversed. P appeals.

   (2) **Issue.** Will the validity of the inter vivos trust be determined under the law of the settlor's domicile?

   (3) **Held.** No. Judgment affirmed.

      (a) Although testamentary trusts are governed by the law of the decedent's domicile, the considerations are different for inter vivos trusts that involve personal property and securities. The practicalities of increasing mobility and business contacts in jurisdictions other than the place of residence lead to the conclusion that New York law applies. Other transfers of personal property are governed by the law of the situs and New York public policy supports the application of the law that would uphold the trust, the intent of the parties.

b) **Recognition of the settlor's choice of law--Shannon v. Irving Trust Co.,** 275 N.Y. 95 (1937).

Shannon v. Irving Trust Co.

   (1) **Facts.** Joseph Shannon, a New Jersey resident, established a trust in New York and appointed Irving Trust Co. (D), a New York corporation, as trustee. The trust beneficiaries, Joseph's wife and his son (P), were also New Jersey residents. The trust stipulated that validity and construction issues were to be determined under New Jersey law, while questions of the trustee's compensation were to be determined under New York law. The trust also contained provisions providing for the accumulation and distribution of the trust corpus that were invalid under New York law. P sought to apply New York law to the trust, which would pay the accumulations to him. The trial court applied the law as stipulated in the trust (New Jersey law). P appeals.

(2)   Issue. When the settlor so stipulates, should the forum apply the law of the settlor's domicile to the issue of the validity of certain provisions of an inter vivos trust?

(3)   Held. Yes. Judgment affirmed.

(a)   The settlor's choice of law ought to be recognized, unless such recognition would violate the forum's strongly held public policy. Here, New Jersey's general policy is substantially the same as New York's, to limit restraints on alienation. Therefore, although New Jersey law reaches a different result, it does not violate New York's public policy.

Wilmington Trust Co. v. Wilmington Trust Co.

c)   Implied intent to apply the law that would validate the trust--Wilmington Trust Co. v. Wilmington Trust Co., 26 Del. Ch. 397 (1942).

(1)   Facts. William Donner, a New York domiciliary, created a personal property trust in New York for the benefit of his family. Dora Donner was succeeded as trustee by a Delaware trust company. By the terms of the trust, the beneficiaries had the power of appointment over certain of the trust assets. Following the appointment of the Delaware trustee, Joseph Donner exercised this power and set up trusts that violated the New York rule against perpetuities but were valid under Delaware law. The trial court upheld the validity of the trust.

(2)   Issue. Will the laws of the jurisdiction that will uphold the trust be applied?

(3)   Held. Yes. Judgment affirmed.

(a)   The intent of the donor is the main determinant of the choice of law in cases involving trusts of personal property. If the donor expresses his intent, it will be given effect so long as the selected jurisdiction has some material connection with the transaction. If the trust instrument is silent as to choice of law, the court will attempt to ascertain the donor's intent. Since the trust agreement provided for the appointment of an out-of-state trustee, there is no reason to deny the application of Delaware law, which the donor apparently intended.

In re Bauer's Trust

d)   The power of appointment when the donor is also the donee--In re Bauer's Trust, 14 N.Y.2d 272 (1964).

(1)   Facts. In 1917, Bauer executed an irrevocable trust in New York, her residence. The trust gave her the income until her death when the remainder would go to her husband. If the husband predeceased her, which was the case, the trust principal was to be distributed according to her will or, if it failed, according to New York intestacy law. Bauer moved permanently to England where she executed a codicil to her will leaving the trust fund to Midland Bank for the benefit of her nieces and an English charity.

(2)   Issue. Will the New York court apply the law of New York applicable at the time the trust was created to test the validity of the foreign codicil?

(3)   Held. Yes.

(a)   Under former New York law, applicable when the trust was created, Bauer had irrevocably given up her power of appointment, though she was both the donor and the donee of the trust. Thus, any attempt in the will or the codicil to exercise the power of appointment was ineffective. The trust corpus will therefore be distributed under the New York laws of intestacy.

(4)   Dissent. The majority arbitrarily and mechanically applied the old rule that the validity of an appointment is governed by the law that would apply to the trust that created that power. When the donor also becomes the donee, it is clear that the donor has the equivalent of ownership and it is irrational to conclude that the donor-donee becomes her own agent to preserve the original trust agreement. Bauer intended English law to apply to her appointment of the property. The appointment was made in England by an English solicitor, designating an English trustee and, in part, English beneficiaries. Therefore New York has no valid interest in defeating Bauer's clear intent.

(5)   Comment. The application of the traditional rule led to an unreasonable result. Most courts would allow sufficient flexibility to give effect to the donor's intent.

e)   **Testamentary trusts—validity--Farmers and Merchants Bank v. Woolf,** 86 N.M. 320 (1974).

(1)   Facts. Mabel Jones, an Arizona resident, willed her residuary estate, in trust, to the Farmers and Merchants Bank (P) in New Mexico, with the provision that, following her brother's death, the corpus of the trust should be paid to Alcoholics Anonymous of San Antonio, Texas. The Bank sought a declaration of the rights of the parties to the trust. The New Mexico trial court upheld the provision for Alcoholics Anonymous under Texas law, although it would have been invalid under Arizona law. Woolf (D), the administrator of the brother's estate, appeals, claiming that Arizona law should have been applied.

(2)   Issue. Did the New Mexico court err in applying Texas law instead of the law of Arizona, the testator's domicile?

(3)   Held. No.

(a)   The Restatement (Second) of Conflicts provides that when the validity of a trust provision created by a will is at issue, the validity will be determined by the law of the state of the testator's domicile at death, unless the trust is to be administered in another state. In that case the law of the state where the trust is to be administered will be applied, if such application is necessary to sustain the validity of the trust. Furthermore, when a testator bequeaths movables to be administered for *charitable purposes* in another state, the disposition is valid if valid under local law, even though it would be invalid under the law of the state of the testator's domicile.

f) **Testator's intent controls the choice of law.** In *Matter of Chappell,* 124 Wash. 128 (1923), the decedent's son sought to set aside trust provisions of decedent's will. Decedent was domiciled in California when he died. The trust provisions of the will involved personal property, the disposition of which is normally governed by the laws of the decedent's domicile. California law would have invalidated the trust and given one-half to the decedent's widow and one-half to the son. The court in Washington, where the property was and where the beneficiaries resided, applied Washington law, which upheld the trust, and the son appealed. The court applied the law which gave effect to the testator's intent. Although the general rule is to apply the law of the decedent's domicile to the disposition of personal property, the testator's intent was clearly to the contrary. Indications of the intent that Washington law should have applied were: (i) the property was located there upon death; (ii) the will was made in Washington and in it decedent referred to himself as being of Seattle, Washington; (iii) most of the trustees resided in Washington; and (iv) the will provided that the trustees who remained in Washington could exercise control in the event others left.

g) **Due process and the notice requirement--Mullane v. Central Hanover Bank & Trust Co.,** *supra.*

4. **Intangibles.**

a. **Introduction.** Since a chose in action has no "situs," courts may refer instead to the document representing the intangible and to its situs. If a document is negotiable, the intangible rights involved are said to be "embodied" in the instrument. Thus, the document is a "thing," and courts exercise jurisdiction based on possession. Choice of law is made by reference to the law of the situs of the instrument. Under the U.C.C., the share of stock is embodied in the stock certificate, which is a negotiable instrument. Certificates are the basis of quasi in rem jurisdiction. The choice of law is the law of the situs in questions involving title to shares. [Morson v. Second National Bank of Boston (below)] However, if there is no document (such as in the debt situation involved in *Harris v. Balk, supra*), then questions as to the assignability of the right involved are governed by the law of the place of transfer. Some courts do make reference to the "situs of the debt" (the domicile of the debtor).

Morson v. Second National Bank of Boston

b. **Stock shares--Morson v. Second National Bank of Boston,** 306 Mass. 588 (1940).

1) **Facts.** Herbert Turner transferred a certificate representing 150 shares of stock in a Massachusetts corporation to Mildred Turner Copperman (D) while they were traveling together in Italy. The transfer would be valid under Massachusetts law but invalid under Italian law. When Herbert Turner died, Morson (P), the administrator of his estate, sought an injunction against the transfer agent of the Massachusetts corporation on the basis that the transfer was invalid. The trial court agreed and entered a decree for P. D appeals.

2) Issue. When stock shares are expressly assignable in a particular manner under the laws of the state of incorporation, should such assignability provision apply to foreign transfers?

3) Held. Yes. Decree reversed.

a) Although transfers of tangible chattels are controlled by the law of the situs, a certificate representing shares of stock is different. The shares themselves are part of the corporate structure created under the laws of the state of incorporation. When the state of incorporation has seen fit in creating the shares to insert in them the intrinsic attribute or quality of being assignable in a particular manner it would seem that that state, and other states as well, should recognize assignments made in the specified manner wherever they are made.

K. FAMILY LAW

1. Marriage.

a. Choice of law rule as to validity of marriage. The validity of a marriage is determined by the law of the place of celebration (where the marriage relationship was entered into) at the time of the marriage—at least when the marriage can be upheld by reference to such law and there is no problem of remarriage following divorce. This is true whether the matter is litigated at the parties' domicile, the place of celebration, or some third state. [Restatement (Second) §283(2)]

1) Rationale. There is a strong interest in upholding marriages. Since people frequently marry in places other than their domicile, the courts will usually uphold a marriage which is valid where entered into, unless the relationship violates some fundamental interest of the parties' real domicile in the health, mores, welfare, or family characteristics of its domiciliaries.

2) Reference to domicile law to uphold marriage. If the marriage would not be valid under the law of the place of celebration, but would be valid under the law of the parties' domicile, then the courts apply the law of the domicile; *i.e.*, basically whichever law (as between place of marriage and domicile) would uphold the marriage (at least when this is not grossly offensive to the public policy or mores of the forum). [Restatement (Second) §283, comment i]

3) Comment. A number of authorities urge that the state of the parties' domicile at the time of the marriage is the state of paramount interest and that reference should always be made to its law, although the law of the place of celebration may control questions of mere form (*e.g.*, license, capacity of person performing the ceremony, etc.). However, the courts have not adopted this position. As will be seen below, the courts instead tend to make reference to whichever law would declare the marriage valid; in their desire to uphold marriages, this often requires application of the law of the place of celebration over the law of the parties' domicile. Moreover, difficulties arise in application of the law of the parties' domicile when the husband and the wife were each domiciled in a different state prior to marriage.

4) Statutes regulating choice of law. Statutes in some states have been interpreted as dictating a contrary result: *i.e.*, under such statutes, marriages by local residents entered into outside the state are invalid if contrary to the laws of the place of marriage, even if the marriage would have been valid under local (domicile) law.

b. Applications.

In re May's Estate

1) Marriages that violate the laws of morality--*In re* May's Estate, 305 N.Y. 486 (1953).

a) Facts. Sam and his niece, Fannie (both New York residents), desired to get married but under New York law such a marriage was incestuous and bore criminal penalties. The couple went to Rhode Island, where the marriage was validly performed. They returned to New York where they lived as husband and wife until Fannie's death. Their daughter objected to Sam's appointment as the administrator of May's estate under a statute which appointed the surviving spouse. The daughter claimed that the marriage was invalid in New York as against public policy. In surrogate's court the marriage was invalidated. The appellate division reversed.

b) Issue. Will the court determine the validity of the marriage according to the law of the place of celebration?

c) Held. Yes. The marriage is valid.

(1) When the public policy of the forum is sufficiently strong against the recognition of a marriage that was valid where celebrated, the forum may choose not to recognize the marriage. Such is not the case here since the statute against the marriage of an uncle and niece did not specify that it should be applied to foreign marriages and the marriage was in accord with the Jewish faith. Therefore no public policy was sufficiently strong to invalidate the foreign marriage.

d) Dissent. The New York statute positively declares a strong public policy against such marriages and this marriage should not be recognized.

e) Comment. If the court's only considerations were those to which its opinion referred, the dissent is a much stronger argument. Most courts would invalidate the marriage. But it appears the court was not sympathetic to the daughter's request and was hesitant to deny Sam (husband of 46 years) appointment as administrator of Fannie's estate.

2)   **Marriages violating the forum's public policy--Wilkins v. Zelichowski,** 26
N.J. 370 (1958).

   a)   **Facts.** Wilkins (P) and Zelichowski (D), both domiciliaries of New
Jersey, ran away to Indiana to marry, where girls of P's age (16) were
allowed to marry. After returning to New Jersey and after having a child,
P sought an annulment on the grounds that the marriage violated New
Jersey's public policy. Under New Jersey's statutory scheme an annulment
of such a marriage could be had if the marriage was not confirmed after
age 18 and if no child of the marriage were involved. If a child was
involved, the child's best interest was to be considered. The trial court
ruled that, under such circumstances, the public policy of New Jersey was
not sufficiently violated to annul the marriage. P appeals.

   b)   **Issue.** May the forum state invalidate the foreign marriage as violative of
its public policy when the marriage was entered?

   c)   **Held.** Yes. Judgment reversed and the annulment is granted.

      (1)   New Jersey's strongly held public policy, as expressed in statute and
by the courts, is against the recognition of foreign marriages of New
Jersey residents under the age of 18. Only New Jersey has an
interest in the marriage, since the parties are New Jersey residents
and only went out-of-state to avoid New Jersey law. The trial court
found that the best interests of the child would not be harmed by
granting the annulment; it should be granted.

   d)   **Comment.** Admittedly the policy considerations in this case are somewhat
different from those in *May*. But policies against incestuous marriages in
New York would seem to be at least as strongly held as policies against the
marriage of minors in New Jersey, the former to protect the unborn and
the latter to protect New Jersey residents from themselves.

3)   **Marriages performed in the forum that violate the domicile's public policy--**
In re **Ommang's Estate,** 183 Minn. 92 (1931).

   a)   **Facts.** Ommang and Seligman, both Wisconsin residents, decided to
marry. However, Seligman could not marry under Wisconsin law until she
had been divorced for an entire year. Therefore they went to Minnesota to
marry and returned to Wisconsin to live. They later separated, and both
ended up living in Minnesota. Ommang died intestate in Minnesota and
Seligman (P) sued to recover as the surviving spouse and sole heir.
Ommang's half-sister (D) claimed that the initial marriage was invalid.
The probate court held that Seligman was not Ommang's wife, but the
appellate court reversed. D appeals.

   b)   **Issue.** Although the marriage was performed in Minnesota to evade
Wisconsin law (the domiciliary state), will the forum apply its own law to
determine the validity of a marriage performed in the forum?

   c)   **Held.** Yes. Affirmed. The marriage is valid.

      (1)   Although states other than the state where the marriage was per-
formed would not need to recognize the marriage, the state where the

marriage was performed must. Since the marriage was performed in Minnesota and is valid under its law, Minnesota will recognize it.

d) **Comment.** A frequent problem arises when either or both spouses were under a prohibition against remarriage within a certain period following a divorce in another state. Here, there is no strong policy to uphold the validity of the second marriage, and the courts' willingness to do so depends on a number of factors: If the divorce is by interlocutory decree only (*i.e.*, a waiting period must expire before the final decree can be obtained), and either party remarries outside the state before the final decree is obtained, the marriage is usually held void. This is because until the final decree is obtained, the first marriage still exists and neither party has capacity to remarry. If the divorce is absolute, but the law of the parties' domicile imposes a prohibition against either spouse remarrying for a certain period of time and one of the spouses remarries outside the state within the prohibited time, the cases are split. Most courts validate the second marriage—*i.e.*, if the marriage was valid under the law of the place of celebration, it will be upheld notwithstanding the prohibition. But there are some cases that hold the new marriage void as violative of the laws of the parties' domicile.

In re Estate of Lenherr

4) **Public policy violations as applied to the incidents of marriage--*In re* Estate of Lenherr,** 455 Pa. 255 (1974).

a) **Facts.** Leo Lenherr, decedent, was divorced on the grounds of adultery committed with Sarah Barney, both of whom were residents of Pennsylvania. They were later married in West Virginia but returned to live in Pennsylvania, where they resided until Leo's death. Pennsylvania law prohibited marriage between adulterers during the life of the former spouse. If the Pennsylvania court recognized the marriage, property held jointly with Leo would pass to Sarah without the imposition of a Pennsylvania inheritance tax.

b) **Issue.** Although such marriages violate Pennsylvania public policy, will the court apply the laws of the state of celebration for purposes of recognizing the tax exemption?

c) **Held.** Yes. The tax exemption will apply.

(1) Pennsylvania has the most significant relationship to the marriage since both Sarah and Leo were residents there before and after the marriage. But the court must balance the policy behind the Pennsylvania law as it relates to the marital exemption against the need for uniformity and predictability obtained by application of the law of the state of celebration. Since invalidation of the marriage will neither deter adulterous conduct nor spare the aggrieved former spouse, the policy behind the Pennsylvania law (to protect the sensibilities of the injured spouse) would not be accomplished by invalidation. On balance, the need for uniformity prevails.

d) **Comment.** Even polygamous or incestuous marriages may be upheld for the purpose of determining certain rights characterized as "incidents" of the marriage relationship. Such has been particularly true in determining property, or other rights, following the death of one of the parties to a marriage. [*See, e.g., In re* May's Estate, *supra*]

2.   Divorce.

a.   **Choice of law governing the grounds for divorce.** Divorce, unlike marriage, is considered to be exclusively a concern of the parties involved and may only be accomplished under the law of the place with which the plaintiff is most intimately connected—the domicile. Since it is possible to establish domicile by showing intent plus residence, the practice of migratory divorces has grown; *i.e.*, persons going to the states having the lowest standards for granting divorces and setting up domicile there expressly for the purpose of obtaining a divorce.

b.   **Basis for jurisdiction to dissolve the marriage.**

1)   **Introduction.** For analytic purposes, it should be noted at the outset that a court in a divorce case may be asked to provide several different kinds of relief—*e.g.*, to declare a dissolution of the marriage; to determine the spouses' property rights; to make orders for the support and maintenance of the dependent spouse and children; to enjoin transfers of property; to award custody of children; etc.

We will first discuss the court's power to grant a divorce—to dissolve the marriage relationship (a status). As will be seen later, entirely different jurisdictional requirements and problems are encountered when the court seeks to grant other or additional relief (personal or property rights).

2)   **Historical background.** The early decisions were in disagreement as to what was required to vest a court with the power to grant a valid divorce. Something in addition to the mere residence or domicile of the plaintiff-spouse was required. Some courts required that both spouses be domiciled locally. Others accepted the so-called "matrimonial domicile"—the last domicile in which the parties lived together as husband and wife—as sufficient basis for jurisdiction, even if one spouse was no longer in the state when the action was brought. [Atherton v. Atherton, 181 U.S. 155 (1898)] While others allowed domicile of the plaintiff-spouse alone, if personal jurisdiction was obtained over the defendant-spouse or if the plaintiff-spouse's separate domicile in the forum was acquired with the consent, or due to the fault (desertion, etc.), of the defendant-spouse. [Haddock v. Haddock, 201 U.S. 562 (1906)]

3)   **Modern rule.** The conflicting positions (above) were resolved by the Supreme Court in *Williams v. North Carolina*, 317 U.S. 287 (1942) ("*Williams I*", *infra*), in which it was held that the domicile of the plaintiff-spouse alone, without any of the additional elements above, provided a complete and sufficient basis for divorce jurisdiction. Thus, a divorce granted by any state in which the plaintiff-spouse was then domiciled is entitled to full faith and credit in every other state.

a)   **Rationale—in rem jurisdiction.** The Court reasoned that a divorce action is a proceeding "in rem"; *i.e.*, the plaintiff-spouse brings the marital relationship (the res) with him when he establishes domicile locally. Having jurisdiction over the res, the local courts can, therefore, dissolve or otherwise adjudicate questions as to the marital relationship.

(1) **"Minimum contacts" requirement.** As discussed earlier, all assertions of state jurisdiction, including in rem jurisdiction, must now be evaluated according to a single "minimum contacts" standard. However, the Supreme Court has indicated this does not mean that the jurisdictional rules governing the adjudication of status are inconsistent with the new standard of fairness. [Shaffer v. Heitner, 433 U.S. 186 (1977)]

Alton v.
Alton

(2) **Domicile requirement--Alton v. Alton,** 207 F.2d 667 (3d Cir. 1953).

    (a) **Facts.** Sonia Alton (W) left Connecticut and went to the Virgin Islands. After residing there for six weeks, she brought suit for divorce in federal court, relying on a Virgin Islands statute providing that six weeks of continuous residency was prima facie evidence of domicile, and that if both parties appeared before the court, divorce could be granted without regard to domicile. David Alton (H) appeared and did not contest. The commissioner recommended divorce on grounds not recognized in the home domicile, but the district court refused to grant it absent further showing of domicile. W appeals.

    (b) **Issue.** Is the statute that reduces domicile requirements valid to establish jurisdiction to grant a divorce?

    (c) **Held.** No. Denial of divorce affirmed.

        1] The statute is invalid either as an attempt to make divorce actions transitory or as an unreasonable interference with the judicial process. The part of the statute eliminating the domicile requirement when both parties appear unjustifiably attempts to do away with domicile as the foundation of jurisdiction. Divorce is a matter of public concern, and the place of domicile has a strong interest in applying its law. Marriage has been determined a "res" for purposes of in rem jurisdiction, but the "res" is present only in the state of domicile. To rule otherwise would not allow states to control the domestic relations of their citizens.

    (d) **Dissent.**

        1] *Statutory prima facie presumption:* This part of the statute is not invalid because the presumption is rebuttable with other evidence. And the court raised a due process objection although H did not assert that he had been denied due process.

        2] *Statutory jurisdiction without domicile:* There is no constitutional dictate that domicile is the only basis for jurisdiction in divorce cases. It is not arbitrary or unfair to base jurisdiction on personal jurisdiction over the parties, rather than in rem jurisdiction over the "res."

        3] *Choice of law problem:* Jurisdiction and choice of law are separate questions. The old approach was to answer both questions with a single inquiry into the domicile of the plaintiff. Here, jurisdiction could be based on a different inquiry. But the choice of law would go in favor of Connecticut since both parties come from Connecticut.

(e) Comments.

1] The Restatement (Second) grants jurisdiction for divorce if either spouse has a relationship with the forum state that makes jurisdiction "reasonable."

2] In *Sosna v. Iowa*, 419 U.S. 393 (1975), the Court upheld the Iowa one-year residence requirement for divorce on the basis that such a requirement fulfills a legitimate state interest—those who seek divorce from the state's courts must be genuinely attached to the state. Also, the residence requirement helps insulate divorce decrees from the likelihood of collateral attack. The majority distinguished between state statutes requiring a durational residency requirement for welfare payments (held unconstitutional because they were based on budgetary or record-keeping considerations alone) and the divorce residence requirement. The dissent would have held the Iowa residence requirement unconstitutional on the basis that it unduly interfered with the right to migrate, resettle, find a new job, and start a new life. While the Court here talks of "residence," it cites with approval *Williams v. North Carolina (Williams II)*, *infra*, for the proposition that judicial power to grant a divorce—jurisdiction, strictly speaking—is founded on domicile.

4) Mexican divorces. In recent years, some Mexican states would grant divorces for almost any reason. Such Mexican divorces where neither spouse personally appeared before the Mexican court have almost always been denied effect in United States courts. When only one spouse appeared, most states have also denied recognition on the basis that neither spouse had domicile in Mexico. But when one spouse was actually before the court and the other appeared either personally or by an attorney, the courts of New York, at least, have given effect to the divorce. [Rosenstiel v. Rosenstiel, Wood v. Wood, 16 N.Y.2d 64, 262 N.Y.S.2d 86 (1965)]

c. Extraterritorial effect of ex parte divorces.

1) Ex parte divorces entitled to full faith and credit.

a) Introduction. Since domicile of the plaintiff-spouse, by itself, is a valid basis for divorce jurisdiction, it follows that courts in such domicile have the power to grant a divorce ex parte—*i.e.*, without personal jurisdiction over the defendant-spouse. Thus, as readily as the plaintiff-spouse can establish a new domicile, she can establish a valid basis for divorce jurisdiction (*e.g.*, the typical "migratory" divorces in Nevada). In such situations, F2 must give full faith and credit to an F1 divorce decree, F1's jurisdiction having been established, even if the plaintiff violated an F2 injunction in proceeding with the suit in F1.

Williams
v. North
Carolina
(Williams I)

b) **Leading case--Williams v. North Carolina (Williams I),** 317 U.S. 287 (1942).

(1) **Facts.** Williams and Hendrix (Petitioners) deserted their spouses in North Carolina and went to live in Nevada for six weeks. Nevada courts determined that they were Nevada domiciliaries, and granted divorces to both Petitioners. Williams and Hendrix were subsequently married and returned to North Carolina where they were prosecuted for bigamy. North Carolina's supreme court affirmed their conviction on the basis of the *Haddock* case (discussed briefly, *supra*)—that personal jurisdiction over the defendant-spouse or that spouse's consent was required. The Supreme Court granted certiorari.

(2) **Issue.** Is an ex parte divorce granted in F1 (where the plaintiff-spouse is domiciled) entitled to full faith and credit in F2?

(3) **Held.** Yes. Judgment reversed.

(a) The old rule that matrimonial domicile remained with the wrongfully deserted spouse and therefore this divorce would be invalid in North Carolina, but valid in Nevada, is reversed. If the plaintiff-spouse is domiciled in F1 and the defendant-spouse in F2, F1 may alter the status of the marriage, even though the defendant-spouse does not appear in F1. The Constitution only requires that the absent spouse be served in a manner reasonably calculated to give actual notice. The F1 judgments are entitled to full faith and credit, although neither defendant-spouse appeared or was served in F1, and F2's public policy was offended.

(4) **Comment.** This case does not decide whether decisions based on a party's residence, rather than domicile, would be entitled to full faith and credit, or whether F2 could find domicile in F1 to be a sham and thereby deny full faith and credit.

2) **Limitation—sufficiency of domicile subject to collateral attack.**

a) **Introduction.** Due to the strong interest of the domicile of the defendant-spouse, the determination of the plaintiff-spouse's domicile in F1 (and, thus, the validity of the F1 divorce jurisdiction) may be collaterally attacked and reexamined in F2. If the defendant-spouse has not appeared in the F1 proceedings, F1's findings as to its own jurisdiction may always be reexamined in F2.

Williams
v. North
Carolina
(Williams II)

b) **Divorce by consent--Williams v. North Carolina (Williams II),** 325 U.S. 226 (1945).

(1) **Facts.** This case is based on the same set of facts as the previous one. On remand, Williams and Hendrix were again convicted of bigamy, this time on the basis that Nevada inappropriately decided their domicile and that Nevada therefore lacked jurisdiction to grant the divorce decree.

(2) **Issue.** Can North Carolina review Nevada's finding as to domicile and, on that basis, deny full faith and credit to the Nevada divorce?

(3) **Held.** Yes. Judgment affirmed.

(a) The previous case decided that the ex parte divorce in F1 was entitled to full faith and credit in F2. But Nevada's judgment as to Petitioners' domicile, on which jurisdiction was based, was not contested. An F1 judgment can be collaterally attacked in F2 on the ground that F1 lacked jurisdiction. Neither the Fourteenth Amendment nor full faith and credit requires that states reach uniform judgments as to domicile; Nevada could legitimately say Petitioners were domiciled there, and North Carolina determine that they were not. Although F2's inquiry cannot be too extreme, a divorce decree is not conclusive as to jurisdictional facts upon which it is dependent.

(b) North Carolina placed the burden of proving the elements of bigamy on the prosecution and the burden of showing the validity of the marriages on the defense. The statement of domicile in the Nevada decree was prima facie evidence of jurisdiction, but the court properly let the jury decide if Petitioners went to Nevada merely to obtain divorces rather than establish domicile.

(4) **Comments.**

(a) The Supreme Court has refrained from establishing any constitutional definition of "domicile" for divorce purposes. Rather, "domicile" is treated as any other jurisdictional fact, so the forum (F2) will usually apply its own standards and concepts in testing the sufficiency of the plaintiff-spouse's domicile in F1. But F1's findings as to the plaintiff-spouse's domicile are entitled to a presumption of validity, and it would violate full faith and credit for F2 to apply some novel or arbitrarily high standards of "domicile" solely to invalidate out-of-state divorces. [Williams II, *supra*]

(b) *Williams II* undermines, to some degree, the *Willliams I* decision, which requires that full faith and credit be given to sister states' divorce decrees. Furthermore, it renders "ex parte divorce proceedings" in F1 subject to the great infirmity that there may always be a subsequent collateral attack on the issue of jurisdiction in a foreign forum (F2).

3) **Note.** F2 will not usually undertake to prosecute the plaintiff-spouse who goes to F1 to get a divorce. The defendant-spouse who wants to contest the divorce has several alternatives:

a) Go to F1 and contest the divorce.

b) Stay in F2 and get an injunction against the plaintiff-spouse proceeding in F1.

c) Bring a declaratory cause of action in F2 to determine who is married to whom.

d. Limitations on collateral attack.

1) Definition of collateral attack. A collateral attack is a challenge to F1's jurisdiction brought in F2.

2) Persons barred from making collateral attacks.

a) Introduction. Collateral attacks in F2 on the validity of an F1 decree ordinarily may be made by any interested person who is not bound by the F1 decree—*e.g.*, the defendant-spouse (assuming he was not subject to F1 personal jurisdiction); a child or heir in a probate proceeding; or the state in a bigamy prosecution. However, certain classes of individuals will not be allowed to make such attack. Because of their relationship to the F1 proceedings, they either will be bound by the F1 decree under the doctrine of res judicata or they will be equitably estopped to attack it. Thus, even though the F1 divorce is based on defective jurisdiction, it still may be binding as against certain parties.

b) Plaintiff in F1. Whichever spouse obtained the F1 divorce decree is bound thereby under res judicata and hence cannot collaterally attack it in F2; *e.g.*, she cannot remarry and then later seek to annul the remarriage on the ground that the F1 divorce was invalid. [Krause v. Krause, 282 N.Y. 355 (1940)]

c) Defendant-spouse who "participated" in F1 proceeding. If the defendant-spouse filed a general appearance or otherwise "participated" in the F1 proceedings, he will be bound by the F1 decree on straight principles of res judicata. Having "participated" in the F1 proceeding, it is no longer an "ex parte" proceeding; he had a chance to fully litigate all issues of the case, including jurisdiction, and he is, therefore, bound by the F1 judgment, whether the issue of jurisdiction was actually litigated or not.

(1) What constitutes "participation." The Supreme Court has never defined this term nor set any minimal standards. All that seemingly is required is such an appearance as affords the opportunity to raise the jurisdiction issue. (It is enough for res judicata purposes that the parties could have litigated the issue, whether or not it was actually litigated.) [Cook v. Cook and Sherrer v. Sherrer, *infra*]

(a) A general appearance filed by authorized counsel on behalf of the nonresident defendant-spouse has been held sufficient "participation" to bar the defendant from later collaterally attacking the F1 decree. [*See* Johnson v. Muelberger, *infra*]

          (b)   But courts may disregard "appearances" that are sham or that are coerced.

       (2)   **Effect—"collusive divorces."** Spouses wishing a "quickie" divorce may proceed in a forum that is not the real domicile of either spouse and that, therefore, has no divorce jurisdiction. Yet, if both spouses "participate" in the F1 proceeding, the F1 judgment is binding on them under res judicata and cannot be attacked by either of them in subsequent proceedings in F1, F2, or elsewhere—*i.e.*, the parties have effectively and fraudulently "conferred jurisdiction" on the F1 court. [*See* Johnson v. Muelberger, *infra*]

d)   **Nonappearing spouse.** The defendant-spouse, not subject to the personal jurisdiction of the F1 court, is not bound by res judicata but he may nevertheless be equitably estopped from challenging the F1 decree if he instigated the F1 proceedings (*e.g.*, H pays W to go to Nevada and get the divorce); or if he has remarried in reliance on the F1 decree, knowing it to be defective.

e)   **Privies.** Persons who are in "privity" with either of the parties before the F1 court will also be bound by the F1 decree. [*See* Johnson v. Muelberger, *infra*]

    (1)   In determining which persons are in "privity" with the parties before the F1 court, the law of F1 applies; *i.e.*, the F1 decree is to receive the same effect in F2 as it would have received in F1.

    (2)   States vary in their rules on privity. For example, some courts hold a child of the divorced parents "privy" to the F1 decree and thus barred from attacking it later in a probate proceeding in F2. But there are contrary decisions.

f)   **"Strangers."** If both spouses are bound by the decree, and there is no fraud involved, third persons will generally not be permitted to attack the decree. [*See* Cook v. Cook, *infra*]

3)   **Applications.**

a)   **The question of jurisdiction fully litigated in F1 is res judicata in F2.** In *Davis v. Davis*, 305 U.S. 32 (1938), H, alleging he was a Virginia domiciliary, instituted a divorce action there. W appeared to contest H's allegations of domicile. The court found for H and entered the decree. In subsequent litigation between H and W in F2, the court there refused to give full faith and credit to the Virginia decree, alleging lack of jurisdiction. The Supreme Court held that, both parties having appeared and the domicile question having been fully argued, the Virginia decision was res judicata.

b)   **Collateral attack following an appearance--Sherrer v. Sherrer,** 334 U.S. 343 (1948).

    (1)   **Facts.** H and W were residents of Massachusetts. W went to Florida, established the statutory residence for divorce, and instituted this proceeding. H appeared by counsel but did not strongly contest

Florida's jurisdiction. The court declared W a domiciliary and granted the divorce. W remarried and moved back to Massachusetts. H then instituted suit in Massachusetts challenging the divorce on the grounds that W was not a Florida domiciliary. The Massachusetts court agreed, and W appeals.

(2) Issue. May H collaterally attack the divorce decree when he appeared in F1 and the jurisdiction issue was litigated in F1?

(3) Held. No. Judgment reversed.

(a) Because H was given every opportunity to litigate all issues in the prior action, due process requirements are satisfied and the jurisdictional issue is res judicata. Full faith and credit bars H from collaterally attacking a divorce decree on jurisdictional grounds when: (i) H participated in the earlier proceeding; (ii) H had full opportunity to contest jurisdiction; and (iii) the decree could not have been so attacked in F1. The fact that H did not contest jurisdiction makes no difference. His own dereliction will not afford him a second chance.

(4) Comment. The doctrine of res judicata generally applies to issues that have been "fully and fairly litigated" in prior proceedings. Note that this concept has been extended by this case to include issues that could have been litigated but actually were not.

Johnson v Muelberger **c) A divorce decree binding on a third party in privity--Johnson v. Muelberger,** 340 U.S. 581 (1951).

(1) Facts. Eleanor was the child of Johnson's first marriage. After his first wife (W1) died, Johnson remarried. Later his second wife (W2) went to Florida and got a divorce. W2 did not reside in Florida long enough to establish statutory residency, but Johnson, a New York resident, sent his attorney to appear in Florida. Johnson then married his third wife (W3). When Johnson died, domiciled in New York, he left all of his property to Eleanor. W3 then elected to take a widow's statutory share. Eleanor contested the validity of Johnson's divorce from W2 (it was clear she had not satisfied the requirements for jurisdiction in Florida) and thus the validity of his marriage to W3. The surrogate determined that Eleanor could not attack W3's status as surviving spouse, and the appellate division affirmed. The court of appeals reversed and held that Eleanor could attack the Florida divorce for lack of jurisdiction, as the divorce only bound the father who appeared. The Supreme Court granted certiorari.

(2) Issue. Is the divorce binding on Eleanor, who did not appear?

(3) Held. Yes. Judgment reversed. The *Sherrer* rationale (*see supra*) is controlling. A collateral attack may not be made if the party attacking the judgment would not be permitted to make such an attack in the courts of the granting state (even if that party was not a party before the F1 court).

(a) No Florida case has been shown to the Court that holds that a child may contest in Florida her parent's divorce decree when the parent was barred from contesting the decree by res judicata.

(b)   In Florida, the child would be found to be in privity with her father, or she would have no standing to collaterally attack the judgment.

d)   Res judicata is presumed--Cook v. Cook, 342 U.S. 126 (1951).

(1)   Facts. H married W and shortly thereafter found out that W was still married to Mann. W secured a divorce from Mann in Florida; then she and H remarried. Later, H brought an annulment proceeding in Vermont, and the court there granted relief on the ground that W's divorce in Florida, and hence their remarriage, was void because W never acquired domicile in Florida. The Vermont court agreed and granted the annulment. The Supreme Court granted certiorari.

(2)   Issue. Absent a showing that Florida's jurisdiction was not litigated in Florida or that Mann was not subject to Florida's jurisdiction, is the divorce entitled to full faith and credit?

(3)   Held. No. Judgment reversed. The Vermont court must give the Florida decree full faith and credit.

(a)   The record does not show what happened in Florida except that the court there gave W a divorce. As far as we know, Mann was a party there.

(b)   If the defendant-spouse appeared in Florida [Sherrer, *supra*], or appeared and admitted W's Florida domicile [Coe v. Coe, 334 U.S. 378 (1948)], or was personally served in the divorce state [Johnson v. Muelberger, *supra*], he would be barred from attacking the decree collaterally, and so would a stranger to the Florida proceedings (H) unless Florida applies a less strict rule of res judicata to the second husband than it does to the first.

(4)   Comments.

(a)   The court said that *Johnson* stood for the proposition that if the defendant-spouse was personally served in F1 the divorce decree there was binding on him—this was only dictum in *Johnson*. The traditional view as to jurisdiction over the subject matter is that if a party defaults (*i.e.*, is personally served but never litigates the issue), the issue is not res judicata (*i.e.*, it can be collaterally attacked). Did the Supreme Court mean what it said?

(b)   Note that *Cook* seems to add a new presumption. The presumption that F1 had jurisdiction is a familiar one—*Williams I*, for example. Here, the second presumption is that F1 had jurisdiction and that this issue is res judicata. Therefore in F2, a party attacking the F1 judgment must show that F1 lacked jurisdiction and that there is no basis for "assuming" that the issue is res judicata. Does this new presumption have wider application than to divorce cases?

e)   Equitable preclusion--Krause v. Krause, 282 N.Y. 355 (1940).

(1)   Facts. H, domiciled in New York, obtained a divorce in Nevada (F1) from W1 and then married W2. W2 brought a suit in New York (F2) for separation and support, and H pleaded the invalidity of their marriage as a defense (*i.e.*, the divorce from W1 was no good since the F1 court had no jurisdiction). The F2 court refused to invalidate the F1 divorce. H appeals.

(2) **Issue.** Will H, as a party to the F1 divorce, be equitably estopped from denying its extraterritorial effect?

(3) **Held.** Yes. Order affirmed. H may not set up the invalidity of the F1 divorce as a defense.

    (a) Even though the F1 divorce was invalid, and therefore H's marriage is not valid, H is estopped from using this as a defense.

    (b) F2 may, on policy grounds, refuse to allow certain persons—those who obtained the decree or acted in reliance on it—to collaterally attack the F1 judgment.

(4) **Comment.** What law governs the question of equitable preclusion?

    (a) In *Cook v. Cook, supra,* when H remarried relying on W's invalid divorce decree from F1, the Supreme Court said that the law of F1 controlled. Of course, *Cook* raises the more general question of how much of the law of F1 relating to res judicata effect must be given full faith and credit in F2.

    (b) *Krause* asks the question, assuming that F1 law would not equitably preclude collateral estoppel attack by certain persons (for example, a child of divorced parents), whether and to what extent F2 can give greater effect to the F1 judgment by applying its own more encompassing notions of equitable preclusion.

  f) **The ramifications of these cases.**

(1) **Collusive divorces.** If the parties are domiciled in one state and lack grounds for a divorce there, they can arrange for one spouse to go to a more hospitable state, establish domicile, bring a divorce action and have the nonappearing spouse arrange for a local attorney to make a general appearance, and thereby get a valid divorce decree that cannot be collaterally attacked in the home state. Note, however, the state of the parties' true domicile is probably not in "privy" and therefore could not be precluded from attacking the F1 decree in a prosecution against one or both of the spouses (assuming they remarried and returned to F2) for bigamy.

(2) **What law governs the issue of res judicata?** Ordinarily, collateral attacks on the validity of the F1 decree may be made by any interested person (for example, the absent spouse). However, certain individuals will not be allowed to make such attacks because their relationship to the F1 decree is said to bind them (res judicata)—the child in *Johnson* and the husband in *Cook,* for example. In reality, the Supreme Court has fashioned its own law to determine when the F1 decree is res judicata, even though no F1 cases are presented demonstrating what effect the F1 decree has in F1. Presumably, if a party could definitely show what effect F1 would give its decree, the Supreme Court would accept this as determinative.

(3) **How does an issue become res judicata?** In each of the above cases, the F2 litigation was on a different cause of action than that decided in F1. By traditional collateral estoppel standards the precise issue being litigated in F2 must have been litigated, decided, and necessary to the decision in F1 before it is res judicata in F2. This point has never been recognized in these cases—it is clear, therefore, that at least in divorce cases the opportunity to have litigated in F1 is enough even though the suit in F2 is on a different cause of action.

(4) **Jurisdiction not res judicata?** Possibly, a fair reading of these res judicata cases is that whenever both parties are before the F1 court, this is a sufficient basis for F1 to exercise jurisdiction, and F2 must therefore recognize the F1 decree as to the issue of jurisdiction. That is, maybe these cases are not res judicata cases at all; they might suggest that there are now two bases for divorce jurisdiction—domicile or both parties before the court. In most instances, it would make little difference which view is taken, but there are some instances when it would. For example, if F1 is seen as having jurisdiction to enter a divorce decree, then F2 must give this determination full faith and credit and would not be able to bring a bigamy prosecution against either spouse who remarried and returned to live in F2.

e. **Basis for jurisdiction as to property or support rights—the "divisible divorce" doctrine.** Without personal jurisdiction over the defendant-spouse, a court in the plaintiff-spouse's domicile may validly dissolve the marital res, but it cannot grant any in personam relief against the absent spouse—*e.g.*, alimony, support, orders to convey property, etc. In other words, the court in the plaintiff-spouse's domicile may have valid jurisdiction for one purpose (to dissolve the marriage) but not for another (awarding support, etc.). This is known as the "divisible divorce" doctrine. [*See* Estin v. Estin, *infra*]

1) **Jurisdiction as to support obligations.**

a) **Personal jurisdiction required over obligor-spouse.** As indicated above, the court generally must have personal jurisdiction over the defendant-spouse to impose an enforceable alimony or support obligation upon him.

(1) **Long arm statutes.** Personal jurisdiction may be based on a valid application of an appropriate forum "long arm" statute; *e.g.*, several statutes provide that jurisdiction may be exercised over a nonresident spouse if the forum was the matrimonial domicile.

(2) **Continuing jurisdiction.** Once personal jurisdiction is obtained, it "continues" as long as the action is pending, enabling a court in a domestic relations case to modify or increase its support order years later without new personal service on the defendant-spouse.

b) **Obligee-spouse's rights cannot be affected without personal jurisdiction.**

(1) **Introduction.** Conversely, without personal jurisdiction over the defendant-spouse, a divorce decree obtained by the plaintiff-spouse may not be effective to terminate that spouse's duty to support the defendant-spouse.

Estin v. Estin   **(2)** **Leading case--Estin v. Estin,** 334 U.S. 541 (1948).

(a) **Facts.** H had been ordered by a New York court (having personal jurisdiction over him) to make monthly payments to W for separate maintenance. H then went to Nevada and obtained an ex parte divorce decree that purported to terminate any future support obligation to W. In subsequent proceedings in New York, H asserted that the Nevada decree had freed him from any further obligation to W. The New York courts held that W was still entitled to payment.

(b) **Issue.** Is Nevada's ex parte decree, which purported to terminate H's support obligation, entitled to full faith and credit in New York?

(c) **Held.** No. Judgment affirmed.

1] The Nevada decree is "divisible"—it is entitled to full faith and credit in New York insofar as it terminates the marital status; but it is ineffective to cut off W's support rights because she was not subject to the personal jurisdiction of the Nevada court.

(d) **Comments.**

1] In *Vanderbilt v. Vanderbilt*, 354 U.S. 416 (1957), the divisibility idea of *Estin* was expanded to encompass the situation where the absent spouse's rights to support could not be affected even though there was no outstanding decree for such at the time of the F1 determination. There, the wife, after the F1 divorce decree, went to another forum and got a determination of support. The Supreme Court held that F1's determination cutting off such rights need not be given full faith and credit in F2.

2] *Query*: What if the plaintiff-spouse sues the defendant-spouse for divorce—is the plaintiff-spouse thereafter precluded from suing for support?

a] If the court had personal jurisdiction over the defendant-spouse, and the plaintiff-spouse did not ask for support, some jurisdictions preclude a later suit on the theory that the plaintiff-spouse cannot split the cause of action.

b] If the court had no personal jurisdiction over the defendant-spouse in the divorce action, the court cannot affect any rights to support; thus, this issue will have to be settled in a separate action by a court having personal jurisdiction over both parties. However, there is a split in authority as to whether support can be granted in a subsequent action because the parties are no longer married.

2) Jurisdiction as to property rights.

a) In personam jurisdiction gives court power to order conveyances of property anywhere.
If the court has personal jurisdiction over both spouses, it can make a complete disposition of the spouses' property claims, even as to assets in other states; *i.e.*, it can order either spouse to make whatever conveyances of title are required and enforce such orders by contempt proceedings if necessary. (As to whether an F1 decree by itself is effective as to land in F2, *see supra*.)

b) In rem or quasi in rem jurisdiction.
Without personal jurisdiction over the defendant-spouse, a local court can exercise in rem or quasi in rem jurisdiction as to his local property only if the forum state is shown to have sufficient "minimum contacts" with the defendant and the subject of the litigation.

c) Effect of ex parte divorce on property rights.
Remember that even without personal jurisdiction over the defendant-spouse, an ex parte divorce is entitled to full faith and credit insofar as it terminates the marriage. [Williams I, *supra*] For example, if W's property rights depend upon her being married to H (*i.e.*, being his "wife" or "widow"), the ex parte divorce will be effective to cut off those property rights.

d) Applications.

(1) Property rights dependent on married status--Simons v. Miami Beach First National Bank, 381 U.S. 81 (1965).

Simons v. Miami Beach First National Bank

(a) Facts.
H and W, New York domiciliaries, separated. W obtained a New York separate maintenance decree. H moved to Florida where he was granted an ex parte divorce. H continued to honor the New York decree until his death. In the subsequent probate action, W argued that the Florida divorce did not abrogate her dower rights. The Florida court disagreed.

(b) Issue.
Are property rights, which depend on married status, extinguished by an ex parte divorce?

(c) Held.
Yes. Judgment affirmed.

1] The former wife is not entitled to dower rights in H's property because the marriage has been effectively dissolved by the ex parte divorce decree. Thus, she was no longer his "wife" at the time of his death (a prerequisite to dower).

(d) Comment.
This decision represents a retreat from the *Vanderbilt* decision, discussed briefly, *supra*.

(2) **Jurisdictional deficiencies.** In *Carr v. Carr*, 46 N.Y.2d 370 (1978), Ann Carr (P), a New York resident, allegedly married decedent, Paul Carr, in Nevada. Since he was in the foreign service, they resided in several countries during their marriage. While residing in Honduras, P left the decedent and eventually established residency in New York. Two years later, the decedent obtained an ex parte divorce in Honduras for abandonment. Barbara Carr (D) claimed that the decedent subsequently married her and petitioned the foreign service for survivor benefits. P brought suit to invalidate the Honduran divorce and establish her right to the survivor benefits. The trial court in New York ruled that it had no jurisdiction over D (who had no contacts with New York) and therefore dismissed P's claim. But the appellate division reversed on the basis that New York had an interest in adjudicating the marital rights of its citizens and New York was as "convenient" as other jurisdictions. The Court of Appeals dismissed for lack of personal jurisdiction over D. The court said P's status as a New York domiciliary did not provide a basis for exercising jurisdiction over the nonresident defendant, and the marital "res" necessary for in rem jurisdiction ends with the death of either marriage partner. Therefore New York would have had to establish that D had sufficient contacts with New York to allow in personam jurisdiction. Since D had no contacts, New York had no jurisdiction.

3. **Annulment.**

a. **Introduction.** The rationale for granting an annulment is that the marriage was never valid due to conditions that existed at the time that the marriage was performed.

b. **Jurisdiction.** Courts differ over the bases that are sufficient to permit a court to exercise jurisdiction.

1) **Place of marriage.** The early cases held that the place where the marriage was performed was the only state having jurisdiction. The rationale was that this was the place that brought the marriage into being and it should be the place determining the validity of the marriage. In addition, the court also had to have personal jurisdiction over both of the spouses. Some states still take this position.

2) **Domicile of the plaintiff-spouse.** Similar to the divorce area, many states exercise jurisdiction when the plaintiff-spouse is domiciled in the state. [*See* Restatement (Second) §76]

3) **Personal jurisdiction.** Some courts have allowed jurisdiction to be exercised when they have had a personal appearance by the plaintiff-spouse or when the plaintiff-spouse has had residence in the state. The rationale is that, unlike divorce (where there is a termination of legal status), annulment involves a situation where no status ever existed. Thus, in personam jurisdiction is sufficient.

a) **Domicile required when one party does not appear--Whealton v. Whealton,** 67 Cal. 2d 656 (1967).

    (1) **Facts.** H married W in Maryland. H, a serviceman, was transferred to California shortly thereafter. H sued for an annulment in California. Because W did not appear, the California court granted a default judgment. W appears to have the default judgment set aside.

    (2) **Issue.** May California annul the marriage when H was not a domiciliary of California and W did not appear?

    (3) **Held.** No. Judgment reversed.

        (a) An annulment differs conceptually from a divorce in that a divorce terminates a legal status (and hence some sort of jurisdiction over that status is required), whereas an annulment establishes that no such status ever existed. Consequently, in annulment actions, simple in personam jurisdiction is sufficient. But the domicile requirement still applies when one party does not appear. Since H did not establish that he was a California domiciliary and W did not appear, California did not have jurisdiction to annul the marriage.

b) **Public policy violations--Wilkins v. Zelichowski,** *supra.*

c. **Choice of law rule.** Normally, the courts apply the law of the place of marriage. The same exceptions apply as the law of marriage; *i.e.,* the court may decline to apply the law of the place of marriage if this law is contrary to the "laws of nature" or "strong public policy" of the forum.

4. Judicial Separation.

a. **Introduction.** Judicial separation is a decree by a court that the plaintiff need not cohabit with her spouse. The marital status is not terminated. Support and maintenance are also normally an issue.

b. **Jurisdiction.**

    1) As to support and maintenance, *Estin, supra,* indicated that personal jurisdiction of the defendant-spouse was necessary to affect property rights. It has been held, however, that quasi in rem jurisdiction is available as to property located in the state when a separate maintenance action is involved.

    2) As to cohabitation, the predominant rule today is that the domicile of the plaintiff-spouse (or other significant contact) is a sufficient basis for a court to exercise jurisdiction. [*See* Restatement (Second) §75]

c. **Choice of law rule.** Normally, the court applies its own law in determining the grounds for separation.

5. **Legitimation.**

   a. **Jurisdiction.**

      1) **Support.** In an action for support against a father during his lifetime (if the child's legitimacy is an issue), most courts now hold that personal jurisdiction over the father is necessary. Some courts hold, however, that such an action is an action in rem (since it is an action seeking to establish a status), and thus the plaintiff's residence or other significant contact with the forum is a sufficient basis for jurisdiction.

      2) **Inheritance.** In an inheritance case, if the question concerns the child's legitimacy, jurisdiction is based on the court's in rem power over the assets located in the state.

   b. **Choice of law.**

      1) **Legitimacy at birth.** The question of legitimacy at birth is a question of whether the parents were married at the time of the birth. Thus the question is one of legitimacy of marriage and is determined according to the rules discussed previously in the section on marriage. Note also that many states now have statutes which provide that even children of invalid marriages are deemed to be legitimate.

      2) **Legitimation after birth.**

         a) **Issue.** A claim may be made that a child whose parents were not married at birth has been legitimated subsequently by her father.

         b) **Restatement position.** The position of the Restatement (Second), section 287, is that the law of the father's domicile at the time of the legitimating acts is the governing law concerning the sufficiency of those acts. This is true even though the acts were done outside the state and even if the child was domiciled elsewhere. Note that some courts apply the law of the father's domicile at the time of the father's death rather than the law of the father's domicile at the time of the legitimating acts.

6. **Adoption of Children.**

   a. **Jurisdiction.**

      1) **Restatement position.** The position of the Restatement (Second), section 78, is that the domicile of the child is the only basis for jurisdiction in adoption proceedings. An exception is permitted if the adopted parents are domiciled locally and the court also has personal jurisdiction over the natural parents or guardian of the child.

      2) **Status approach.** On the basis that the issue is one of status (that of parent and child), some courts have exercised jurisdiction when the child is residing within the state and the forum state is also the domicile of the adoptive parents. Thus in these situations, courts

have not found it necessary that jurisdiction be obtained over the natural parents. The idea is that the res (the child) is before the court, giving it power to act in rem.

3) **Residency of child in forum state.** Some have suggested that the mere residence of the child in the forum state is a sufficient basis for jurisdiction.

4) **Notice to the natural parents.** In *Armstrong v. Manzo*, 380 U.S. 545 (1965), the Supreme Court held that the natural parents must be given adequate notice and an opportunity to be heard in adoption proceedings. This is a requirement of due process.

b. **Choice of law rule.** The forum always applies its own law since adoption is a statutory proceeding.

7. **Custody.**

a. **Jurisdiction.**

1) **Introduction.** The position of the Restatement (Second), section 79, is that a court may exercise jurisdiction whenever the child is residing or is physically present within the forum state, or when all persons having claim to custody are before the court. Thus, courts in two or more states may have concurrent jurisdiction. One court may exercise jurisdiction on the basis of the residence of the child; another court may exercise jurisdiction concurrently on the basis of having all persons with a claim to custody before the court. The case of *Sampsell v. Superior Court*, 32 Cal. 2d 763 (1948), held that the court having the "most substantial interest" in the case (generally the court where the child is present) should be the court to exercise jurisdiction in this kind of situation. The earlier view was that courts could exercise jurisdiction only when the domicile was within the forum state. The Supreme Court has not ruled clearly on what constitutes a sufficient basis for jurisdiction to determine custody. In fact, its decision in *May v. Anderson* has only confused the matter greatly.

a) **Personal jurisdiction required--May v. Anderson,** 345 U.S. 528 (1953).

May v. Anderson

(1) **Facts.** H and W, Wisconsin domiciliaries, separated, and W took the children to Ohio to contemplate her future. W decided she would not return the children. H subsequently sued for divorce and custody in Wisconsin. W was served but did not appear. Divorce and custody were granted to H, and the children were returned to Wisconsin. But when they visited W, she again refused to return them. H sued in Ohio for a writ of habeas corpus to have the children returned.

(2) **Issue.** Is the Wisconsin ex parte decree, granting custody to H, entitled to full faith and credit in Ohio, when the Wisconsin court had no personal jurisdiction over W?

(3) Held. No. Ohio does not have to recognize the custody decree.

    (a) Child custody proceedings are primarily disputes between the parents as to the right to custody of the children, which is an in personam right. Thus, personal jurisdiction over both parents is the requisite basis for jurisdiction; domicile of the children is irrelevant.

(4) Concurrence (Frankfurter, J.). The Full Faith and Credit Clause does not require Ohio to accept the disposition made by Wisconsin. Children have a very special place in life, which the law should reflect. A state has a responsibility for the welfare of children such that it is not foreclosed by a prior adjudication by another state at another time.

(5) Dissent (Jackson, Reed, JJ.). Domicile of one parent and the children should be sufficient to bestow jurisdiction for purposes of establishing custody. The jurisdictional test for custody ought to be the same as for divorce, not the same as for money judgments.

Quenzer v.
Quenzer

b) **Interplay of state and federal statutes--Quenzer v. Quenzer,** 653 P.2d 295 (1982).

    (1) Facts. Nola Quenzer (P) and Fred Quenzer (D) were divorced in Texas in 1975 and custody of their daughter was awarded to P. Shortly after the divorce, P moved to Oregon with the result that D was unable to exercise his visitation rights. In 1979, P moved to Alaska, and in June of 1980, while the daughter was visiting D in Texas, D filed a motion in the Texas district court seeking a modification in the custody award. P instituted a habeas corpus proceeding in the Texas court and the Texas court ordered D to return the child to P, who had taken up permanent residence in Wyoming. In January of 1981, trial was held on the modification issue and the court ruled that custody should be granted to D. The court found that it had jurisdiction, that P had not been a continuous resident of any state for six months preceding the filing of the action, that no court had or has continuing jurisdiction of the suit or of the child, and that Texas was the most convenient forum to determine the best interests of the child. In February of 1981, P commenced this action in Wyoming. The Wyoming court found that it had jurisdiction under the Wyoming Uniform Child Custody Jurisdiction Act and that the mother was the proper person to have custody of the child. D appeals, claiming that the Parental Kidnapping Prevention Act of 1980 prevents the Wyoming court from modifying the modification decree entered by the Texas court.

    (2) Issue. Is the Wyoming court prevented from modifying the Texas decree by the provisions of the Parental Kidnapping Prevention Act?

    (3) Held. No. Judgment of the lower court affirmed.

        (a) We recognize that when a child custody determination is made consistently with the provisions of the Act, that determination is required to be enforced according to its terms by the courts of every other state. A state court's determination is consistent with the Act only if the court had jurisdiction under the laws of such state and if one of four conditions is met: (i) the state is the home state of the child on the date the proceedings are commenced; (ii) no other state has jurisdiction under (i) and the child and her parents have a significant connection with the state; (iii) the child is present in the state; and (iv) no other state has jurisdiction under these conditions and it is in the best interest of the child that the forum state assume jurisdiction. If a court meets one of these conditions, the court has continuing jurisdiction pursuant to the Act. We hold that the Texas determination did not meet any of these conditions and, therefore, that the Wyoming court was not foreclosed from modifying the Texas decree.

(b) Under the provisions of the Wyoming Uniform Child Custody Jurisdiction Act, which are similar to those of the Parental Kidnapping Prevention Act, Wyoming is justified in its exercise of jurisdiction. Wyoming is now the home state of the child; she and her mother have resided in the state for more than six months. In addition, there now exists a significant connection with the state and substantial evidence of the child's care, protection, and relationship is available in Wyoming.

(c) We also hold that the Wyoming statute requiring recognition and enforcement of modification decrees made by courts of another state is not applicable. Under the statute, another state's custody decrees will not be modified unless it appears that the court that rendered the decree no longer has jurisdiction under standards similar to those in the Wyoming Uniform Child Custody Act. At the time Wyoming exercised its jurisdiction, the Texas court no longer had jurisdiction and Wyoming was the child's home state under the Wyoming Uniform Act. We conclude that Wyoming was the forum with the most significant connections with the child.

2) **Uniform Child Custody Jurisdiction Act.** All states have enacted the Uniform Child Custody Jurisdiction Act ("UCCJA") or its successor, the Uniform Child Custody Jurisdiction and Enforcement Act ("UCCJEA"), which provide one court with continuing jurisdiction over a child.

3) **Notice.** The Supreme Court held in *Stanley v. Illinois*, 405 U.S. 645 (1972), that natural parents must be given notice and an opportunity to be heard in any proceeding affecting custody of the child. In *Stanley*, the specific facts were that the unwed father was held entitled to notice of a hearing concerning his fitness as a parent in an action to determine custody of the child on the death of the mother.

8. **Enforcement of Support Orders.**

a. **Introduction.** A difficult issue as to "finality" is raised when an F1 alimony or child support decree is sought to be enforced in F2 and it appears that the decree is subject to modification in F1. (Those few alimony decrees that are not subject to modification are treated as "final" judgments and, hence, will be enforceable in F2 both as to amounts already due thereunder and as to all future payments.) Since the vast majority of alimony decrees are subject to modification on a showing of "changed circumstances," the question becomes: To what extent should the forum enforce the foreign alimony or child support decree?

b. **Past due installments.** At least when the accrued installments are no longer modifiable under the law of F1, full faith and credit applies; *i.e.*, the amounts past due under the F1 alimony or child support decree will be treated as sufficiently "final" for full faith and credit purposes, so that they can be enforced in F2, like any other money judgment.

1) **Note.** A different result may be obtained if the judgment was rendered in a state which allows retroactive modification of alimony or child support orders.

c. **Future installments.** From a constitutional standpoint, full faith and credit need not be given to future modifiable installments under an F1 alimony or child support order. *Rationale*: The fact that F1 reserved the power to modify its decree as to future installments means that the order is not "final" in F1.

d. **Applications.**

Kulko v.
California
Superior
Court

1) **Jurisdiction over nondomiciliary parent of a child domiciled in the forum--Kulko v. California Superior Court,** 436 U.S. 84 (1978).

a) **Facts.** Sharon Kulko (P) and her former husband, Ezra Kulko (D), both residents of New York, were married in California during D's three-day stopover on his way to Korea. Both continued to be domiciled in New York and lived there continuously for several years until they separated. The marriage produced two children who, under a written separation agreement drawn up in New York, were to remain in the custody of D except on specific holidays. P obtained a divorce decree in Haiti that retained the provisions of the separation agreement. P moved to San Francisco and both children subsequently decided they wanted to live with P rather than remain in D's custody in New York. One child had lived with P for about three years when the other decided he would also like to live with P. One month after his arrival, P commenced this suit to modify the Haitian divorce decree such that she got custody of the children and increased child support. D moved to quash service on the ground of lack of personal jurisdiction, but the motion was denied.

b) **Issue.** May the California state courts exercise in personam jurisdiction over a nonresident, nondomiciliary parent of a minor child domiciled in the state?

c) **Held.** No. Judgment reversed.

(1) A father who agrees, in the interest of family harmony and his children's preferences, to allow them to spend time in California

can hardly be said to have "purposefully availed himself" of the "benefits and protections" of California laws.

    (2)   The cause of action arises from D's personal, domestic relations, not from any commercial transactions.

    (3)   D has not received sufficient benefits from his children's presence in California to warrant personal jurisdiction under the "fair play and substantial justice" standard.

2)   **Final judgment for a lump sum payment.** *See Lynde v. Lynde, supra.*

3)   **Disposition binding on a nonresident third party.** *See Yarborough v. Yarborough, supra.*

4)   **Past due alimony not retroactively modifiable.** *See Barber v. Barber, supra.*

5)   **Modifiable decrees when both parties are before the court.** *See Worthley v. Worthley, supra.*

6)   **Personal jurisdiction requirement.** *See Estin v. Estin, supra.*

7)   **Support obligation accrued in other state--State of California v. Copus, 158 Tex. 196 (1958).**

> State of California v. Copus

    a)   **Facts.** In 1936, D's mother (Mrs. Copus) was adjudged mentally ill in California and committed to a state institution. Under a California statute, D was required to support his incompetent mother. In 1951, he moved to Texas, where the state of California (P) brought suit to compel D to continue support payments. The trial court required D to make up and continue payments on the grounds that D's move did not discharge his liability created by California law.

    b)   **Issue.** Will D be held liable in Texas for support payments accruing following his move to Texas?

    c)   **Held.** No. Judgment reversed.

        (1)   California law cannot create a legal obligation on a Texas citizen. But enforcement of the California law for the period that D was a California domiciliary does not violate Texas public policy. Therefore D will have to pay all payments that accrued within the four years (the California statute of limitations) prior to this action and that accrued while D was a California domiciliary.

    d)   **Dissent.** Texas should not become a haven for those seeking to escape their support obligations. D's obligation is continuing and should not be discharged merely by a move to Texas. Admittedly, the case would be easier had California complied with the Uniform Support Act.

e.   **Reciprocal Support Legislation.**

1) **Full Faith and Credit for Child Support Orders Act.** Under this Act, full faith and credit must be given to another court's child support order if the parties had reasonable notice and an opportunity to be heard. [28 U.S.C. §1738B]

2) **Uniform Interstate Family Support Act.** Under the Uniform Interstate Family Support Act ("UIFSA"), enacted in all 50 states, an F1 support order is subject to the same enforcement procedures in F2 as if it had been issued in F2. However, UIFSA limits the ability of F2 to modify the original support order. F2 can only enforce the order, unless the parties no longer reside in F1 or agree in writing that F2 may assert jurisdiction to modify the order.

9. Marital Property Interests.

a. **Introduction.** Marital property is that interest that a spouse acquires in real and personal property as a result of marriage. There are two basic systems under which states provide for marital property interests—common law (which prevails in most states) and community property. Common law protects the marital property interest by allowing a surviving spouse a portion of the decedent spouse's estate, which portion is not subject to reduction by testamentary disposition. The community property system provides that each spouse acquires, inter vivos, a one-half interest in community property (generally property acquired during marriage) that must be recognized upon dissolution of the marriage by death or divorce. "Conflicts" problems arise in litigating "marital interest" disputes because of the differences in the two systems and inconsistencies among the states applying either system.

b. **Applications.**

Rozan v.
Rozan

1) **Decisions that affect out-of-state land--Rozan v. Rozan,** 49 Cal. 2d 322 (1957).

a) **Facts.** W sued H for divorce, support, custody, and division of their community property. H and W became domiciled in California in July 1948. In 1949, H purchased properties in North Dakota, which were community property under California law. H, apparently in an attempt to defraud W of her community property interest, transferred the North Dakota property to his nephew. The California trial court ruled that W was entitled to 65% of the North Dakota property.

b) **Issue.** Did the forum exceed its jurisdiction when it granted a judgment affecting title to land in another state?

c) **Held.** No. Judgment affirmed, but modified.

(1) Although a court cannot directly determine title to land in another state, when the parties are before the court it can compel execution of conveyance between the parties according to its own law. In a majority of states, such actions are "res judicata" as to the rights and equities between the parties. This judgment would therefore be entitled to full faith and credit in North Dakota. However, to actually effect the change of title in North Dakota, W must bring an action on this judgment in that state. This judgment cannot actually transfer the property; it transfers only an entitlement that may be enforced in North Dakota. The judgment is so modified.

    d)   **Comment.** Compare *Fall v. Eastin*, *supra*, to which the court referred. In that case, the court decided that one state cannot directly affect title to land in another state. Does this decision violate that principle?

2)   **Property transferred to the forum with intent that forum law apply--Wyatt v. Fulrath,** 16 N.Y.2d 169 (1965).

Wyatt v. Fulrath

    a)   **Facts.** H and W were domiciliaries of Spain who deposited cash and securities in New York banks for safekeeping during the Spanish revolution. Under New York law, the accounts were held in joint ownership with rights of survivorship, as the parties agreed. But Spanish community property law voided such survivorship rights on the principle that one spouse could dispose of no more than one-half of the total estate. When H died in 1957, W took all the New York accounts and even transferred some additional money from London to New York. When W died in 1959, Wyatt (P), representing H's estate, sued Fulrath (D), representing W's estate, for the interest in the New York accounts that would not have gone to W under Spanish law.

    b)   **Issue.** May New York apply its own law to accounts placed in New York by foreign domiciliaries?

    c)   **Held.** Yes.

        (1)   Although the laws of the domicile are usually applied to these situations, New York, on grounds of its public policy, has the right to determine whether it will apply its own law to property placed in New York by foreign domiciliaries. If the parties clearly intended that New York law apply, New York will recognize that intent, even though the parties never were in New York. Therefore the property in the New York accounts upon H's death passed to W by right of survivorship. But the property transferred from London will be controlled by local law because that property was not transferred to New York with the expectation that New York law would apply to its disposition.

    d)   **Dissent.** The court should not ignore the rule that the law of the decedent's domicile controls the disposition of personal property and that the law of the matrimonial domicile controls property and contract rights between H and W. Besides, the fact that the parties signed standard forms that provide for right of survivorship (largely for the benefit of the bank creating the account) does not sufficiently evidence the parties' intent that New York law apply.

3) **Distinction between vested and survivorship rights--Estate of O'Connor,** 218 Cal. 518 (1933).

    a) **Facts.** H and W were domiciled and married in Indiana. H deserted W and went to California where he died, leaving his property (worth about $200,000) to a third person. In the California administration proceedings, W claimed a one-third interest allowed under Indiana law. The trial court sustained a demurrer to W's claim on the grounds that W had not acquired a vested right in H's property. W appeals.

    b) **Issue.** Must a community property state, where the decedent was domiciled at death, recognize a marital property interest that did not vest prior to the decedent's removal from the state of matrimonial domicile?

    c) **Held.** No. Demurrer affirmed.

        (1) In common law jurisdictions such as Indiana, W has an expectancy as heir when H dies, but W does not have vested ownership rights in H's personal property. There is a difference between an inchoate right (an expectancy) that gives a spouse a right to marital property only upon death of the other spouse and a vested right that gives a spouse ownership rights in marital property upon marriage. While the latter is not divested upon change of domicile, the former is subject to the law of the decedent's domicile at death. Since W concedes that the property would be "separate property" under California's community property scheme, W has no claim to it.

4) **Application of forum law to property acquired elsewhere--Addison v. Addison,** 62 Cal. 2d 558 (1965).

    a) **Facts.** H and W were married in Illinois, a common law state. When they moved to California, a community property state, they had acquired assets valued at $143,000, only a small part of which H claimed as his own prior to marriage. W obtained a divorce on the grounds of adultery. California had passed a statute that upon divorce or separate maintenance actions, property acquired outside the state that would have been community property if acquired in California would be quasi-community property, to be distributed one-half to each, unless divorce was granted for adultery or cruelty, in which case the court could exercise its discretion. W sued for division of the quasi-community property, but the trial court ruled the statute unconstitutional. W appeals.

    b) **Issue.** May the forum where the parties are domiciled constitutionally apply its own community property law to marital property acquired in another state that does not recognize community property?

    c) **Held.** Yes. Judgment reversed.

        (1) This quasi-community property statute is constitutional because it does not alter a vested property right merely on a change of domicile, as did statutes that have been held to violate "due process." Under the statute here, the property interest changes character only if the parties petition the California court for dissolution of the marriage. H had a full hearing and was found guilty of adultery. California had

sufficient interest in protecting W to distribute the property under its community law process.

    (2)   H also alleged violation of the "privileges and immunities" clause, but that clause is not violated if there is a valid reason for discrimination between citizens of one state and citizens of another. W had lost the protection of the common law state and needed California's protection.

L.   ADMINISTRATION OF DECEDENTS' ESTATES

1.   **Introduction.** The material here primarily concerns jurisdiction and the effect of judgments in probate proceedings involving local and foreign administrations.

2.   **Location of Administration.** There are several possible locations for the appointment of an executor and the probate of a will (or the appointment of an administrator if decedent died intestate):

    a.   **Domicile.** The Restatement (Second) indicates that the domicile of the decedent at death is a proper place to administer the estate. The administration here is known as the "principal" administration; the administration of assets located any place else is known as "ancillary" administration.

    b.   **Location of assets.** The Restatement also indicates that administration may occur wherever the decedent left any property, whether it be movable or immovable.

3.   **Administrator's Power Outside the State.** The general rule is that an administrator in one state has no power to act outside the state in which she has been appointed.

    a.   **Exception.** The Restatement (Second) indicates an exception to the general rule in the case of the protection of personal property prior to the appointment of ancillary administrators. Prior to her appointment, the domiciliary administrator may take possession of personal property and her administration of such will be recognized in other states.

    b.   **Power to sue.** However, the common law rule has been that an administrator cannot sue outside the state of her appointment. This is often an impractical rule, and some states have changed this result by statute.

4.   **Judgments and Their Effects Against Administrators.** Since normally an administrator in one state cannot sue or be sued in another state, a judgment in F1 is generally of no effect in a suit involving an administrator in F2. [Restatement (Second) §356] Therefore, if a plaintiff wins a judgment in F1 against the administrator there, it can only be enforced against the assets being administered in F1; if the plaintiff loses in F1, he can take his cause of action and sue in F2.

5. General Applications.

a. **Ancillary probate proceedings--Milmoe v. Toomey,** 123 U.S. App. D.C. 40 (1966).

    1) **Facts.** Milmoe's (P's) daughter, a member of the Peace Corps in Washington, D.C., rented a car there to travel to her home in New York. P's daughter was killed in an auto accident in Pennsylvania, as was a couple from Illinois. Toomey (D) was appointed by the D.C. court as an ancillary administrator in D.C. of the couple's rights in P's daughter's insurance policy on the rented car. P objects to the appointment on the grounds that the D.C. court lacked jurisdiction.

    2) **Issue.** May the forum institute ancillary probate proceedings if the personal property of a nondomiciliary is located in the forum?

    3) **Held.** Yes. D's appointment is upheld.

        a) By statute D.C. has the right to conduct an ancillary administration of the decedent's personal property located in D.C. Since the insurance policy, which is personal property, was purchased there and both the rental company and the insurance company are located there, it is subject to D.C. jurisdiction. A pending tort action in another state does not affect D.C.'s jurisdiction to appoint an administrator or probate the policy. The tort action essentially becomes a forum non conveniens case in which the judge decides whether D.C., Pennsylvania, or New York is the most appropriate forum.

b. **Appointment revoked for lack of domicile--*In re* Fischer's Estate,** 118 N.J. Eq. 599 (1935).

    1) **Facts.** The decedent died intestate in New Jersey survived by her husband and a brother. The husband was appointed administrator of his wife's estate based on his representation that she had been domiciled in New Jersey. Her brother (P) petitioned the New York court to be appointed as the decedent's administrator claiming that the decedent was domiciled in New York at the time of her death. The husband became mentally deranged and Mermelstein (D) was appointed in his stead and entered an appearance and answer in the proceeding. Under New Jersey intestate succession law, decedent's husband was entitled to all her property, but under New York law, P was entitled to a portion. D and the husband appeared in New York, where the issue of the decedent's domicile was fully and fairly litigated. The court found that the decedent was domiciled in New York and appointed P administrator. P petitioned the New Jersey court to be appointed as ancillary administrator in New Jersey.

    2) **Issue.** Is the New York decision entitled to full faith and credit such that New Jersey cannot continue to administer the decedent's estate?

    3) **Held.** Yes.

      a)   D's letters of administration are revoked in New Jersey and P is granted ancillary administration there. The law of the decedent's domicile governs intestate succession and that state must conduct general probate. Since all the parties appeared in New York and litigated the issue of the decedent's domicile, the New York final decree is entitled to full faith and credit in New Jersey. By New Jersey statute, the general or domiciliary administrator has the prior right to ancillary administration in New Jersey. The initial appointment of D in New Jersey is not binding on P since P did not appear to litigate the issue of domicile.

c.   **Relitigation of domicile by a nonparty.** *See Riley v. New York Trust Co.,* *supra.*

d.   **The problem of double liability--Wilkins v. Ellett, Administrator,** 108 U.S. 256 (1883).

Wilkins v. Ellett, Administrator

    1)   **Facts.** Decedent died in Alabama. The administrator appointed in Alabama collected a debt owed to the decedent from Wilkins (D), a Tennessee employer. Later, Ellett (P) was appointed in Tennessee as administrator of the same estate. When P sought recovery of the debt, D raised the defense of prior payment. The jury found that the decedent was domiciled in Tennessee and ordered payment. D appeals.

    2)   **Issue.** If a debtor voluntarily pays a debt in a state outside the state of the decedent's domicile, will the debt against the estate be discharged?

    3)   **Held.** Yes. Judgment reversed.

        a)   Succession to personalty is governed by the law of the decedent's domicile, which is also the proper place for principal estate administration. But ancillary jurisdiction may be had anywhere the decedent had property, although an administrator may sue to recover debt only where he has taken out administration. If a debtor voluntarily enters a state and pays an appointed administrator, the debt is discharged everywhere. The fact that the decedent was later found to be domiciled in Tennessee does not change the result.

    4)   **Comment.** Generally, courts will protect bailees, custodians, or debtors from double liability potentially caused by payment to out-of-state personal representatives if they have (i) no notice of a local personal representative and (ii) no actual notice of local creditors.

e.   **Aggregation of debts from several states allowed when decedent insolvent-- Estate of Hanreddy,** 176 Wis. 570 (1922).

Estate of Hanreddy

    1)   **Facts.** Decedent died testate in his state of residence, Illinois, where his widow (W) was appointed executor. W was also appointed executor of decedent's Wisconsin assets in an ancillary proceeding. In both states, the decedent's resident debts exceeded his resident assets. But the decedent's Wisconsin assets would cover about 90% of his Wisconsin debts, while his Illinois assets would only cover about 10% of his Illinois debts. W petitioned the Wisconsin court to allow her to aggregate the assets and pay creditors in both states an equal percentage. The Wisconsin court held that

the Wisconsin assets were a fund out of which Wisconsin creditors were to be fully paid before any could be applied to foreign debt and that the court lacked jurisdiction to consider foreign claims.

2) **Issue.** If the debts in several states are exceeded by the resident assets, may the court aggregate the assets so as to pay the creditors of each state equally?

3) **Held.** Yes. Judgment reversed.

a) Generally, resident debts are paid from resident assets in each state of administration, whether primary or ancillary. But if the decedent's total assets are less than his total liabilities, equity requires such aggregation.

Lenn v. Riche **f.** **Assets in ancillary forum as security for debts owing to ancillary forum's residents--Lenn v. Riche,** 331 Mass. 104 (1954).

1) **Facts.** Bonn gave a valuable painting to P in Germany. P loaned it back to Bonn in France for exhibit and preservation. Bonn died in France, where his wife was named "universal legatee." She refused to return the painting to P, and P brought this suit against decedent's ancillary administrator (D) in Massachusetts. P recovered, but D claims that under French law, P would have to bring suit against her personally and not the ancillary administrator.

2) **Issue.** Will the court where ancillary probate occurs allow its residents to secure foreign-made debts with the assets present in the forum?

3) **Held.** Yes. Judgment affirmed.

a) Although Bonn's debt arose in France, P may enforce it against the estate's assets in Massachusetts, since P is a Massachusetts resident. In Massachusetts, the administrator (D) is liable to suits on the debts of the deceased owing to Massachusetts creditors, who are entitled to secure such debts with the decedent's assets in Massachusetts.

Ghilain v. Couture **g.** **Exception to rule that administrator may not sue outside state where appointed--Ghilain v. Couture,** 84 N.H. 48 (1929).

1) **Facts.** Decedent, a resident of Massachusetts, was killed in an auto accident in New Hampshire. Ghilain (P), general administrator in Massachusetts, sued Couture (D), a New Hampshire driver, in New Hampshire for wrongful death. The New Hampshire statute required such actions to be brought by the "administrator of the deceased party." The trial court granted recovery to P. D appeals on the ground that P was the decedent's administrator only in Massachusetts, where P was appointed, and not in New Hampshire.

2) **Issue.** Will the court interpret the statutory language to include administrators not appointed in the forum?

3) **Held.** Yes. Judgment affirmed.

a) The purpose of the rule that an administrator cannot sue outside the state of his appointment is to protect resident creditors from withdrawal of the decedent's assets to another state. The wrongful death statute in question clearly would not have incorporated a rule whose sole justification was to protect local creditors, an entirely different matter. The denial of the right to sue must rest on some principle of public policy and in this situation there is no public policy reason to deny P the right to sue.

h. **Long-arm statute does not wither upon death of decedent--Eubank Heights Apartments, Ltd. v. Lebow,** 615 F.2d 571 (1st Cir. 1980).

Eubank Heights Apartments, Ltd. v. Lebow

1) **Facts.** In 1972, Saul Lebow executed in Massachusetts a limited partnership agreement and six promissory notes. Eubank Heights Apartments (P), the payee, was a Texas partnership created under Texas law and with its principal office in Texas. Lebow, a Massachusetts resident, died in March 1973, and his wife (D) was appointed executrix. P did not learn of Lebow's death until 1974 and then exercised its right to make the notes payable in Texas by notifying D. In December 1974, P brought suit on the notes in Texas naming the Estate of Saul Lebow as defendant. D made no response after being served and a default judgment was entered against the estate. P brought an action on the judgment against D in the district court of Massachusetts and was granted summary judgment, from which D appeals.

2) **Issue.** Was the judgment obtained in Texas valid against estate assets in Massachusetts?

3) **Held.** Yes. Judgment affirmed.

a) In *Saporita v. Litner*, a Massachusetts creditor obtained a judgment in Massachusetts against a Connecticut executor. The Massachusetts court upheld this procedure and we here hold that since Texas would likely honor a Massachusetts judgment, Massachusetts could not refuse to recognize the Texas judgment.

6. **Applications When the Decedent Is Insolvent.**

a. **Discrimination against nonresident creditors--Blake v. McClung,** 172 U.S. 239 (1898).

Blake v. McClung

1) **Facts.** An English mining company doing business in Tennessee became insolvent. Several classes of creditors filed claims in Tennessee against the company, including British creditors, Ohio creditors, a Virginia corporation, and Tennessee creditors. By Tennessee statute, Tennessee creditors had priority in the distribution of the company's assets. The nonresident creditors objected to the subordination of their interests to those of resident creditors. The state court applied the statute and gave the Tennessee creditors priority. That judgment was appealed to the United States Supreme Court.

2)   **Issue.** Is the Constitution violated when, in an insolvency proceeding, the forum grants a preference in the local assets to resident creditors?

3)   **Held.** Yes. Judgment reversed in part.

   a)   The Tennessee statute violates the "privileges and immunities" of the nonresident creditors. A state may take possession of the assets of a foreign corporation doing business within its borders. But the interests of out-of-state creditors cannot be subordinated to those of resident creditors in the distribution of the assets. A state may retain assets of a corporation to prevent injustice to its citizens, but it may not discriminate against outsiders in so doing.

4)   **Comment.** The Federal Bankruptcy Act has solved most conflicts problems by supplanting the old state receivership administration of insolvent estates. But it does not apply to municipal, insurance, or banking corporations, which are still hampered by interstate conflicts problems.

Morris v.
Jones

b.   Full faith and credit applied to foreign debt resolution--Morris v. Jones, 329 U.S. 545 (1947).

1)   **Facts.** Chicago Lloyds conducted an insurance business in several states including Illinois and Missouri. Jones (P) sued Chicago Lloyds in Missouri for malicious prosecution and false arrest. Prior to judgment, Chicago Lloyds became insolvent; Morris (D) was appointed as its statutory liquidator in Illinois, and the Illinois court issued a stay against all suits against Chicago Lloyds. Under D's direction, counsel withdrew from the Missouri suit. P was granted a default judgment in Missouri, which P sought to have enforced against D in Illinois. The Illinois courts refused, and P appeals.

2)   **Issue.** Is the Missouri judgment entitled to full faith and credit in Illinois?

3)   **Held.** Yes. Judgment reversed.

   a)   The Missouri judgment merely established the nature and amount of P's claim; it does not order distribution of the insolvent's assets. Since these issues are distinct, Illinois must recognize the debt but does not need to immediately enforce its payment. Since the Missouri court had jurisdiction over the subject matter and the parties, the issue of the amount of the debt is res judicata. If D wanted to argue that the Illinois decree was entitled to full faith and credit in Missouri, he should have raised that defense in the Missouri court.

4)   **Dissent** (Frankfurter, Black, Rutledge, JJ.). The real issue is whether a state may require out-of-state creditors (whose debts have not been reduced to judgment) to prove to the state's satisfaction that they are entitled to payment. The principle of full faith and credit should not be mechanically applied to the detriment of powers reserved to the states by the Constitution. The court should also consider the hardship of requiring out-of-state creditors to appear. On balance, the judgment should be affirmed.

c. **Receivers granted extraterritorial powers--Converse v. Hamilton,** 224 U.S. 243 (1912).

1) **Facts.** A Minnesota corporation became insolvent and a receiver was appointed. A Minnesota statute provided for double liability of the stockholders. The court levied on the corporation's stockholders for the full par value of their shares and directed Converse (P), the receiver, to prosecute such actions. P brought suit in Wisconsin to levy on the Wisconsin stockholders, who were not made parties to the Wisconsin suit. Hamilton (D), a Wisconsin stockholder, successfully defended on the grounds that enforcement violated Wisconsin policy.

2) **Issue.** Must Wisconsin grant full faith and credit to the Minnesota judgment that allowed P to sue for double liability outside of Minnesota?

3) **Held.** Yes. Judgment Reversed.

a) D's liability is not a penal liability imposed against the corporation; it is a contractual liability to the corporation's creditors. The receiver has greater power than most common law receivers who are merely arms of the court; in this case, the receiver is the quasi-assignee and representative of the creditors to whom D owes a contractual obligation. The judgment in Minnesota was not in the nature of a personal judgment to which D is subject without being a party. Rather, the judgment was a statement of the corporation's contractual obligations to its creditors which the corporation adequately defended.

d. **Statutory denial of full faith and credit--Broderick v. Rosner,** 294 U.S. 629 (1935).

1) **Facts.** New York had a statute imposing personal liability upon stockholders and granting the Superintendent of Banks (P) the power to sue anywhere to enforce such liability when a bank became insolvent. P exercised this prerogative following administrative resolution of a bank's insolvency and levied against the bank's stockholders in New Jersey. The New Jersey court refused to levy against its residents, relying on a statute that denied jurisdiction unless all creditors and stockholders were made party to the suit. This was a practical impossibility, and P appeals.

2) **Issue.** May the New Jersey statute operate to deny full faith and credit to the New York administrative decision concerning the liability of the shareholders?

3) **Held.** No. Judgment reversed.

a) New Jersey cannot deny full faith and credit to the New York decision by passing a statute that effectively denies jurisdiction to enforce foreign judgments in New Jersey. The liability incurred by the stockholders is contractual and assessment of it is an incidence of incorporation in New York. Since New Jersey courts possess general jurisdiction over the subject matter and New Jersey policy cannot control, New Jersey must enforce the New York decision.

M. NONCORPORATE BUSINESS ASSOCIATIONS: AGENCY AND PARTNERSHIP

1. **Introduction.** This section deals primarily with the choice of law problems in determining the rights and responsibilities of a principal or partner vis-a-vis some third party with whom an agent or partner has done business. It also covers conflicts problems in disputes among partners or between an agent and the principal.

2. **The First Restatement Approach.**

   a. **General choice of law rule.** The liability of the principal or partner vis-a-vis a third party will be governed by the law where the agent, principal, or partner performed the acts in question.

Mercier v.
John Hancock
Mutual Life
Insurance Co.

   b. **Law where agent acts governs--Mercier v. John Hancock Mutual Life Insurance Co.,** 141 Me. 376 (1945).

      1) **Facts.** Mercier (P) sued to recover on a life insurance policy procured in Maine. The insurance company (D) refused to pay on the basis that the insured materially misrepresented his physical condition when he made application and failed to disclose his diabetic condition and that his brother had tuberculosis. P contended that the agent was informed of the diabetes but assured the insured that there was no need to mention it in the application and that the agent had not inquired as to the brother's health. The evidence was contradictory, so the judge let the jury decide. Judgment was for P. D appeals.

      2) **Issue.** Will the law where the agent acts govern the issue of whether the principal is bound?

      3) **Held.** Yes. Judgment affirmed.

         a) Although D contends that this is a Massachusetts contract and therefore not subject to Maine law, the agency (and not the contract) is at issue. Since the acts of the agent occurred in Maine, Maine's law, which provides that D may not rely as a defense on misrepresentations known to the agent, applies. The court adopts the First Restatement position that the principal is bound by the acts of the agent (acting with apparent authority), and the issue of authorization is governed by the law where the agent acts.

3. **The Restatement (Second) Approach.**

   a. **General rules.**

      1) **Liabilities between agent and principal.** Agencies are usually created by contract. In such situations, the contractual liabilities between the principal and the agent will be governed by the law of the state with the "most significant relationship to the parties and the transaction," the same as other contracts. [Restatement (Second) §291]

2) **Contractual liabilities vis-a-vis third parties.** Whether a principal is bound by action taken on his behalf by an agent in dealing with a third person is determined by the local law of the state which, with respect to the particular issue, has the most significant relationship to the parties and the transaction.

4. Applications.

a. Contracts to create a partnership in another state--First National Bank of Waverly v. Hall, 150 Pa. 466 (1892).

First National
Bank of
Waverly
v. Hall

1) **Facts.** Hall (D), among others, agreed to finance a New York toy factory for Crandall (D) in return for payments, a share of the profits until the loan was paid, and a security interest in the machinery and fixtures of the business. The agreement was made in Pennsylvania. When Crandall defaulted on notes owing to First National Bank of Waverly (P), P sued to hold both Hall and Crandall jointly liable as partners. Hall defended on the grounds that the contract with Crandall denied that they were partners and that Hall did not participate in the management of the business. P contests a decision which applied New York law.

2) **Issue.** Should the issue of creation of a partnership be governed by the law that would govern the agreement between Crandall and Hall?

3) **Held.** Yes. Judgment affirmed.

a) The issue of the creation of this partnership would be governed by the law where the factory was being built (New York). The trial court appropriately applied New York law to conclude that the contract between Hall and Crandall did not create a partnership as to third persons.

4) **Comment.** Contract formation issues are generally governed by the laws of the state where the contract was entered (Pennsylvania). This case apparently was decided on agency principles, which require the application of the law where the agent acted (New York).

b. Reasonable reliance on a foreign limited partner--Barrows v. Downs & Co., 9 R.I. 446 (1870).

Barrows v.
Downs & Co.

1) **Facts.** Barrows and Meriden Britannia Company (Ps) are suing Downs & Co. (D), a Cuban partnership, to recover past due accounts. Service could be had only on William Downs, who claims that he was only a "special" (limited) partner under Cuban law. Ps offer evidence that William came to New York and represented himself as a general partner and therefore Ps contend that D is liable for the full amount.

2) **Issue.** Is an agent who conducts business as a general partner liable under the laws where the agent conducted the business?

3) **Held.** Yes. Judgment for Ps in the full amount of the debt.

a)   If a general partner (or someone representing himself as such) goes abroad to conduct business, he is liable for the whole amount. This is true although under the law where the partnership is located (Cuba), the agent is only a "special" or limited partner.

c.   **A shareholders' derivative suit--Greenspun v. Lindley,** 36 N.Y.2d 473 (1975).

1)   **Facts.** Greenspun and others (Ps) sought to bring a shareholders' derivative suit against a Massachusetts real estate investment trust of which Lindley (D) was a trustee. Contrary to the trust agreement, the trustees had appointed an insurance company (in which several of the trustees were officers) to manage the trust. Ps sought to recover excessive management fees and profits realized by the defendant trustees. The trial court dismissed on the grounds that Massachusetts law required the plaintiff to make direct demands on the trustees before commencing suit. The appellate division affirmed. Ps appeal.

2)   **Issue.** Will Massachusetts law apply to the relationship between a Massachusetts business entity and its foreign shareholders?

3)   **Held.** Yes. Order affirmed.

a)   The declaration of trust expressly provides that Massachusetts law should apply; the shareholders voluntarily invested in the Massachusetts trust; and there are practical advantages to deciding the rights of the shareholders under a single body of law. However, this does not mean that another state's law could not be applied if significant contacts were proven. Under Massachusetts law, the shareholders in the trust will be treated as shareholders in a Massachusetts corporation and therefore must meet the conditions precedent to institution of a shareholders' derivative suit.

N. CORPORATIONS

1.   **Approaches.**

a.   **Traditional approach.** Traditionally, all rights and obligations respecting a corporation were deemed "created" by the law of the place of its incorporation, and reference was therefore made to its laws.

b.   **Most significant relationship approach.** The Restatement (Second) continues to apply the law of the state of incorporation to many conflicts questions, such as the creation and dissolution of a corporation and the liability of its shareholders for assessments.

c.   **Policy-oriented approaches.** Again, these approaches do not treat choice of law issues respecting corporations differently from other choice of law issues.

2.   Common Issues.

a.   **Capacity to sue.** The general choice of law rule applies; capacity is determined by the law of the state of incorporation. [*See* FRCP 17(b)]

1)   **State "qualification" requirements.** Keep in mind that if a foreign corporation is doing business locally, it must "qualify" in the state (pay local filing fees, etc.) and comply with local, nondiscriminatory regulations. If it fails to do so, it may be denied the right to sue or defend itself in local courts.

2)   **Constitutional limitation.** Such regulations cannot constitutionally be applied to corporations that do not operate regularly within the state, and whose intrastate activities are merely "fleeting events" in otherwise purely interstate business transactions.

3)   **Applications.**

a)   **State qualification requirements--Eli Lilly & Co. v. Sav-On-Drugs, Inc.,** 366 U.S. 276 (1961).

Eli Lilly & Co. v. Sav-On-Drugs, Inc.

(1)   **Facts.** Eli Lilly (P), an Indiana corporation, sued Sav-On-Drugs (D), a New Jersey corporation, in New Jersey to enjoin D from selling P's products below the contractually fixed minimum retail price. D moved to dismiss on the grounds that P had not met the New Jersey statutory requirement that, for a foreign corporation to sue in New Jersey, it had to obtain a certificate authorizing it to do business in the state. P opposed the motion on the grounds that its business was entirely interstate and therefore New Jersey could not regulate it without violating the Commerce Clause. Both the trial court and the New Jersey Supreme Court ruled that P was involved in intrastate commerce and granted the motion to dismiss.

(2)   **Issue.** May the forum apply state qualifications to a corporation involved in both interstate and intrastate commerce?

(3)   **Held.** Yes. Affirmed.

(a)   It is well established that New Jersey cannot place requirements on wholly interstate sales to New Jersey wholesalers; however, New Jersey can place requirements on foreign corporations who are involved in intrastate commerce. Although P is primarily an interstate wholesaler, the court would have to ignore reality to conclude that P was not doing business in New Jersey. It staffs an office in Newark with 18 "detailmen" who travel intrastate soliciting wholesale business directly, encouraging retailers to purchase from intrastate wholesalers, and taking orders that they transfer to intrastate wholesalers.

(b) P also contends that the suit arises out of the interstate aspects of its business, but its contract with D is "separable" from any particular interstate sale.

(4) Concurrence (Harlan, J.). The difference between P's activities in New Jersey and purely interstate "drumming" (which cannot be regulated by the state) is that P has done more than solicit direct sales from itself (as an out-of-state seller); P has solicited local sales by its local wholesalers.

(5) Dissent (Douglas, Frankfurter, Whittaker, Stewart, JJ.). The issue here is whether an interstate business can be subjected to a state licensing system. The majority draws a superfluous distinction between "drumming up" interstate trade by direct contact to wholesalers (which is not subject to state regulation) and soliciting such business indirectly by contact with retailers.

b) Appointment of an agent as an undue burden on interstate commerce. *See Sioux Remedy Co. v. Cope, supra.*

Union Brokerage Co. v. Jensen

c) A federal license that failed to immunize against state regulation-- Union Brokerage Co. v. Jensen, 322 U.S. 202 (1944).

(1) Facts. Union Brokerage (P), a North Dakota corporation, was licensed under federal statute to do business in Minnesota. However, P had not obtained a certificate that was required by Minnesota statute before P could have access to Minnesota courts. P attempted to sue two former employees in Minnesota for breach of fiduciary duty. The trial court dismissed because P had not obtained a Minnesota certificate. P appeals on the basis that the Minnesota statute (which required filing, paying a fee, and appointing an agent) was an undue burden on a federally licensed instrumentality.

(2) Issue. Does the fact that P is federally licensed immunize P against nondiscriminatory state regulation?

(3) Held. No. Judgment affirmed.

(a) The fact that the federal government has licensing privileges over those engaged in the commonhouse brokerage business does not preclude the state from imposing nondiscriminatory regulations for the purpose of protecting its citizens in the course of business with outsiders. The state and the federal regulations operate in separate spheres.

b. Corporate powers and liabilities. Most questions as to a corporation's powers, purposes, capacity to contract or hold title to property, regulation of internal affairs, etc., fall under the general choice of law rule, *i.e.*, referring to the law of the place of incorporation. [Restatement (Second) §302]

c. Liabilities of officers, directors, and controlling shareholders. The law of the place of incorporation applies to acts that affect the corporate structure issues (*e.g.*, liability for issuing "watered" stock or dividends from illegal source).

[Restatement (Second) §309] However, if claims involve transactions, such as seizing a corporate opportunity, making a contract, or committing a tort, the forum or some other state may have an interest in regulating this conduct. [Restatement (Second) §301]

1) Thus, in determining questions of alter egos (whether officers and directors are personally liable for corporate debts), reference may be to the place of contracting rather than the place of incorporation. [Restatement (Second) §302]

3. Limitation—Forum Statutes or Public Policy.

a. **Introduction.** The general choice of law rule (law of state of incorporation) will not be applied to uphold some transaction that would be contrary to the forum's own statutes or strong public policy. Actually, this limitation reflects the shift in case law, which recognizes that a state other than that of incorporation may have a legitimate interest in regulating the affairs of a foreign corporation.

b. **Applications.**

1) **The forum's control over foreign corporations--German-American Coffee Co. v. Diehl,** 216 N.Y. 57 (1915).

German-American Coffee Co. v. Diehl

a) **Facts.** German-American Coffee Co. (P), a New Jersey corporation that conducted its business primarily in New York, sued in New York to recover an illegal dividend from one of its directors. In New Jersey, the corporation could not sue its directors, but New York allowed such actions. A New York statute also provided that foreign corporations and their officers, directors, etc. doing business in New York were subject to the same liabilities as applied to New York corporations and their officers, directors, etc. The trial court decided that the statute was constitutional and allowed P to sue in New York. D appeals.

b) **Issue.** May the forum court allow a cause of action that is not recognized in the state of incorporation?

c) **Held.** Yes. Judgment affirmed.

(1) When a foreign corporation comes into a state and transacts business there, it must obey that state's laws, and for many purposes the laws of the state of incorporation are to be disregarded. In modern times, when corporations are organized on paper in one state and conduct their business in another, public policy demands that the state where business is conducted be invested with a measure of control—even when the prohibited acts occur in the state of incorporation but have repercussions where business actually takes place. In effect, a state that is not the state of incorporation may impose conditions on the right to do business in the state.

Western
Airlines, Inc.
v. Sobieski

2) **Application of the forum's public policy--Western Airlines, Inc. v. Sobieski,** 191 Cal. App. 2d 399 (1961).

    a) **Facts.** Western Airlines (P), originally a California corporation, desired to eliminate cumulative voting for directors. Cumulative voting was required in California and included in the provisions of the articles of incorporation. A corporation was therefore established in Delaware (where cumulative voting was not required) to acquire Western's assets. The California Commissioner of Corporations would allow a shareholder vote on the issue of cumulative voting only on condition that before amending Western's articles of incorporation (which provided for cumulative voting) in Delaware, a hearing would be held in California to determine the "fairness" of the amendment. When the hearing was later held, the Commissioner ruled that the amendment was "unfair" and disallowed it. Despite the fact that Western's major business remained in California, P objects to the Commissioner's ruling.

    b) **Issue.** If the major thrust of P's business remained in California, may the California court refuse to enforce the law of the state of incorporation (Delaware) when enforcement would violate its strong public policy?

    c) **Held.** Yes. Ruling upheld.

        (1) We refuse to permit a Delaware corporation to solicit shareholder approval for the amendment to its articles of incorporation that would eliminate cumulative voting for directors. Even though the amendment would be permitted under Delaware law, California has a legitimate interest in the matter—the corporation's principal business is in California and many shareholders reside here; the corporation, in fact, does not transact any business in Delaware. Hence, California law (prohibiting such amendment) applies.

Edgar v.
MITE Corp.

3) **State statute imposes burden on interstate commerce; interest balancing test--Edgar v. MITE Corp.,** 457 U.S. 624 (1982).

    a) **Facts.** MITE Corp. and its wholly owned subsidiary, MITE Holdings, Inc. (P), are Delaware corporations with their principal offices in Connecticut. James Edgar (D), Secretary of State of Illinois, is charged with enforcement of the Illinois Act regulating any takeover offer for the shares of a target company. A target company is defined as a corporation or other issuer of securities of which Illinois shareholders own 10% of the class of equity securities subject to the offer, or for which two of the following three conditions are met: the corporation (i) has its principal executive office in Illinois, (ii) is organized under the laws of Illinois, or (iii) has at least 10% of its stated capital and paid-in surplus represented within the state. Under the Act, the secretary may call a hearing within the 20-day waiting period prior to registration of the offer to adjudicate the fairness of an offer, and a hearing must be held if requested by a majority of the target company's outside directors or if requested by Illinois shareholders who own 10% of the class of securities subject to the offer. If a hearing is held, the secretary may deny registration if he finds the tender offer fails to provide full and fair disclosure, is inequitable, or would work a fraud upon the offerees.

P initiated a cash offer for all outstanding shares of Chicago Rivet by filing with the S.E.C. in compliance with the Williams Act but did not comply with the Illinois Act. On the day of its offer, P requested a declaratory judgment that the Illinois Act was preempted by the Williams Act and violated the Commerce Clause and further requested a temporary restraining order and injunctions prohibiting D from enforcing the Illinois Act. The district court found the Illinois Act invalid under the Commerce Clause. D appeals.

b)   **Issues.**

(1)   Is the Illinois Act preempted by the Williams Act?

(2)   Does the Illinois Act violate the Commerce Clause?

c)   **Held.** (1) Yes. (2) Yes. Judgment affirmed.

(1)   Even when a state statute regulates interstate commerce indirectly, under the *Pike v. Bruce Church* test, the burden imposed upon that commerce must not be excessive in relation to the local interests served by the statute. The Illinois Act purports to give that state the power to determine whether a tender offer may proceed anywhere and is, therefore, unconstitutional.

(2)   None of the reasons advanced by D in support of the Illinois Act outweigh its burden on interstate commerce. The shareholders' position is not enhanced in any way not already provided for by the Williams Act, and the Illinois Act may in fact increase the risk that a tender offer will fail due to potential delays imposed. Insofar as regulating the internal affairs of an Illinois corporation, tender offers do not implicate the internal affairs of a target company. Furthermore, the reach of the Illinois Act goes beyond Illinois corporations in that it applies to tender offers for any corporation for which 10% of the outstanding shares are held by Illinois residents.

4)   **Legitimate state concerns reflected--CTS Corp. v. Dynamics Corp. of America,** 481 U.S. 69 (1987).

CTS Corp.
v. Dynamics
Corp. of
America

a)   **Facts.** The "Control Share Acquisitions Chapter" of the Indiana Business Corporation Law applies to corporations that: (i) are incorporated in Indiana, (ii) have at least 100 shareholders, (iii) have their principal office or substantial assets in Indiana, (iv) have either 10,000 or 10% of their shareholders being Indiana residents, or (v) have more than 10% of their shares owned by Indiana residents. When the acquisition of shares in a company covered by the Act would bring the acquiror's voting power above specified levels, voting rights will not accompany the acquisition unless a majority of the preexisting shareholders agree. Dynamics Corp. made a tender offer that would have raised its ownership in CTS above the level specified by the Act. Dynamics sought declaratory relief and both the district court and court of appeals found that the Indiana statute was preempted by the Williams Act and that it violated the Commerce Clause.

b)   **Issues.**

(1)   Does the Indiana statute violate the Commerce Clause?

(2)   Is the Indiana statute preempted by the Williams Act?

c)   **Held.** (1) No. (2) No. Judgment reversed.

(1)   The Indiana statute has the same effects on tender offers whether or not the offeror is a domiciliary or resident of Indiana. Also, the statute does not affect interstate commerce by subjecting activities to inconsistent regulations. So long as each state regulates voting rights only in the corporations it has created, each corporation will be subject to the law of only one state. It is a firmly established principle of corporation law that a state has the authority to regulate domestic voting rights of shareholders. The Indiana statute applies only to corporations incorporated in Indiana that have a substantial number of shareholders in Indiana; every application of the Act will affect a substantial number of Indiana residents whom Indiana indisputably has an interest in protecting.

TABLE OF CASES

(Page numbers of briefed cases in bold)

Notes

Publications Catalog

Publishers of America's Most Popular Legal Study Aids!

All Titles Available At Your Law School Bookstore.

Gilbert Law Summaries are the best selling outlines in the country, and have set the standard for excellence since they were first introduced more than twenty-five years ago. It's Gilbert's unique combination of features that makes it the one study aid you'll turn to for all your study needs!

Accounting and Finance for Lawyers
Professor Thomas L. Evans, University of Texas

Basic Accounting Principles; Definitions of Accounting Terms; Balance Sheet; Income Statement; Statement of Changes in Financial Position; Consolidated Financial Statements; Accumulation of Financial Data; Financial Statement Analysis.
ISBN: 0-15-900382-2   Pages: 136 $19.95

Administrative Law
By Professor Michael R. Asimow, U.C.L.A.

Separation of Powers and Controls Over Agencies; (including Delegation of Power) Constitutional Right to Hearing (including Liberty and Property Interests Protected by Due Process, and Rulemaking- Adjudication Distinction); Adjudication Under Administrative Procedure Act (APA); Formal Adjudication (including Notice, Discovery, Burden of Proof, Finders of Facts and Reasons); Adjudicatory Decision Makers (including Administrative Law Judges (ALJs), Bias, Improper Influences, Ex Parte Communications, Familiarity with Record, Res Judicata); Rulemaking Procedures (including Notice, Public Participation, Publication, Impartiality of Rulemakers, Rulemaking Record); Obtaining Information (including Subpoena Power, Privilege Against Self-incrimination, Freedom of Information Act, Government in Sunshine Act, Attorneys' Fees); Scope of Judicial Review; Reviewability of Agency Decisions (including Mandamus, Injunction, Sovereign Immunity, Federal Tort Claims Act); Standing to Seek Judicial Review and Timing.
ISBN: 0-15-900000-9   Pages: 278 $20.95

Agency and Partnership
By Professor Richard J. Conviser, Chicago Kent

Agency: Rights and Liabilities Between Principal and Agent (including Agent's Fiduciary Duty, Right to Indemnification); Contractual Rights Between Principal (or Agent) and Third Persons (including Creation of Agency Relationship, Authority of Agent, Scope of Authority, Termination of Authority, Ratification, Liability on

Agents, Contracts); Tort Liability (including Respondeat Superior, Master-Servant Relationship, Scope of Employment). Partnership: Property Rights of Partner; Formation of Partnership; Relations Between Partners (including Fiduciary Duty); Authority of Partner to Bind Partnership; Dissolution and Winding up of Partnership; Limited Partnerships.
ISBN: 0-15-900327-X   Pages: 149 $17.95

Antitrust
By Professor Thomas M. Jorde, U.C. Berkeley, Mark A. Lemley, University of Texas, and Professor Robert H. Mnookin, Harvard University

Common Law Restraints of Trade; Federal Antitrust Laws (including Sherman Act, Clayton Act, Federal Trade Commission Act, Interstate Commerce Requirement, Antitrust Remedies); Monopolization (including Relevant Market, Purposeful Act Requirement, Attempts and Conspiracy to Monopolize); Collaboration Among Competitors (including Horizontal Restraints, Rule of Reason vs. Per Se Violations, Price Fixing, Division of Markets, Group Boycotts); Vertical Restraints (including Tying Arrangements); Mergers and Acquisitions (including Horizontal Mergers, Brown Shoe Analysis, Vertical Mergers, Conglomerate Mergers); Price Discrimination— Robinson-Patman Act; Unfair Methods of Competition; Patent Laws and Their Antitrust Implications; Exemptions From Antitrust Laws (including Motor, Rail, and Interstate Water Carriers, Bank Mergers, Labor Unions, Professional Baseball).
ISBN: 0-15-900328-8   Pages: 210 $18.95

Bankruptcy
By Professor Ned W. Waxman, College of William and Mary

Participants in the Bankruptcy Case; Jurisdiction and Procedure; Commencement and Administration of the Case (including Eligibility, Voluntary Case, Involuntary Case, Meeting of Creditors, Debtor's Duties); Officers of the Estate (including

Trustee, Examiner, United States Trustee); Bankruptcy Estate; Creditor's Right of Setoff; Trustee's Avoiding Powers; Claims of Creditors (including Priority Claims and Tax Claims); Debtor's Exemptions; Nondischargeable Debts; Effects of Discharge; Reaffirmation Agreements; Administrative Powers (including Automatic Stay, Use, Sale, or Lease of Property); Chapter 7- Liquidation; Chapter 11-Reorganization; Chapter 13-Individual With Regular Income; Chapter 12- Family Farmer With Regular Annual Income.
ISBN: 0-15-900442-X   Pages: 311 $21.95

Business Law
By Professor Robert D. Upp, Los Angeles City College

Torts and Crimes in Business; Law of Contracts (including Contract Formation, Consideration, Statute of Frauds, Contract Remedies, Third Parties); Sales (including Transfer of Title and Risk of Loss, Performance and Remedies, Products Liability, Personal Property Security Interest); Property (including Personal Property, Bailments, Real Property, Landlord and Tenant); Agency; Business Organizations (including Partnerships, Corporations); Commercial Paper; Government Regulation of Business (including Taxation, Antitrust, Environmental Protection, and Bankruptcy).
ISBN: 0-15-900005-X   Pages: 277 $17.95

California Bar Performance Test Skills
By Professor Peter J. Honigsberg, University of San Francisco

Hints to Improve Writing; How to Approach the Performance Test; Legal Analysis Documents (including Writing a Memorandum of Law, Writing a Client Letter, Writing Briefs); Fact Gathering and Fact Analysis Documents; Tactical and Ethical Considerations; Sample Interrogatories, Performance Tests, and Memoranda.
ISBN: 0-15-900152-8   Pages: 216 $18.95

Civil Procedure
By Professor Thomas D. Rowe, Jr., Duke University, and Professor Richard L. Marcus, U.C. Hastings

Territorial (Personal) Jurisdiction, including Venue and Forum Non Conveniens; Subject Matter Jurisdiction, covering Diversity Jurisdiction, Federal Question Jurisdiction; Erie Doctrine and Federal Common Law; Pleadings including Counterclaims, Cross-Claims, Supplemental Pleadings; Parties, including Joinder and Class Actions; Discovery, including Devices, Scope, Sanctions, and Discovery Conference; Summary Judgment; Pretrial Conference and Settlements; Trial, including Right to Jury Trial, Motions, Jury Instruction and Arguments, and Post-Verdict Motions; Appeals; Claim Preclusion (Res Judicata) and Issue Preclusion (Collateral Estoppel).
ISBN: 0-15-900429-2   Pages: 410 $22.95

Commercial Paper and Payment Law
By Professor Douglas J. Whaley, Ohio State University

Types of Commercial Paper; Negotiability; Negotiation; Holders in Due Course; Claims and Defenses on Negotiable Instruments (including Real Defenses and Personal Defenses); Liability of the Parties (including Merger Rule, Suits on the Instrument, Warranty Suits, Conversion); Bank Deposits and Collections; Forgery or Alteration of Negotiable Instruments; Electronic Banking.
ISBN: 0-15-900367-9   Pages: 166 $19.95

Community Property
By Professor William A. Reppy, Jr., Duke University

Classifying Property as Community or Separate; Management and Control of Property; Liability for Debts; Division of Property at Divorce; Devolution of Property at Death; Relationships Short of Valid Marriage; Conflict of Laws Problems; Constitutional Law Issues (including Equal Protection Standards, Due Process Issues).
ISBN: 0-15-900422-5   Pages: 161 $18.95

LAW SCHOOL LEGENDS SERIES

America's Greatest Law Professors on Audio Cassette

We found the truly gifted law professors most law students can only dream about — the professors who draw rave reviews not only for their scholarship, but for their ability to make the law easy to understand. We asked these select few professors to condense their courses into a single lecture. And it's these lectures you'll find in the Law School Legends Series. With Law School Legends, you'll get a brilliant law professor explaining an entire subject to you in one simple, dynamic lecture. The Law School Legends make even the most difficult concepts crystal clear. You'll understand the big picture, and how all the concepts fit together. You'll get hundreds of examples and exam tips, honed over decades in the classroom. But best of all, you'll get insights you can only get from America's greatest law professors!

Administrative Law

Professor Patrick J. Borchers
Albany Law School of Union University

TOPICS COVERED: Classification Of Agencies; Adjudicative And Investigative Action; Rulemaking Power; Delegation Doctrine; Control By Executive; Appointment And Removal; Freedom Of Information Act; Rulemaking Procedure; Adjudicative Procedure; Trial-Type Hearings; Administrative Law Judge; Power To Stay Proceedings; Subpoena Power; Physical Inspection; Self Incrimination; Judicial Review Issues; Declaratory Judgment; Sovereign Immunity; Eleventh Amendment; Statutory Limitations; Standing; Exhaustion Of Administrative Remedies; Scope Of Judicial Review.
4 Audio Cassettes
ISBN: 0-15-900189-7 $45.95

Agency & Partnership

Professor Thomas L. Evans
University of Texas

TOPICS COVERED: Agency: Creation; Rights And Duties Of Principal And Agent; Sub-Agents; Contract Liability — Actual Authority: Express And Implied; Apparent Authority; Ratification; Liabilities Of Parties; Tort Liability — Respondeat Superior; Frolic And Detour; Intentional Torts. Partnership: Nature Of Partnership; Formation; Partnership By Estoppel; In Partnership Property; Relations Between Partners To Third Parties; Authority of Partners; Dissolution And Termination; Limited Partnerships.
4 Audio Cassettes
ISBN: 0-15-900351-2 $45.95

Antitrust

Professor Thomas D. Morgan
George Washington University Law School

TOPICS COVERED: Antitrust Law's First Principle; Consumer Welfare Opposes Market Power; Methods of Analysis; Role of Reason, Per Se, Quick Look; Sherman Act §1: Civil & Criminal Conspiracies In Unreasonable Restraint Of Trade; Sherman Act §2: Illegal Monopolization, Attempts To Monopolize; Robinson Patman Act Price Discrimination, Related Distribution Problems; Clayton Act §7: Mengers, Joint Ventures; Antitrust & Intellectual Property; International Competitive Relationships; Exemptions & Regulated Industries; Enforcement; Price & Non-Price Restraints.
4 Audio Cassettes
ISBN: 0-15-900341-5 $39.95

Bankruptcy

Professor Elizabeth Warren
Harvard Law School

TOPICS COVERED: The Debtor/Creditor Relationship; The Commencement, Conversion, Dismissal, and Reopening Of Bankruptcy Proceedings; Property Included In The Bankruptcy Estate; Secured, Priority And Unsecured Claims; The Automatic Stay; Powers Of Avoidance; The Assumption And Rejection Of Executory Contracts; The Protection Of Exempt Property; The Bankruptcy Discharge; Chapter 13 Proceedings; Chapter 11 Proceedings; Bankruptcy Jurisdiction And Procedure.
4 Audio Cassettes
ISBN: 0-15-900273-7 $45.95

Civil Procedure

By Professor Richard D. Freer
Emory University Law School

TOPICS COVERED: Subject Matter Jurisdiction; Personal Jurisdiction; Long-Arm Statutes; Constitutional Limitations; In Rem And Quasi In Rem Jurisdiction; Service Of Process; Venue; Transfer; Forum Non Conveniens; Removal; Waiver; Governing Law; Pleadings; Joinder Of Claims; Permissive And Compulsory Joinder Of Parties; Counter-Claims And Cross-Claims; Ancillary Jurisdiction; Impleader; Class Actions; Discovery; Pretrial Adjudication; Summary Judgment; Trial; Post Trial Motions; Appeals; Res Judicata; Collateral Estoppel.
5 Audio Cassettes
ISBN: 0-15-900322-9 $59.95

Commercial Paper

By Professor Michael I. Spak
Chicago Kent College Of Law

TOPICS COVERED: Types Of Negotiable Instruments; Elements Of Negotiability; Statute Of Limitations; Payment-In-Full Checks; Negotiations Of The Instrument; Becoming A Holder-In-Due Course; Rights Of A Holder In Due Course; Real And Personal Defenses; Jus Teril; Effect Of Instrument On Underlying Obligations; Contracts Of Maker And Indorser; Suretyship; Liability Of Drawer And Drawee; Check Certification; Warranty Liability; Conversion Of Liability; Banks And Their Customers; Properly Payable Rule; Wrongful Dishonor; Stopping Payment; Death Of Customer; Bank Statement;

Check Collection; Expedited Funds Availability; Forgery Of Drawer's Name; Alterations; Imposter Rule; Wire Transfers; Electronic Fund Transfers Act.
3 Audio Cassettes
ISBN: 0-15-900275-3 $39.95

Conflict Of Laws

Professor Patrick J. Borchers
Albany Law School

TOPICS COVERED: Domicile; Jurisdiction—In Personam, In Rem, Quasi In Rem; Court Competence; Forum Non Conveniens; Choice Of Law; Foreign Causes Of Action; Territorial Approach To Choice/Tort And Contract; "Escape Devices"; Most Significant Relationship; Governmental Interest Analysis; Recognition Of Judgments; Foreign Country Judgments; Domestic Judgments/Full Faith And Credit; Review Of Judgments; Modifiable Judgments; Defenses To Recognition And Enforcement; Federal/State (Erie) Problems; Constitutional Limits On Choice Of Law.
4 Audio Cassettes
ISBN: 0-15-900352-0 $39.95

Constitutional Law

By Professor John C. Jeffries, Jr.
University of Virginia School of Law

TOPICS COVERED: Introduction; Exam Tactics; Legislative Power; Supremacy; Commerce; State Regulation; Privileges And Immunities; Federal Court Jurisdiction; Separation Of Powers; Civil Liberties; Due Process; Equal Protection; Privacy; Race; Alienage; Gender; Speech And Association; Prior Restraints; Religion—Free Exercise; Establishment Clause.
5 Audio Cassettes
ISBN: 0-15-900373-3 $45.95

Contracts

By Professor Michael I. Spak
Chicago Kent College Of Law

TOPICS COVERED: Offer; Revocation; Acceptance; Consideration; Defenses To Formation; Third Party Beneficiaries; Assignment; Delegation; Conditions; Excuses; Anticipatory Repudiation; Discharge Of Duty; Modifications; Rescission; Accord & Satisfaction; Novation; Breach; Damages; Remedies; UCC Remedies; Parol Evidence Rule.
4 Audio Cassettes
ISBN: 0-15-900318-0 $45.95

Copyright Law

Professor Roger E. Schechter
George Washington University Law School

TOPICS COVERED: Constitution; Patents And Property Ownership Distinguished; Subject Matter Copyright; Duration And Renewal; Ownership And Transfer; Formalities; Introduction; Notice, Registration And Deposit; Infringement; Overview; Reproduction And Derivative Works; Public Distribution; Public Performance And Display; Exemptions; Fair Use; Photocopying; Remedies; Preemption Of State Law.
3 Audio Cassettes
ISBN: 0-15-900295-8 $39.95

Corporations

By Professor Therese H. Maynard
Loyola University Law School

TOPICS COVERED: Ultra Vires Act; Corporate Formation; Piercing The Corporate Veil; Corporate Financial Structure; Stocks; Bonds; Subscription Agreements; Watered Stock; Stock Transactions; Insider Trading; 16(b) & 10b-5 Violations; Promoters; Fiduciary Duties; Shareholder Rights; Meetings; Cumulative Voting; Voting Trusts; Close Corporations; Dividends; Preemptive Rights; Shareholder Derivative Suits; Directors; Duty Of Loyalty; Corporate Opportunity Doctrine; Officers; Amendments; Mergers; Dissolution.
4 Audio Cassettes
ISBN: 0-15-900320-2 $45.95

Criminal Law

By Professor Charles H. Whitebread
USC School of Law

TOPICS COVERED: Exam Tactics; Volitional Acts; Mental States; Specific Intent; Malice; General Intent; Strict Liability; Accomplice Liability; Inchoate Crimes; Impossibility; Defenses; Insanity; Voluntary And Involuntary Intoxication; Infancy; Self-Defense; Defense Of A Dwelling; Duress; Necessity; Mistake Of Fact Or Law; Entrapment; Battery; Assault; Homicide; Common Law Murder; Voluntary And Involuntary Manslaughter; First Degree Murder; Felony Murder; Rape; Larceny; Embezzlement; False Pretenses; Robbery; Extortion; Burglary; Arson.
4 Audio Cassettes
ISBN: 0-15-900279-6 $39.95

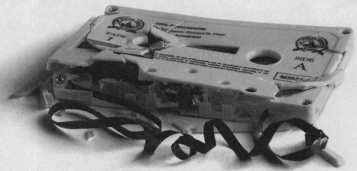

Legalines

Legalines gives you authoritative, detailed briefs of every major case in your casebook. You get a clear explanation of the facts, the issues, the court's holding and reasoning, and any significant concurrences or dissents. Even more importantly, you get an authoritative explanation of the significance of each case, and how it relates to other cases in your casebook. And with Legalines' detailed table of contents and table of cases, you can quickly find any case or concept you're looking for. But your professor expects you to know more than just the cases. That's why Legalines gives you more than just case briefs. You get summaries of the black letter law, as well. That's crucial, because some of the most important information in your casebooks isn't in the cases at all … it's the black letter principles you're expected to glean from those cases. Legalines is the only series that gives you both case briefs and black letter review. With Legalines, you get everything you need to know—whether it's in a case or not!

Administrative Law
Keyed to the Breyer Casebook
ISBN: 0-15-900169-2   176 pages $19.95
Keyed to the Gellhorn Casebook
ISBN: 0-15-900170-6   186 pages $21.95
Keyed to the Schwartz Casebook
ISBN: 0-15-900171-4   145 pages $18.95

Antitrust
Keyed to the Areeda Casebook
ISBN: 0-15-900405-5   165 pages $19.95
Keyed to the Handler Casebook
ISBN: 0-15-900390-3   158 pages $18.95

Civil Procedure
Keyed to the Cound Casebook
ISBN: 0-15-900314-8   241 pages $21.95
Keyed to the Field Casebook
ISBN: 0-15-900415-2   310 pages $23.95
Keyed to the Hazard Casebook
ISBN: 0-15-900324-5   206 pages $21.95
Keyed to the Rosenberg Casebook
ISBN: 0-15-900052-1   284 pages $21.95
Keyed to the Yeazell Casebook
ISBN: 0-15-900241-9   206 pages $20.95

Commercial Law
Keyed to the Farnsworth Casebook
ISBN: 0-15-900176-5   126 pages $18.95

Conflict of Laws
Keyed to the Cramton Casebook
ISBN: 0-15-900331-8   113 pages $16.95
Keyed to the Reese (Rosenberg) Casebook
ISBN: 0-15-900057-2   247 pages $21.95

Constitutional Law
Keyed to the Brest Casebook
ISBN: 0-15-900338-5   172 pages $19.95
Keyed to the Cohen Casebook
ISBN: 0-15-900378-4   301 pages $22.95
Keyed to the Gunther Casebook
ISBN: 0-15-900060-2   367 pages $23.95
Keyed to the Lockhart Casebook
ISBN: 0-15-900242-7   322 pages $22.95

Constitutional Law (cont'd)
Keyed to the Rotunda Casebook
ISBN: 0-15-900363-6   258 pages $21.95
Keyed to the Stone Casebook
ISBN: 0-15-900236-2   281 pages $22.95

Contracts
Keyed to the Calamari Casebook
ISBN: 0-15-900065-3   234 pages $21.95
Keyed to the Dawson Casebook
ISBN: 0-15-900268-0   188 pages $21.95
Keyed to the Farnsworth Casebook
ISBN: 0-15-900332-6   219 pages $19.95
Keyed to the Fuller Casebook
ISBN: 0-15-900237-0   184 pages $19.95
Keyed to the Kessler Casebook
ISBN: 0-15-900070-X   312 pages $22.95
Keyed to the Murphy Casebook
ISBN: 0-15-900387-3   207 pages $21.95

Corporations
Keyed to the Cary Casebook
ISBN: 0-15-900172-2   383 pages $23.95
Keyed to the Choper Casebook
ISBN: 0-15-900173-0   219 pages $21.95
Keyed to the Hamilton Casebook
ISBN: 0-15-900313-X   214 pages $21.95
Keyed to the Vagts Casebook
ISBN: 0-15-900078-5   185 pages $18.95

Criminal Law
Keyed to the Boyce Casebook
ISBN: 0-15-900080-7   290 pages $21.95
Keyed to the Dix Casebook
ISBN: 0-15-900081-5   103 pages $15.95
Keyed to the Johnson Casebook
ISBN: 0-15-900175-7   149 pages $18.95
Keyed to the Kadish Casebook
ISBN: 0-15-900333-4   167 pages $18.95
Keyed to the La Fave Casebook
ISBN: 0-15-900084-X   202 pages $20.95

Criminal Procedure
Keyed to the Kamisar Casebook
ISBN: 0-15-900336-9   256 pages $21.95

Decedents' Estates & Trusts
Keyed to the Ritchie Casebook
ISBN: 0-15-900339-3   204 pages $21.95

Domestic Relations
Keyed to the Clark Casebook
ISBN: 0-15-900168-4   119 pages $16.95
Keyed to the Wadlington Casebook
ISBN: 0-15-900377-6   169 pages $18.95

Estate & Gift Taxation
Keyed to the Surrey Casebook
ISBN: 0-15-900093-9   100 pages $15.95

Evidence
Keyed to the Sutton Casebook
ISBN: 0-15-900096-3   271 pages $19.95
Keyed to the Waltz Casebook
ISBN: 0-15-900334-2   179 pages $19.95
Keyed to the Weinstein Casebook
ISBN: 0-15-900097-1   223 pages $20.95

Family Law
Keyed to the Areen Casebook
ISBN: 0-15-900263-X   262 pages $21.95

Federal Courts
Keyed to the McCormick Casebook
ISBN: 0-15-900101-3   195 pages $18.95

Income Tax
Keyed to the Freeland Casebook
ISBN: 0-15-900361-X   134 pages $18.95
Keyed to the Klein Casebook
ISBN: 0-15-900383-0   150 pages $18.95

Labor Law
Keyed to the Cox Casebook
ISBN: 0-15-900238-9   221 pages $18.95
Keyed to the Merrifield Casebook
ISBN: 0-15-900177-3   195 pages $20.95

Property
Keyed to the Browder Casebook
ISBN: 0-15-900110-2   277 pages $21.95
Keyed to the Casner Casebook
ISBN: 0-15-900111-0   261 pages $21.95
Keyed to the Cribbet Casebook
ISBN: 0-15-900239-7   328 pages $22.95
Keyed to the Dukeminier Casebook
ISBN: 0-15-900432-2   168 pages $18.95
Keyed to the Nelson Casebook
ISBN: 0-15-900228-1   288 pages $19.95

Real Property
Keyed to the Rabin Casebook
ISBN: 0-15-900262-1   180 pages $18.95

Remedies
Keyed to the Re Casebook
ISBN: 0-15-900116-1   245 pages $22.95
Keyed to the York Casebook
ISBN: 0-15-900118-8   265 pages $21.95

Sales & Secured Transactions
Keyed to the Speidel Casebook
ISBN: 0-15-900166-8   202 pages $21.95

Securities Regulation
Keyed to the Jennings Casebook
ISBN: 0-15-900253-2   324 pages $22.95

Torts
Keyed to the Epstein Casebook
ISBN: 0-15-900335-0   193 pages $20.95
Keyed to the Franklin Casebook
ISBN: 0-15-900240-0   146 pages $18.95
Keyed to the Henderson Casebook
ISBN: 0-15-900174-9   162 pages $18.95
Keyed to the Keeton Casebook
ISBN: 0-15-900406-3   252 pages $21.95
Keyed to the Prosser Casebook
ISBN: 0-15-900301-6   334 pages $22.95

Wills, Trusts & Estates
Keyed to the Dukeminier Casebook
ISBN: 0-15-900337-7   145 pages $19.95

Call To Order: 1-800-787-8717 or Order On-Line at http://www.gilbertlaw.com

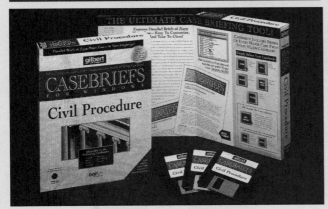
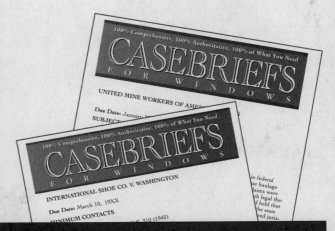

on the Internet!

www.gilbertlaw.com

Pre-Law Center
Learn what law school is really like including what to expect on exams. Order your free 32-page color catalog and a free 88-page sample of Gilbert Law Summaries for Civil Procedure — the most feared first year course!

Bookstore
Review detailed information on over 200 of America's most popular legal study aids — Gilbert Law Summaries, Legalines, Casebriefs, Law School Legends audio tapes and much more. Order on-line!

gilbert LAW SUMMARIES

Past Exam Library
Browse hundreds of past exams from law schools across the country. Test your knowledge with true/false, multiple choice, short answer, essay – all of the question types (with answers!) you'll see on your midterm and final exams. Includes exams from some of the country's greatest law professors. If you can pass their exams — you can pass any exam!

100 NEW EXAMS!

Links to Law Sites
Links to hundreds of law-related sites on the web, including:
- Legal Publications
- International Law
- Legal Research
- Department of Justice
- Legal Employment
- Legal Associations

Order Products On-line!
Fast, easy and secure on-line ordering is now available 24 hours per day, 7 days per week!

Employment Center
E-mail the Job Goddess with your job search questions, and download a free copy of *The Myths of Legal Job Searches: The 9 Biggest Mistakes Law Students Make.* View content from some of America's best selling legal employment guides, including *Guerrilla Tactics For Getting The Legal Job Of Your Dreams* and *The National Directory of Legal Employers.*

THE JOB GODDESS

Wanted! Student Marketing Reps
Become a campus representative and earn hundreds of dollars of free product from Gilbert Law Summaries, Legalines, Casebriefs and more! Join our national marketing program and help promote America's most popular legal study aids at your law school!

1st Year Survival Manual
A must-read for 1L's! Learn how to prepare for class, how to handle class discussions, and the keys to successful exam performance — plus much more!

Taking the Bar Exam?
Learn how to make the transition from law school exams to the bar exam — including what to expect on the MBE, MPT, MPRE, MEE and state essay exams.

Welcome Center
Whether you're about to enter law school or you're already under way, we've created this site to help you succeed!

Employment Guides

A collection of best selling titles that help you identify and reach your career goals.

Guerrilla Tactics for Getting the Legal Job of Your Dreams
Kimm Alayne Walton, J.D.

Whether you're looking for a summer clerkship or your first permanent job after school, this revolutionary book is the key to getting the job of your dreams!

Guerrilla Tactics for Getting the Legal Job of Your Dreams leads you step-by-step through everything you need to do to nail down that perfect job! You'll learn hundreds of simple-to-use strategies that will get you exactly where you want to go. You'll Learn:

- The seven magic opening words in cover letters that ensure you'll get a response.
- The secret to successful interviews every time.
- Killer answers to the toughest interview questions they'll ever ask you.
- Plus Much More!

Guerrilla Tactics features the best strategies from the country's most innovative law school career advisors. The strategies in *Guerrilla Tactics* are so powerful that it even comes with a guarantee: Follow the advice in the book, and within one year of graduation you'll have the job of your dreams … or your money back!

Pick up a copy of *Guerrilla Tactics* today … you'll be on your way to the job of your dreams!

ISBN: 0-15-900317-2   **$24.95**

Proceed With Caution: A Diary Of The First Year At One Of America's Largest, Most Prestigious Law Firms
William R. Keates

Prestige. Famous clients. High-profile cases. Not to mention a starting salary approaching six figures.

In *Proceed With Caution*, the author takes you behind the scenes, to show you what it's really like to be a junior associate at a huge law firm. After graduating from an Ivy League law school, he took a job as an associate with one of New York's blue-chip law firms.

He also did something not many people do. He kept a diary, where he spelled out his day-to-day life at the firm in graphic detail.

Proceed With Caution excerpts the diary, from his first day at the firm to the day he quit. From the splashy benefits, to the nitty-gritty on the work junior associates do, to the grind of long and unpredictable hours, to the stress that eventually made him leave the firm — he tells story after story that will make you feel as though you're living the life of a new associate.

Whether you're considering a career with a large firm, or you're just curious about what life at the top firms is all about — *Proceed With Caution* is a must read!

ISBN: 0-15-900181-1   **$17.95**

The Official Guide To Legal Specialties
Lisa Shanholtzer

With *The Official Guide To Legal Specialties* you'll get a behind the scenes glimpse at dozens of legal specialties. Not just lists of what to expect, real life stories from top practitioners in each field. You'll learn exactly what it's like to be in some of America's most desirable professions. You'll get expert advice on what it takes to get a job in each field. How much you'll earn and what the day-to-day life is really like, the challenges you'll face, and the benefits you'll enjoy. With *The Official Guide To Legal Specialties* you'll have a wealth of information at your fingertips!

Includes the following specialties:

Banking	Intellectual Property
Communications	International
Corporate	Labor/Employment
Criminal	Litigation
Entertainment	Public Interest
Environmental	Securities
Government Practice	Sports
Health Care	Tax
Immigration	Trusts & Estates

ISBN: 0-15-900391-1   **$17.95**

Beyond L.A. Law: Inspiring Stories of People Who've Done Fascinating Things With A Law Degree
National Association for Law Placement

Anyone who watches television knows that being a lawyer means working your way up through a law firm — right?

Wrong!

Beyond L.A. Law gives you a fascinating glimpse into the lives of people who've broken the "lawyer" mold. They come from a variety of backgrounds — some had prior careers, others went straight through college and law school, and yet others have overcome poverty and physical handicaps. They got their degrees from all different kinds of law schools, all over the country. But they have one thing in common: they've all pursued their own, unique vision.

As you read their stories, you'll see how they beat the odds to succeed. You'll learn career tips and strategies that work, from people who've put them to the test. And you'll find fascinating insights that you can apply to your own dream, whether it's a career in law or anything else!

From Representing Baseball In Australia. To International Finance. To Children's Advocacy. To Directing a Nonprofit Organization. To Entrepreneur.

If You Think Getting A Law Degree Means Joining A Traditional Law Firm — Think Again!

ISBN: 0-15-900182-X   **$17.95**

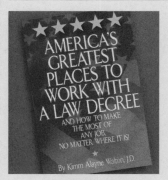

America's Greatest Places To Work With A Law Degree
Kimm Alayne Walton, J.D.

"Where do your happiest graduates work?" That's the question that author Kimm Alayne Walton asked law school administrators around the country. Their responses revealed the hundreds of wonderful employers profiled in *America's Greatest Places To Work With A Law Degree*.

In this remarkable book, you'll get to know an incredible variety of great places to work, including:

- Glamorous sports and entertainment employers — the jobs that sound as though they would be great, and they are!
- The 250 best law firms to work for between 20 and 600 attorneys.
- Companies where law school graduates love to work and not just as in-house counsel.
- Wonderful public interest employers – the "white knight" jobs that are so incredibly satisfying.
- Court-related positions, where lawyers entertain fascinating issues, tremendous variety, and an enjoyable lifestyle.
- Outstanding government jobs, at the federal, state, and local level.

Beyond learning about incredible employers, you'll discover:

- The ten traits that define a wonderful place to work … the sometimes surprising qualities that outstanding employers share.
- How to handle law school debt, when your dream job pays less than you think you need to make.
- How to find — and get! — great jobs at firms with fewer than 20 attorneys.

And no matter where you work, you'll learn expert tips for making the most of your job. You'll learn the specific strategies that distinguish people headed for the top … how to position yourself for the most interesting, high-profile work … how to handle difficult personalities … how to negotiate for more money … and what to do now to help you get your next great job!

ISBN: 0-15-900180-3   **$24.95**

About The Author

Kimm Alayne Walton is the author of numerous books and articles including two national best seller's — *America's Greatest Places To Work With A Law Degree* and *Guerrilla Tactics For Getting The Legal Job Of Your Dreams*. She is a renowned motivational speaker, lecturing at law schools and bar associations nationwide, and in her spare time, she has taken up travel writing, which has taken her swimming with crocodiles in Kakadu, and scuba diving with sharks on the Great Barrier Reef.

THE JOB GODDESS

E-mail the Job Goddess with your own legal job search questions!

Visit www.gilbertlaw.com for details.

Call To Order: 1-800-787-8717 or Order On-Line at http://www.gilbertlaw.com